LEE COUNTY LIBRARY
SANFORD, N. C.

W9-ADV-748

LA SALLE

The Life and Times of An Explorer

BIOGRAPHIES BY JOHN UPTON TERRELL

ZEBULON PIKE
The Life and Times of An Adventurer.
New York; 1968.

JOURNEY INTO DARKNESS
The Story of Cabeza de Vaca.
New York; 1962.

FURS BY ASTOR
A History of John Jacob Astor and the American Fur Trade.
New York; 1963.

BLACK ROBE
*Pierre Jean deSinet, First Missionary in the
Rocky Mountain Region.*
New York; 1964.

FAINT THE TRUMPET SOUNDS
The Life and Trial of Major Reno.
New York; 1966.

ESTEVENICO THE BLACK
Discoverer of Arizona and New Mexico.
Los Angeles; 1968.

LEE COUNTY LIBRARY
SANFORD. N. C.

LA SALLE

The Life and Times of an Explorer

JOHN UPTON TERRELL

Weybright and Talley

NEW YORK

© by John Upton Terrell 1968
All rights reserved, including the
right to reproduce this book or portions
thereof in any form.

Published simultaneously in the United States by
WEYBRIGHT AND TALLEY, INC.
3 East 54th Street,
New York, New York 10022
and in Canada by
CLARKE, IRWIN & COMPANY, LIMITED,
Toronto and Vancouver

Library of Congress Catalog Card No. 68-28272
PRINTED IN THE UNITED STATES OF AMERICA

LA SALLE

The Life and Times of An Explorer

LEE COUNTY LIBRARY
SANFORD, N. C.

I ✤ ✤ ✤

THEY APPEARED in canoes, on a late fall day of 1668, before the palisade of the Seigneury St. Sulpice, which stood where the clear icy waters of the St. Lawrence widened, pushing back the thick dark forests, to form Lake St. Louis.

They were Seneca Iroquois, perhaps nine or ten men, women, and children, well wrapped in deerskins and fine furs of beaver and otter and fox, and they had a few pelts to trade to the young man in buckskin who came out to meet them.

His name was René-Robert Cavelier, Sieur de la Salle. Although standing slightly under six feet in height, he gave evidence of abundant physical strength in the broadness of his shoulders and the thickness of his limbs. His hair was long and shiny black and brushed the nape of a sturdy neck in the manner of a *courier du bois* who had been long in the wilderness. His sun-darkened

[1]

face was narrow, the nose slightly convex and long, the lips firm and straight.

Nothing could have been termed remarkable about him, except his eyes. Large and intensely dark, they gazed from under heavy slanting brows, much like those of a bloodhound, and in them fires alternately smouldered and flamed. The eyes reflected his emotions, and these changed quickly and frequently as he listened to men talk, as he became enraptured by some private hope, engrossed by the prospects inherent in some dream, or angered by the adversities of a situation he must face.

Numerous Indians stopped at the Seigneury St. Sulpice. Only some eight miles above the fortress-settlement of Montreal, it was a good location for a fur trading post, and easily reached on relatively calm lake waters. But the arrival there of the little band of Seneca Iroquois was not to be included among the commonplace comings and goings of the forest people who might be traveling up or down the river.

The visit of these Seneca Iroquois was important for a special reason.

Out of it came events which dramatically affected the history of North America, which drastically transformed the course of empire in the immense regions, still unknown to white men, that reached, no one knew how far, into the setting sun.

2 ⚜ ⚜ ⚜

THAT SENECAS, or any of the Iroquois peoples, could travel openly and in relative safety down the Valley of the St. Lawrence was due to the provisions of a treaty consummated, after lengthy negotiations, in the summer of 1667. For years previously the scourge of the St. Lawrence region, the Iroquois had been severely punished by strong colonial forces, and some regular troops sent from France, under Governor Daniel de Rémy, Sieur de Courcelle, and the famed old soldier, Lieutenant-General Alexandre de Prouville, Marquis de Tracy.

Four of the Iroquois Five Nations had sued for peace, convinced of the futility of fighting men who poured from ships like grains of sand, all dressed alike, advancing as a moving wall, and firing together in a single peal of thunder a devastating hail of lead. The Mohawks, however, had continued their defiance for some time. At last, they were soundly defeated in a campaign in which their towns and their winter supplies (in New York State) were destroyed and they were sent fleeing for their lives. They, too, came to realize that war against the French could no longer be profitable, and they had sent chiefs to Quebec to sign the treaty of peace with the other tribes of the Iroquois alliance.

The Senecas who stopped at the Seigneury St. Sulpice that fall day of 1668 asked for permission to camp there. La Salle granted it without hesitation. Trade with them would amount to little—indeed, if they remained long he would lose money, for he would be obliged to furnish them with foodstuffs—but his willingness to let them stay as long as they desired derived not so much from generosity or hospitality as from a totally unsentimental objective.

Curiosity seethed in La Salle. He was aware that these Indians were members of a tribe that wandered through a land of which little—almost nothing, it might be said—was known, a country far south and west of the few main water routes which had been opened from Montreal by *couriers du bois et pères* to the northern rivers and fresh water seas of the western interior.

An insatiable student of the history of Indian peoples, an unrelenting seeker of new information about them, La Salle had come to know that when the Senecas were first encountered by Europeans their homeland had been in western New York State between Seneca Lake and the Geneva River. About the middle of

[3]

the seventeenth century, only two decades before La Salle's arrival in Canada, the Iroquois had conquered the Eries and the Neuters, and, during the years immediately following, the Senecas had extended their villages westward along the south shore of Lake Erie, into Ohio and western Pennsylvania.*

Questions marched in close parade through La Salle's inquisitive mind. What kind of a country was this into which they had migrated? What were the possibilities for fur trade? How many people dwelt there and in adjoining territories? How accessible was it by water? By land? What kinds of game abounded in it? Was it flat? Mountainous? Forested? Barren?

The Senecas stayed at the Seigneury St. Sulpice through the winter, and during those long bitter months they gave their answers in numerous councils to the interrogations their host so assiduously pursued. They told him they had moved into a rich country, not as cold as Canada. The opportunities for fur trade were incomparable. It could be reached easily by either water or land. Much of it contained rolling, beautiful hills bordered by luxuriant meadows. Buffalo flourished, along with countless kinds of other game, the fresh water lakes and streams swarmed with fish, and the air was alive with birds. As to people, the Senecas themselves were numerous, having absorbed many conquered enemies, and other large tribes lived beyond them to the south and west who were wealthy in the products of the earth. How far the land extended no one could say, for it ran away to the stars.

While all this information was stimulating and pleasing to the ears, an innate prudence caused La Salle to refrain from swallowing it as unadorned fact. Indians not only had a penchant for boasting of the grandeur and bountifulness of their homeland, but they were not averse to telling a white man whatever they believed he was most desirous of hearing.

La Salle could find no reason, however, to harbor reserva-

* Modern names are applied to geographical areas throughout this work.

tions about one segment of the intelligence imparted by the Senecas. It came in a few simple statements which stirred in him at once a strong feeling that he was hearing the unvarnished truth.

Their country could be easily gained, said the Senecas, by the St. Lawrence and Lakes Ontario and Erie. A short distance south of these lakes rose the headwaters of a river that attained a size beyond calculation. It flowed in the course the sun moved. So far away was its end that a journey of eight or nine moons would be required to reach it. The river lost itself at last in a distant sea, the waters of which, they had heard, were warm and of a reddish color.

The Seneca name for the river was Ohio.

. . . . *a sea of warm waters of a reddish color.*

La Salle was filled with intense excitement. These descriptive words themselves warranted the assumption—which he quickly elevated to a conviction—that the mouth of the Ohio was upon the Gulf of California, known to him by the name Vermilion Sea.

In all the decades that had passed since the voyages of Columbus, the supreme objective of adventurers striking along the immense land mass of North America had been to find a water passage through it. Each search had ended upon impregnable coasts or endless reaches of arctic ice. Now the old dream had been revived in him, given new life that was enhanced by the infusion of seemingly indubitable geographical factors.

In long and profound meditations, La Salle sought to discover a reciprocal relationship for each fragment of knowledge he possessed, each tale and each claim he had heard. There were many, and not a few of them brought forth aggravating questions with puzzling aspects for which he strove in rapt absorption to find satisfactory answers.

His contemplation sometimes carried him to far horizons. *Voyageurs, couriers du bois,* and missionaries with whom he had talked had related to him that in their journeys up the Ottawa, to

[5]

the French River, to Georgian Bay, and the northernmost fresh water lakes, they had heard from Algonquians and other tribes of a large river called the Mississippi. None of these wilderness travelers had ever seen the Mississippi, however, and all they had been able to learn of it had been that it lay somewhere west—always a great distance farther to the west—of the routes they had traversed. But all of them had felt certain it existed, whatever its location and wherever it went.

That the Mississippi of the Algonquians and the Ohio of the Senecas were not one and the same was a conclusion which La Salle considered irrefutable in the light of the available evidence. The fur traders and the priests had heard of the Mississippi when they were obviously far north of Seneca territory. The name had not been mentioned in the talks at the Seigneury St. Sulpice, and he reasoned that, in all probability, this omission would not have occurred had his visitors been familiar with it. The existence of the Mississippi had not been established, and, unless he was being grossly deceived, which he was unwilling to believe, the same thing could not be said of the Ohio. The Senecas not only knew where its tributaries rose and where each entered the main stream, but they knew the course it took, and, most significant of all, they knew of its ending.

The Senecas had no name for the sea of reddish color, but if this was a regrettable hiatus in their accounts, La Salle refused to look upon it as a portent of grievous frustration he would suffer. The indestructible belief that his reasoning was sound—if not his irrepressible enthusiasm and soaring hopes—precluded his dwelling upon possible adversities and disappointments. He had no more time to devote to apprehension than he did to being hesitant in carrying out the plans taking shape in his thoughts. Even if it should be found that the Ohio did not reach the Vermilion Sea, an investigation of it was justified, no matter what length of time the journey consumed, for it must run through a land rich in furs, a land never seen by white men. And both that land and the river bisecting it had endings . . . somewhere.

La Salle would never be accused of having disregarded an opportunity to make an important geographical discovery or of having ignored a chance to gain a commercial advantage.

As he impatiently waited for the winter to pass, he pondered the steps which he understood must be taken before a venture of any kind could be launched. He had not been in Canada a sufficient time to acquire more than superficial knowledge of the political complexities which beset the colonial government, but he had been there long enough to appreciate fully the extent to which civil regulations and ecclesiastical laws intruded upon the everyday lives of both temporary and permanent residents, be they officials, small shopkeepers, poor farmers, common laborers, prominent shipowners, affluent businessmen, or wealthy traders. Inasmuch as circumvention of these restrictions was hardly possible—and he fully realized that in his case such an attempt would be not only imprudent but perilous—his progress would be measured by his ability to withstand and surmount them.

Official sanction was required for any type of enterprise, stationary or transient, large or small. In this case, it took the form of a license to move. No man—and most assuredly not an uninfluential settler like him—could engage in an unauthorized exploration without laying himself open to severe reprisals. The right to discover was privileged, not the prerogative of any adventurous citizen who chose to wander in the wilderness. As to the fur trade, it was subject to controls and concessions decreed in Versailles. While these royal edicts were not infrequently defeated by stratagems devised by dishonest functionaries, they were nevertheless the laws of the land, and their enforcement to the greatest possible extent was rigorously attempted by the high authorities whose actions and records were open to scrutiny by superiors in France.

La Salle had no way of anticipating the attitudes which the

Governor and the Intendant, Jean Talon, both of whom he must consult, would display toward him in Quebec, although the unqualified confidence he held in himself made it inconceivable to him that he would fail to obtain their approval of his plan, once he had been accorded proper audiences with them. He could, however, feel certain of the reactions which would come from other quarters when the nature of the enterprise he wished to undertake had been disclosed. The fur merchants, for example, would suspect his motives, fearful that he had concocted some scheme to benefit from illegal trade with Indians, and would seek to prevent his voyage. The Jesuit hierarchy undoubtedly would register objections to it in accordance with their policy of opposing any exploration in the west in which they would not participate and over which they could not exercise strong control.

It was at best not a promising outlook, but even before the ice of the St. Lawrence had completely broken, La Salle was descending the river with a crew of oarsmen in a longboat, en route to the seat of the colonial government.

3 ⚜ ⚜ ⚜

AS LA SALLE traveled toward Quebec in the early spring of 1669, he had passed by no more than half a year his twenty-fifth birthday. He had been in Canada less than three years. In that short period of time he had acquired a seigneury of no small proportions, he had become a fur trader of modest attainments, he had hewn fields out of the forest, and he had become landlord and director of a growing settlement of artisans and farmers with sizable broods of children.

The seigneury had been awarded to him by the Seminary of St. Sulpice, the members of which not only dominated the religious affairs of Montreal, but were in reality the feudal lords, the civil rulers, and the legal proprietors of the island on which the city stood. Ownership of the land had given him a desirable security and the pleasure of envisioning, if he chose to do it, a promising future for himself, but it had brought him neither peace nor contentment. On the contrary, his progress and the prospect of increasing affluence had added new fuel to every desire he possessed and new ferment to the inherent restlessness which on numerous past occasions had made life miserable for him.

His intelligence, his seemingly boundless energy, an avowed patriotism, and an unmistakably sincere desire to contribute to the development of the colony, had endeared him to the Sulpicians, and especially to the Abbé de Queylus, the Seminary's head. Similar esteem and respect were seldom reflected in the attitudes of trading house operators and the proprietors of mercantile establishments. These recognized in him—not without considerable misgiving—business capabilities rarely demonstrated by one so young and inexperienced. However, this was a situation he found both bearable and amusing.

La Salle had left Montreal on his Quebec mission prepared to sacrifice, if necessary, every advantage he held, every asset he had acquired, to carry out the idea which had taken complete control not only of his mind but of his heart. It was not basically a new idea, for it had existed in him in vague and rough form even before he had left France. But now he had brought it to a state of refinement, he had given it substance and an unequivocal definition.

He had emigrated to Canada with certain explicit objectives. Not the least of them was to make money, but acquisition of a fortune was by no means his uppermost ambition. That, without question, was to become an explorer, and, in the light of the popular pattern of his time, exploration meant, first, attempting to discover a water passage usable for commercial enterprises to some point on the western sea from which carriers could continue to the Orient, and, second, to open unknown regions to profitable development and trade.

[9]

With good reason, after his arrival, La Salle had proceeded directly to Montreal. His elder brother, Jean, was already there, having two years previously entered the Sulpician Order to become a wilderness missionary. While the affection they held for each other had never been more than perfunctory—they had corresponded hardly at all—the presence of close kin in the wild and strange land was to a somewhat bewildered young man who had known nothing but a sheltered existence an advantage he felt it would be unwise to disregard. Besides, La Salle had little money, a condition which made it imperative that he find inexpensive quarters, and he recognized his pressing need for counsel. He felt he could safely assume that his brother would not refuse to provide him with shelter, but he could not be certain, as he reflected upon the dissensions of their past relationship, that any advice he received would be either sound or acceptable to him. Yet, whatever he might find there, the seminary appeared to be the most logical destination, and he headed for it.

He had been right.

His brother welcomed him with the cold reserve that he had anticipated, but his reception by the Superior, Abbé de Queylus, was warm and enthusiastic. Extraordinarily discerning, a man of vision that was matched by inordinate ambition, as totally unselfish as he was devout, de Queylus quickly recognized in La Salle the type of settler he so fervently had hoped might be found for the community.

La Salle could not have reached Montreal at a more propitious moment. Under de Queylus's direction, the seminary had embarked on a program of securing new residents and developing the island, not, however, for the sole purpose of improving its economy. They wanted as much to strengthen defenses, for they feared that the treaty of peace with the Iroquois would not long endure. Tradition and past events, if nothing else, were basis enough for an expectation that violations would occur.

All possible measures of protection had been taken. In addition to the small fort of stone, in which the military commander and a few soldiers were quartered, the town's windmill, the Hôtel-Dieu or hospital, the buildings of the seminary and the church, as well as almost every house, had been equipped with loopholes, stout doors, and enclosures, but these improvements were not sufficient to enable the inhabitants to withstand an attack in force by the Iroquois.

The Sulpicians had conceived the idea of establishing a line of small settlements around the perimeter of the island which might serve as outposts and from which warnings of an invasion could be sent in time to permit the town to gird itself. To accomplish this development they had announced a policy of awarding tracts of land to dependable and worthy settlers.

La Salle had not been long in Montreal before de Queylus made him an extremely generous offer; without the investment of a *livre* he became owner of a seigneury which would appreciate greatly in value as Montreal grew. There was, however, one serious drawback to the gift. The land which the wily Abbé had selected for him was the most dangerously located in the colony, completely exposed to attack from the forests that bordered Lake St. Louis. Persons residing on it would be the first to bear the brunt of a surprise assault. But La Salle did not dwell upon this adverse aspect of his good fortune, considering it outweighed by other factors. The site was ideal for commercial and agricultural developments, and with his customary zest he set to work at once to implement them.

His announcement that to each qualified farmer or craftsman who wished to join him he would assign a farm of sixty arpents with a perpetual annual rent of only thirty *sous* soon brought applicants anxious to take advantage of the low charges. He laid out a village common, and adjoining it he reserved for himself an estate of four hundred and twenty arpents, on it erecting several

buildings, his living quarters, stables, and a trading post. Around these structures he built a strong palisade into which all residents could retreat at the sounding of an alarm.

These labors and activities might normally have been accepted as indications of a profound desire to create a permanent and profitable establishment. Nothing could have been more untrue in the case of La Salle. If the actual extent of his interest in developing his seigneury was a debatable matter, it was an incontestable fact that he entertained no visions of himself one day living there in a grand manor house, surrounded by lush and peaceful fields and herds. This was made apparent in several ways.

One of his first acts after reaching Montreal had been to begin an intensive study of Indian tongues, and he quickly demonstrated an extraordinary talent as a linguist. Within two years he had learned to speak Iroquois with considerable fluency and to a lesser extent had become conversant in other Indian languages and dialects.

On at least three occasions he had interrupted his activities at the seigneury, entrusting the work of building to others, and had journeyed into the bleak forest and lake country north of the St. Lawrence Valley. These trips, brief as they were, served to confirm the belief he already held that nothing was to be gained by more extensive penetrations in that direction, and his gaze became fastened on the west and southwest.

He made no secret in meetings with the priests of the seminary and other residents of Montreal of his conviction that the future of New France and the fur trade lay in regions still to be opened. In the west, perhaps far beyond any point yet reached by white men, over trails and along rivers still unknown, lay the common destiny of the empire and its people in the New World.

His preoccupation with the idea of finding a waterway to China, and his unshakable belief that it existed, would bring more than critical opinions of his rationality. Guests in his rude home or customers in his trading post who were subjected to lengthy discourses on the subject were inspired to give the nickname "La Petite Chine" to his seigneury. In time to come, men who had served with him and had deserted him would adopt it. It would come into official usage—a memorial of dubious quality—when, in 1670, an ordinance would designate the Seigneury St. Sulpice as "the habitations that are known as 'la petite Chine.'" And that name it would thereafter bear.

Neither criticism nor ridicule inflicted upon him by others troubled La Salle's thoughts in the spring of 1669 as he descended the St. Lawrence to Quebec.

4 ✣ ✣ ✣

DURING THE first fifteen years of his life, Robert Cavelier had known neither poverty nor hardship. In an examination of his character, this circumstance of his boyhood environment has a relevancy that might not be expected. To conditions prevalent in the early lives of men who achieve fame and distinction are usually attributed the intellectual and social attitudes and habits they display as adults. This cannot be postulated in the case of La Salle.

His background reflected little of his way of thinking, nor did it influence him in any way in pursuing with indomitable perseverance the earthly course he charted for himself.

Personal poverty, chastity, and obedience were the cardinal ecclesiastical vows of the Jesuits. If the latter two were adhered to with commendable diligence by the missionaries sent to North America, the first was not always observed within the letter of its intent. Not a few of the men of the cloth in New France acquired wealth, through land, furs and other means, although most of them absolved themselves of these transgressions with deathbed acts of charity.

Impecuniousness, both during the years he wore a Jesuit

habit and after he had withdrawn from the order, was a condition
with which La Salle was thoroughly familiar. But he never inti-
mated that he felt the burden of them was unfairly inflicted or
undeserved. Quite the other way around, he saw his lack of funds
as an aggravating detriment to progress, temporary, of course, and
he never doubted that he would not fail to remove it. His self-
confidence, if not his blind courage itself, dissipated that state of
mind. Indeed, he feared no economic force, and assuredly not one
created by competitors or the exigencies which faced him as the
result of his own behavior.

Endowed with a good name and a superior education, he was,
nevertheless, completely at ease among men of lesser stations and
advantages. He had the facility of walking on common ground
with persons of all levels. Snobbishness, a feeling of superiority,
or excessive vanity were not to be found in him. Yet, he had an
uncountable number of enemies. He was hated more than he was
liked, reviled more than he was praised, denounced and condemned
more than he was commended and defended.

It would be very convenient to explain the vilification and
malicious attacks to which he was subjected with the assertion that
even the men closest to him did not understand him. If such an
explanation contains a element of truth, it would not constitute the
whole truth. Far from it. A large part of La Salle's misfortunes
and the disparagements he suffered came as the result of qualities
inherent in him, and acts he himself performed.

It was his way on occasions to withdraw into himself, as if he
were unaware of the existence, anywhere on earth, of other mortals.
His prolonged silences were often mistaken for animosity. His
unwavering dedication to duty and to plan was not infrequently, in
the eyes of those encountering it, a signal of vengefulness. He
expected spiritual fealty from men who were no more than laboring horses. He expected intellectual reactions from persons who
had no capacity to respond in such a way, whose powers of reasoning were sharply limited, who not only did not understand what

he was trying to do but could not comprehend his reasons for doing it.

As for his chastity, it must be presumed that his youthful habits met the stringent demands of the religious order he had entered. Freedom from the vows left no ecclesiastical restrictions upon his private life, and there can be no question about his physical capabilities or his virility. He would be accused of immoral conduct, of attempting to seduce a friend's wife, but the sources of these accusations were almost invariably persons plotting to discredit him for their own gain.

No man of his time who did not abandon all pretensions of being white would enter further into the world of the Indians than La Salle. No contemporary of his would understand better the Indian ways of life, nor hold a greater respect for the doctrines which guided the red man. It follows, therefore, that he was completely aware that the wilderness peoples, among whom he spent the greater part of his adult years, were as matter-of-fact about biological functions as they were about war or hunting. He knew that spiritual and physical significance were welded into the basis of their understanding and their beliefs. Codes varied among tribes, as did religious ceremonies, but neither hypocrisy nor inflexible standards were extraordinary influences on their actions.

In the view of these Indians, a man's desire for a woman was as normal, and as expected, as the rising of the sun. The missionaries who adhered to their vow of celibacy presented an enigma which the Indian mind was unable to solve. Moreover, to proffer an attractive bedmate to an honored guest was, in the tenets of most Indians, a supreme gesture of hospitality and a symbol of high esteem. In a strictly religious sense, La Salle was not a missionary. Indeed, he was a most rigorous opponent of the policies and programs promulgated by the Jesuits. But neither was he a man of reprehensible moral attributes. Both his wishes and his attempts to provide advantages for the Indians, to create the economic and military safeguards they so desperately needed, to establish peaceful relationships between warring tribes, were as pronounced, as profound, and as sincere, as those of any man garbed in a black or gray robe.

Evidence that his emotions, whatever form they took and whenever they stirred him, were subjugated by greater fires in his blood is seemingly incontrovertible. Strikingly absent from his letters, from the accounts of persons associated with him, and official and unofficial records, are hints of romantic attachments, of *affaires d'amour*.

More precise statements may be made about the third and last vow, obedience. If its true definition meant anything to him, its effect on him was insignificant. His defiance of the principles, theorems, and concepts which the Jesuits strove to drive into him made his mentors despair. He was not irreligious, but neither was his brain a sponge that would absorb any fluid applied to it. His intellect equaled, if not surpassed, that of many of his teachers. He coldly rejected what did not appear to be realistic and truthful, and he would not be swayed by forces that usually shape and govern the mental processes of fanatics. He knew what he wanted, and, when he was thwarted, instead of surrendering, he turned from his masters and went his own way.

5 ❧ ❧ ❧

LA SALLE WAS born in the Parish of St. Herbland in Rouen. The home of the Caveliers, who for several generations had enjoyed affluence and position, stood in the Rue de la Grosse Horloge.

The *acte de naissance* in the civil records of the parish states that he was baptized on the 22nd day of November, 1643. Thus, he might have entered the world on that date or on the previous day.

He was the son, the register notes, of the "honorable Jean

Cavelier and Catherine Geest." Named as his godfather and god-mother were "Nicholas Geest and Marguerite Morice."

The Caveliers' money came from wholesale establishments operated by both La Salle's father and his uncle Henri. The family had a long history of commercial success. They were not nobles, but they were not without political influence, and members of both the Caveliers and the Geests had held diplomatic and government posts.

A short distance from the cobbled streets and industrial com-motion of Rouen, in the peaceful beauty of the Seine Valley, the Caveliers maintained a country manor and farm, called La Salle. It was customary for wealthy French burghers to honor a son by awarding him a title that included the name of a prized estate. To René-Robert Cavelier, therefore, was appended, Sieur de la Salle.

He was the second son of Jean and Catherine Geest Cavelier. His elder brother, also named Jean, early dedicated himself to the priesthood, and he achieved his ambition to become a missionary in New France. Nicholas, the youngest son, became a lawyer. Of the only daughter of the Caveliers little is known. She was the wife of Nicholas Crevel, Counselor to the King and Master of Government Accounts in Rouen. The sons of both Nicholas and Madame Crevel would have roles in the dramatic life of their famous uncle Robert.

The Caveliers could well afford tutors for their young chil-dren, and they adopted this means of insuring themselves that their sons and daughter received thorough training and instruction, not only in the common subjects of reading, writing and ciphering, but in manners, social mores, and deportment. They were enlight-ened parents, fully appreciative of the advantages and opportunities education opened to young persons. The commerce of busy Rouen was the outside world of Jean Cavelier. Transactions in cloth and foodstuffs and chemicals and furnishings occupied his daily life and brought him wealth. But he did not permit the calloused practices of business to intrude upon the warm, congenial, and gentle atmosphere of his home. Similarly, Catherine Cavelier, a woman of refinement and graciousness, kept her mind, as she did the shutters of her fine old house, securely closed against bad taste, gaucherie and inelegance.

From the beginning of his life, La Salle knew the safety, comforts, and kindnesses to be found only in a well-ordered home occupied by persons of culture. Vulgarity, roistering, and undisguised wickedness existed about him in the brawling and filthy streets and slums of the ancient city, but his knowledge of them as a youth came from hearsay and not from personal experience.

If his father had entertained the hope that La Salle would, one day, assume the helm of the lucrative Cavelier enterprises, it was soon destroyed. La Salle would never be prejudiced against, nor even show a dislike for, the environment or the requisites one must accept in the world of commerce and trade. Indeed, he would demonstrate extraordinary business proclivities, and he would become one of the most shrewd and successful traders of New France. It was not that he did not care for a commercial career, but that he cared more for other things.

In his boyhood he was drawn toward books. The subjects for which he showed a preference were geography, history, and religion, in that order. His precociousness was probably best illustrated, however, in his natural gift for mathematics, which was revealed early in his youth. These inclinations and his obvious intellectual capacity led both his first teachers and his parents to feel certain that he was destined to become a lawyer or diplomat. This may have been a reasonable assumption, but La Salle soon left no doubt of its erroneousness.

He was fifteen years old when he was accepted in the school which the Jesuits conducted in Rouen. His choice of a college, while having the sanction of his mother and father, was his own, and he had good reasons for making it. Books, and probably more than any others the *Jesuit Relations*, had aroused in him a determination to embark as soon as possible on a life of adventure. But it was not at this time his ambition to become only an explorer. He wanted to be of service to others, to his church as well as his country. This desire reveals the influence which the stirring tales to be found in the *Relations* had upon him. They not only fired his blood but stimulated his religious zeal.

As a youth of fifteen he reasoned that through the Jesuits he could be certain to achieve his twin goals of adventure and worthy service to God, and he applied himself diligently to his studies. La Salle took the vows of the Society of Jesus at the age of sixteen. He was then studying at the Jesuit novitiate in La Flèche, to which he had been transferred shortly after entering the college at Rouen. The rapidity of his progress was so great that when he was eighteen he was adjudged qualified to teach and was sent to Alençon as an instructor of boys. Thereafter followed assignments in Tours and Blois.

If La Salle was qualified academically to teach, he was not a good teacher. During his tenures as an instructor it became plain that his strong will, his impatience, his independent nature, his energy, would never permit him to be successful as the master of dull-witted boys on the hard benches of a Jesuit classroom.

No one understood this better than La Salle himself. As the dreary months dragged on, teaching became intolerable to him. Considerable effort was expended by his superiors to bend him to accept the rigid rules and demands of the order, to no avail.

La Salle made several requests to be sent as a missionary to North America, but each was denied. Individuality of the kind that marked him had first to be destroyed before he could become acceptable for a wilderness mission, where little control over him could be exercised. Next, La Salle asked Jean Paul Oliva, the General of the Jesuit Order, to permit him to go to Portugal to undertake special studies in the exact sciences. This request also was refused.

In 1665, after nearly seven years of struggling against his own discontent and the rigid prescriptions of the Society of Jesus, La

Salle submitted his resignation. It was a step that only a fearless and determined young man would have taken. For he found himself suddenly penniless, without a career, without prospects of employment, and, in a manner of speaking, without the protection of a dependable roof.

His father had died, and the estate he left had been probated in a manner that placed La Salle in the position of a disinherited member of the Cavelier family. This situation, however, had not been the result of scheming by either of his brothers, his sister, his cousins, the Plets of Paris, or his uncle Henri, to cut him out of a share of the Cavelier money. It was brought about by the laws of France, and the oaths he had taken when he joined the Jesuits.

French statutes prohibited novices and priests who had sworn to adhere to ecclesiastical poverty from claiming an inheritance from one who died while they were members of a clerical order. The legal books had been closed on his father's estate before La Salle had shed his Jesuit habit, and neither his brother, Nicholas, nor his sister, having gained control of the family funds, was disposed to hand an equal share to him. The most they would do, since his mother had no legal authority in the matter, was to allow him a small sum amounting to four hundred dollars a year.

He might have gone to work in some mercantile establishment, perhaps even one of those owned by his uncle or his cousin, François Plet, but he was no more fitted for the unexciting life of a bourgeois merchant than he was for the narrow rigid life of a teacher in a Jesuit school. He would have been unable to contain himself for a moment selling cooking utensils, suitings, bed covers or ladies' apparel. He might have obtained a government post, but he shrank from the thought of such a dull existence.

La Salle saw no possible future for himself in France. With no more than a few hundred *livres* in his pocket, he sailed, in the spring of 1666, for Canada.

6 ⚜ ⚜ ⚜

NEITHER GOVERNOR COURCELLE nor Intendant Talon had met La Salle before he arrived in Quebec on a day late in May in 1669, but they were not unaware of his ambitions and his capabilities. This knowledge had been acquired through several different channels. They had obtained information about his qualities and his enterprise from the Abbé de Queylus. They had heard more about him from the Jesuits, and particularly from the Vicar-Apostolic, François Laval-Montmorency. The Jesuits had reasons, or thought they had them, to keep an eye on one who had taken their vows as a youth and had renounced them in favor of a wild life as an adventurer. And Courcelle and Talon had received news of him, probably in the form of complaints or warnings, from traders and other businessmen who knew him and who had been impressed, if not alarmed, by his perspicacity, volubility, and startling intentions.

Courcelle, who had been governor since 1665, was neither very shrewd nor very forceful in performing the administrative functions of his office. As a soldier, he was even less capable. He had arrived in Canada at a time when the menace of the Iroquois made mandatory an expedition against them. Courcelle had launched it with untrained troops to support a few Canadians experienced in fighting Indians in the dead of winter. Except for the fact that the Iroquois had been somewhat impressed by the show of power, it was a failure. Not until a larger force of well-disciplined and trained men, commanded by General Tracy, had waged a second campaign was the desired result, a treaty of peace, achieved.

Courcelle, however, was not altogether inept. He was smart enough to accept Talon's advice on fiscal and civil problems, and they were for a time a successful team. Differences over policies and the division of authority would lead them to a serious clash, but when La Salle came before them they were working for the most part in harmony.

Jean Talon was about forty years of age when the brilliant French administrator, Jean Baptiste Colbert, arranged to have a new post established for the government of New France, that of Intendant. Talon, who had already shown himself to be a man of rare competence while chief commissary of the French military and Intendant of the Province of Hainault, was selected for the important colonial position.

During his tenure in Canada—he would serve two terms there between 1665 and 1672—Talon would lay the stones of a solid economic foundation on which New France would build, prosper, and expand. He was not an aristocrat, not a soldier, not a lawyer, not a missionary, not an explorer. He was simply a good business-man. But he was also a man of vision and understanding. This unusual combination made him especially well fitted for his office. His loyalty to the empire, his compassion for the common people, and his determination to serve their best interests, were profound and without limit.

Bringing new settlers across the ocean, he well understood, was not in itself enough to develop the economy. Expansion itself was not enough. Sound money, good homes, opportunities for farmers, artisans, and merchants to progress and secure their families, good stores, good inns, a dependable food supply—not to mention an honest government—all were bricks which must be built into the colony's foundation, and, without all of them strongly cemented together weaknesses would develop which might well result in its collapse.

Courcelle and Talon listened courteously and attentively to the young man from the Seigneury St. Sulpice. They admired his forthright manner, his air of confidence, and his ability to present his case with clarity and conviction.

La Salle had among his natural gifts the instincts and thoroughness which a successful trial lawyer must possess, and long before he had completed the hundred and fifty mile trip to Quebec he had repeatedly rehearsed the arguments he would make. He delivered them in a calm and convincing manner that would have graced a diplomat *par excellence*.

The plan he wished to carry out was in no way grandiose. On the contrary, it was modest. But above all it was practicable. He asked permission to lead a small expedition to find the Ohio River, the river he believed ran to the western sea.

That was it.

The approval of both Courcelle and Talon was quickly obtained, but, as La Salle had anticipated, each had reservations.

Courcelle brought up the matter of an expedition the Sulpicians were organizing. It was their intention to send missionaries to the Northwest, among the Nipissings, the Shawnees, or tribes beyond these peoples which they had heard lived in unholy and unchristian darkness. It was the Governor's thought that the two expeditions might well be combined, and in that manner obtain protective strength which might be needed.

La Salle was well informed concerning the plans of the Sulpicians. They were jealous of the progress already made by the Jesuits in reaching the Indians of the Northwest and establishing missions among them. Only a single mission had been built by the Sulpicians. It stood at Quinte on the north shore of Lake Ontario. The ascendancy of the Jesuits to a position in which they were in virtual control of all soul-saving and other ecclesiastical matters, and in which they wielded a powerful influence over the Quebec government, had stirred in the Sulpicians a profound resentment, and they proposed to gain some ground for themselves.

La Salle shrewdly sensed that Courcelle had set his mind to effect the union. Mildly, he remarked that the homes of the Nipissings and the Northwest tribes were not exactly in the direction he proposed to take in his search for the Ohio.

Courcelle agreed. He had already thought of that, and he

would arrange with the Sulpicians to change their plans, so that they would go with La Salle to explore for the great river. Missions could wait. Territorial discoveries which might be of great value were more important, at the moment at least, to the colony.

Fearing that Courcelle might be deeply aggravated and might withdraw his approval if he voiced strong opposition to the amalgamation, La Salle reluctantly agreed to combine the expeditions.

Now the practical-minded Talon had something to say. Valuable as they might be, explorations cost money. To speak frankly, there was no assurance that in finding the Ohio River La Salle would do the colony a beneficial service. It was obviously very far away. And Indians, as La Salle well knew, had a habit of concocting tales they thought white men would enjoy hearing.

Moreover, Talon went on, for years stories had been heard about immensely rich copper mines which allegedly existed at the head of the Great Lakes. The previous year he had sent an expedition, led by a young man named Louis Joliet, in search of them. Joliet had not yet returned, and it was not known whether he had been successful in his quest. The treasury of the colony did not contain unlimited resources. In fact, the opposite was true. Talon was willing that La Salle should go to look for the great river, but he did not feel that he was justified in defraying with public money the costs of the expedition.

La Salle was ready for the contingency. He would pay the costs of his journey out of his own pocket.

He did not add that he was virtually penniless, having spent every *livre* he possessed in building and developing his seigneury. But neither did he reveal that he had a plan to meet the necessary expenses of his project.

Talon and Courcelle were both relieved and satisfied. The Governor signed letters patent authorizing the exploration.

La Salle and his crew wasted no time in setting their longboat against the spring flood of the St. Lawrence, on their way back to Montreal.

[26]

As soon as he arrived there, La Salle called on the Abbé de Queylus. In order that he might bear the cost of his expedition, he proposed that the Abbé buy back the seigneury which the Sulpician Seminary had so generously awarded him.

Not a little surprised, and even more disappointed, the Abbé demurred. He wanted to keep a brilliant young man like La Salle in Montreal. But, at last, swayed by La Salle's salesmanship, de Queylus agreed to authorize the Seminary to purchase a part of the seigneury. It was his private thought that if La Salle continued to own the major part of the property he would be certain to return to it.

Realizing that this was the best bargain he could obtain from the seminary, La Salle accepted it, and requested that instead of cash he be given equipment and merchandise. The amount to be paid by de Queylus under the agreement—certainly no less than one thousand *livres* and probably no more than fifteen hundred— was not enough for La Salle. He estimated that he would need three times that sum.

Promptly he went in search of a buyer for the remainder of his landholdings, and he found him in Jean Milot, a prosperous ironmonger, who paid him twenty-eight hundred *livres*.

Some of the Sulpicians, notably his brother, accused him of violating their trust, of dealing unfairly with them, and of forcing the seminary to buy back what had been given him for nothing. The charges were unjust. He had made no promise to hold the land for a specified period, no promise that he would not dispose of it. Moreover, de Queylus had taken back only a part of the seigneury, and the amount he had paid La Salle—in equipment and supplies—was much less than the value of the improvements which La Salle had made on the property. This was, incidentally, also true of the price Milot had paid for the part of the seigneury he purchased. The ironmonger had got a bargain.

But La Salle was not to be deterred by reproaches or criticisms reflecting upon his character. He felt that he had obtained

[27]

enough goods and money to enable him to start, and he was willing to face whatever end fate might have in store for him should they prove to be insufficient. He had no fear of failure or the future.

As the month of July began, both he and the Sulpicians were preparing their boats.

7 ✤ ✤ ✤

IT WOULD not have been in keeping with La Salle's nature to have participated passively in an exploit he did not completely control. To be the moved and not the mover, to share a command, to have his ideas and his orders subjected to opposition, especially from men motivated by prejudice and fanaticism, were conditions which profoundly irritated him. Had he been able to have found a means of preventing the merger of his expedition with that of the Sulpicians he most assuredly would have employed it.

His attitude was not a reflection of a personal dislike for any of the companions he was obliged to accept, for he had no such feeling. Perspicacity was an asset with which La Salle was abundantly blessed. He was making a voyage of discovery, with the correlative purpose of assessing trade possibilities. The Sulpicians would give first thought to soul-saving. However, having no alternative but to proceed as Courcelle and Talon had decreed, he made every effort to conceal his true feelings behind a mask of congeniality and the pretense of cooperation. He was not successful.

The leader of the Sulpician company was the priest, François Dollier de Casson, a man of gigantic stature and immense physical strength. He stood at least six inches over six feet, and with one arm easily could raise more than a hundred-weight above his head. Twenty-nine years old, he had been in New France only three years. His arrival in Quebec had preceded by only a week the

[28]

start of General Tracy's campaign against the Iroquois, and he volunteered at once to accompany it.

Dollier de Casson knew well the horrors of war. He had been a captain in the French cavalry, and he had served gallantly under Marshal Turenne. He had resigned his commission to become a priest with the hope that he could be of service to the victims of barbarous fighting. The Sulpician order, which he had joined in Nantes, considered him ideally fitted to serve as a missionary and sent him across the Atlantic.

A man of great courage, calm under fire, and capable of bearing patiently seemingly unendurable hardships, he had plunged into the American wilderness with the troops being sent against the Iroquois only a few days after he had first stepped ashore from France.

Dollier de Casson was no more pleased than La Salle by the request of Courcelle and Talon that the expeditions be combined, and that La Salle's quest in search of the Ohio be made the first order of business. His eyes burned with religious ardor when he thought of the great numbers of heathens to be converted in the northwest, but, like La Salle, he hesitated to register strenuous objections, and he, too, disguised his disappointment in outward amiability, displaying the attitude that he wished for nothing more than to assist in making the exploration successful. The Lord, he believed, would forgive his deception and be patient with him.

With Dollier de Casson would go Father René de Brehand de Galinée, skilled as a surveyor, and thought to be an accomplished observer. It was his duty to make a map of the expedition's route, and prepare a narrative of its accomplishments.

The Sulpicians had equipped three canoes and had engaged seven watermen, one of whom was a Dutchman who professed to speak Iroquois. The party of nine assembled at the Seigneury St. Sulpice, where La Salle was making his own preparations. He had purchased four canoes and had employed fourteen *couriers du bois*.

He also had arranged with several of the Seneca Iroquois who had spent the winter with him to serve as guides; they would travel in two of their own canoes.

The combined groups—twenty-three Frenchmen and French-Canadians, among them not a few who carried Indian blood in their veins, one Dutchman, and several Senecas—in nine heavily loaded canoes, pushed off from the shore of Lake St. Louis on the morning of July 6, 1669, and headed into the torrent of the mighty St. Lawrence.

For the remainder of the month they alternately fought the current and portaged around the innumerable rapids. It was a struggle which both astonished and appalled Galinée as he scribbled, often in pain and always in weariness, his daily notes.

The heat of August was upon the company by the time they emerged from the river and entered Lake Ontario. Now the first serious dissension between the Sulpicians and La Salle occurred. Dollier and Galinée proposed that they follow the north shore of the lake to the mission at Quinte and get advice from their brothers stationed there. La Salle flatly rejected the idea, pointing out that summer would soon be gone and there was no time to be lost in carrying out their primary objective. He announced that if Dollier and Galinée wished to go to Quinte, they would go alone, for he would engage their men. The priests capitulated, and the company moved on along the south shore of the lake.

Fortunately, it remained calm, and by August 9, they paddled into Irondequoit Bay. A large group of Senecas was encamped there, and they expressed great pleasure at seeing the white men and priests. All the visitors were invited to be guests in their main village, which they said was located only a day's journey to the south.

La Salle discovered that his knowledge of Iroquois dialects was insufficient to make himself fully understood by these Senecas. Moreover, the Dutchman whom the Sulpicians had engaged as an interpreter was unable to translate Iroquois—if he could understand it—into French. He knew only a few words of English, and no one could speak Flemish. The problem might have been solved if the Jesuit, Father Fremin, had been at his post, which was at the Seneca village, but at the time he was off in the woods on a religious mission.

However, through his Seneca friends who had come from St. Sulpice with him, and by the aid of gestures and stumbling translations, La Salle was able to explain the purpose of his journey. Most of all he wanted guides to lead him to the headwaters of the Ohio, and, being assured that they would be furnished to him, he accepted the invitation to visit the main village.

Intuitively, he was cautious, and took only Galinée and eight watermen with him. Dollier and the others were left to guard the canoes on the lake shore.

The village was reached after several hours of travel on August 12 through the lovely countryside just northwest of the beautiful Finger Lakes. It was a large settlement containing some hundred and fifty bark houses, and incomparably filthy. In the absence of Father Fremin, one of his Indian assistants agreed to serve as interpreter, but this arrangement brought little more success than the councils at the lake had produced.

After being welcomed by the Seneca leaders, the visitors were shown into a large house and told it was to be their quarters. Then followed a constant flow of gifts and feasts of dog and maize seasoned with nut and sunflower oils. As a grand gesture, the Senecas brought in a young man of eighteen or nineteen who had been captured in warfare against an enemy tribe. It was announced that for the special entertainment of the guests, he would be slowly tortured to death.

Galinée vigorously protested, and made an effort to purchase the captive, but the Senecas, appearing to be offended by the offer, proceeded with their program. The torture was carried on for six hours, while the villagers, men, women and children, danced about and yelled with glee. Red hot gun barrels were applied to the most sensitive parts of the victim's body, he was pelted with stones and coals, strips of flesh were torn from him, his eyes were gouged from his head, his testicles were cut out, his arms and legs were not only seared but broken. At last the body was torn apart, cut up, and the pieces of flesh passed about the throng and eaten with obvious enjoyment. After this horrible spectacle, the balance of the night was made a terror by Indians beating on the walls and roofs of the guests' lodge with sticks, assertedly to frighten away evil spirits.

La Salle soon understood that he had made a serious mistake in coming to the town. The evil spirits to be driven away were not of the supernatural world; they were the living people about him and his men. Through the servant of Father Fremin he learned that some of the Seneca leaders favored killing him in retaliation for the recent murder of a Seneca by three Montreal soldiers and the killing by three Frenchmen of several Oneida Iroquois in order to steal their furs.

The Senecas would furnish no guides to take La Salle to the Ohio. He began to suspect that their failure to abide by this promise was due, at least partially, to extraneous forces. Fremin appeared to have considerable influence with the Seneca leaders. His assistant seemed to be opposed to La Salle's going any farther to the south. Perhaps word had come to him from the Jesuit to block the advances by the Sulpicians. The assistant, as well as other Senecas, bluntly warned La Salle that if he went to the Ohio he and all his men would be killed by members of other tribes in that region. It was La Salle's conviction that the Senecas themselves, and not other Indians, would do the killing. Indeed, he had begun to fear that his death would occur before he could escape.

For four weeks, La Salle and the eight men with him were in the position of being captive guests, realizing that an attempt to break away might well result in disaster. During this time, he had come to know an Iroquois whose home was at Otinawatawa, a village near the head of Lake Ontario. The Ohio, this Indian maintained, could be more easily reached by striking south from Lake Erie. With this information in mind, La Salle informed the Senecas that he had changed his plans, and had abandoned all thought of traveling southward from their village. This seemed to placate them and to quell their talk of killing him. They released him, and he and his men hastened to rejoin their waiting companions.

8 ✤ ✤ ✤

THANKFUL TO be reunited after so many harrowing days, the entire company pushed off without further delay westward along the south shore of Lake Ontario. The Iroquois from Otinawatawa served as their guide. September was half gone when they crossed the mouth of the Niagara River. They could hear the distant roar of the great falls, but they did not stop to visit it.

On September 24, they reached Otinawatawa, which was located near the present Hamilton, Ontario. The information conveyed by the Iroquois in the Seneca village was confirmed by others there. La Salle's company was well received, and they sensed no danger from this band of Iroquois. Moreover, to demonstrate their good will toward the white men, they presented La Salle with a Shawnee captive. This man, said the Iroquois, was familiar with the route to the Ohio. His name was Nika.

It was a welcome turn of circumstances, and La Salle urged speed in departing. They were on the verge of leaving Otinawatawa when an event occurred which not only forced a change of plan but caused dissension which could not be resolved.

Out of the forest came two Frenchmen. The identity of one of them remains in doubt, but the other was a young man named Louis Joliet.

Like La Salle, Joliet, a native Canadian, had spent some time as a novice of the Jesuits. He, too, driven by an irrepressible urge for adventure, and an unconquerable desire to become an explorer, had abandoned his career as a priest. A man of extraordinary capability as a woodsman, pronounced intelligence, and uncommon courage, he had soon won a name as a *voyageur*. Talon had chosen him to investigate the reports that copper mines were to be found beyond Lake Superior. Joliet had not been successful in locating the deposits, largely because of Indian warfare then raging in the remote area. It was from this journey that he was returning.

The meeting with La Salle was an accident which would not have occurred under ordinary circumstances. Coming from Lake Erie, Joliet might have been expected to take the Niagara portage to Lake Ontario. He had, instead, followed the advice of his Indian guide, who feared that enemies might be encountered at the portage, and who had taken a more circuitous route up the Grand River and its tributaries to the westernmost shore of Lake Ontario. This trail had brought them to Otinawatawa.

Joliet had been in the region to which Dollier and Galinée had intended to go, and where they had hoped to establish a mission, before they had been induced to change their plan by Courcelle and Talon. He gave the Sulpician priests a copy of a map he had made, but, even more significant, he told them of large tribes beyond the inland seas, among them the powerful Potawatomis, who knew nothing of Christianity and who dwelt in heathenish darkness.

A light of exaltation shone in the eyes of the gigantic Dollier. He saw the meeting with Joliet as a manifestation of God's wish that they abandon the search for the Ohio and proceed to the northern lakes to minister to Indians so grievously in need of spiritual instruction.

Nothing La Salle could say would change Dollier's mind. If he proceeded at all, he and Galinée would go only one way, to the country of the fifth inland sea. La Salle argued that Jesuits were already there, that they had built missions in the area, and that they would not welcome the competition of the Sulpicians. His arguments were to no avail.

Then, declared La Salle, if Dollier would not listen to reason, he and Galinée must go alone, for none of the watermen could be induced to go with them, not being foolish enough to travel in a small group into such dangerous country, where, as Joliet had stated, tribal wars were raging.

La Salle was more optimistic than correct. Some men of each group did not care to go any way but toward the St. Lawrence. La Salle and Dollier made little effort to persuade them to stay, and they departed. How many left is not a matter of record, but, whatever their number, they reached Montreal late in November exhausted and half-starved, only to be severely denounced as deserters.

La Salle, however, had no desire to part with the Sulpicians on unfriendly terms, and he resorted to a stratagem to make it appear that even if he were to bow to the wishes of Dollier that the entire expedition point for Lake Superior, he would not be able to go. He feigned illness, complaining that he had contracted a fever. Under such conditions he would not wish to undertake a long and arduous journey. He would, after a short rest, have to return to Montreal.

This, of course, was not true. He had no intention of retreating a mile. He had invested every sou he possessed in the expedition to discover the Ohio. He had sold his seigneury. He would have arrived in Montreal penniless and homeless. Yet, even in the face of this unpleasant prospect, he might have turned back if he had believed the barriers ahead were insurmountable. He made no claim to infallibility in sensing danger, to an incomparable ability to judge and understand a situation. The truth was that he saw himself standing exactly where he had wanted to be, in full command of his own small company, obligated to give no consideration whatsoever to the wishes and opinions, and, least of all, the demands, of others. The odds against him were no greater than they had been at the beginning of the game.

As if he could see into La Salle's thoughts, Galinée bluntly rejected La Salle's protestations of illness, expressing the opinion that if any indisposition existed in him at all it had been caused by nothing more infectious than the sight of a rattlesnake on a rock adjacent to his path. Dollier, however, refused to think La Salle deceitful. Nor would he permit himself to indulge in prolonged arguments. The mountainous priest saw his own earthly path clearly illuminated by a heavenly light. He and Galinée would go on their way as the Lord had commanded, if necessary with no more than Indians to guide them.

Joliet and his companions vanished into the woods. Dollier said mass. The men received the sacrament. Then the two priests and their guide (or guides) pushed off on the Grand River, en route to Lake Erie.

La Salle and his men turned back along the south shore of Lake Ontario, not on their way home, but to find a river that would lead them southward to the Ohio.*

No document has been found to show the course La Salle

---

* Dollier and Galinée were forced by severe fall weather to establish a camp at Long Point, below Port Rowan, on Lake Erie. They spent the winter of 1669–70 there. In the spring they resumed their journey. At the western end of Lake Erie, they lost most of their equipment and their altar service in a storm. Having had all they wanted of the tempestuous Lake Erie, they elected to travel northward with the intention of falling in with the Ottawas, who each year went to Montreal with furs by a northern route. They passed through Lake St. Clair, camping where the city of Detroit would rise, and paddled along the eastern shore of Lake Huron to Georgian Bay. They passed inside Manitoulin Island, and, late in May, 1670, reached the Jesuit mission of Saint Marie du Saut at the entrance to Lake Superior. Glad to speed them on their homeward journey, the Jesuits furnished them a French *voyageur* as a guide. They reached Montreal on June 18, 1670.

took when he turned south from Lake Erie into a land completely unknown to white men. Traveling in light canoes, he and his company would have been able to ascend and descend small streams with comparative ease. But, if their route cannot be reported in detail, there can be no mistake about its ending. It took them, in the late fall of 1669, to the Beautiful River of the Senecas.

The Ohio had been found.

And it ran as the Senecas had told him it did: from the rising to the setting sun, through a land of great beauty and richness.

He floated down it, still filled with the dream of reaching the Vermilion Sea, but, as the year ended, his advance was interrupted by strong rapids. La Salle had reached the site of Louisville.

There his great dream was forever shattered. There his conviction that the Ohio reached the Vermilion Sea was forever destroyed.

Indians living in the vicinity left no doubt in him that only a short journey would be required to reach the place where the Ohio entered an even larger river.

The larger river came from the north, and Indians dwelling upon its banks called it Mississippi.

9 ✤ ✤ ✤

DESPITE THE disheartening disappointment, La Salle was eager to press on, but prevailing circumstances forced him to abandon the idea. Storms lashed the region, bringing snow and temperatures well below the freezing point. His men were stricken with fear at the thought of advancing farther into an unknown land under conditions that might prove to be as severe as those obtaining in the Valley of the St. Lawrence during the winter months. Most of them were simple men, not possessing inordinate bravery, not intrepid explorers, not seeking personal fame. Whatever discoveries might be made in a continuation of the expedition, they were aware they would receive none of the glory and none of the riches that might be acquired. They wanted only to turn back, to go home.

And go home they did. In a single night, all but one slipped away and disappeared. The one who remained was Nika, the Shawnee hunter.

La Salle understood that any attempt to descend the Ohio and the Mississippi with only a single companion upon whom he could depend would be worse than foolhardy. It would be suicidal. He was well versed in the history of the Spanish on the Mississippi. If the distance they had advanced up it remained indeterminate, the river itself had been marked on Spanish maps for a hundred and fifty years. As early as 1519, the daring Spanish navigator, Pineda, had noted the delta of an immense river while sailing along the coast of the Gulf of Mexico. A decade later, the little makeshift boats of Narvaez—one of whose lieutenants was Cabeza de Vaca—had fought their way in the same area through and around a torrent of fresh water coming from the north as they sailed to disaster on the coast of Texas.

The Spanish controlled the lower reaches of the Mississippi at least, if not a much longer part of its course, and the prospect of imprisonment and possible execution at their hands convinced La Salle of the wisdom of turning back.

One of the few records extant pertaining to this period of La Salle's adventures was prepared by the historian, Abbé Renadout. Several years later, after having talked with La Salle in France, he would write that, after encountering the rapids at Louisville, La Salle had disembarked and had "followed a plateau which might have led him far, and thereon met a few Indians. Far away yonder, they informed him—" below the falls and marshes "—the river would gather itself together again to form one stream. He then resumed his way, but so bereft of strength were the twenty-three or twenty-four men who had followed him thus far that they left him

during the night and fled to New Holland or New England. . . .
He was left in the great wilderness, some four hundred leagues distant from home. His courage did not fail him and he retraced his
way *up the stream*, deriving his subsistence from herbs, hunting, and
whatever was given him by Indians he encountered on the way."

"Twenty-three or twenty-four" men did not desert La Salle,
for there had been only twenty-one white watermen with the combined expeditions from the start, and some of them had returned
home from Lake Ontario. But whatever the number of the deserters
at the falls of the Ohio, except for the devoted and loyal Nika,
La Salle was alone.

The course he followed northward from the Ohio in the
winter of 1669–70 remains as much concealed from history as does
his route to the river from Lake Erie. No assertion was ever made,
either by him or by those in his confidence, that at that time he
descended the Ohio to its junction with the Mississippi.

The famed *voyageur*, Nicholas Perrot, one of the most competent and daring adventurers of early French Canada, would
record in his memoirs that he met La Salle on the Ottawa River
in the spring of 1670. La Salle, wrote Perrot, was in the company
of several Iroquois hunters.

In traveling from the falls of the Ohio to the Ottawa—the
shortest airline distance would have been considerably greater than
six hundred miles—La Salle could have followed several routes.
It would be illogical to suggest that he paddled across Lake Erie
in a canoe. But he could have ascended the Wabash and the
Tippicanoe and have portaged to a stream running into the Kankakee. This would have put him in touch with source waters of the
Illinois. Or he could have followed the Wabash to its uppermost
reaches, near Fort Wayne, and have made his way to the Maumee,
which enters Lake Erie at Toledo. It was asserted by some early
historians that La Salle did descend the Ohio as far as the Wabash
before turning back, but the contention lacks supporting evidence.

Further, from the Ohio he could have ascended either the

Miami, the Scioto, or the Muskingum, and traveled by various water courses and portages to the eastern end of Lake Erie, circled the western end of Lake Ontario, and continued by numerous routes, possibly through Lake Simcoe, to waters flowing to the Ottawa. He might have passed through the Straits of Detroit to Lake Huron, followed its eastern shore to Georgian Bay, ascended the French River, and portaged to the Ottawa. This was a route he had heard about from Joliet.

Whatever the case, La Salle was the first white man to see the Ohio, to break a trail between it and the Great Lakes. Therefore, he brought with him new geographical knowledge of the interior of the continent, of its great central rivers, of its inhabitants, its resources, and its climate to the civilized world.

He had, as well, demonstrated his boldness and his skill as an explorer. And he had traversed the great distance of his return journey with only a few Iroquois hunters with whom he had made friends.

When Perrot met him on the Ottawa River, La Salle was on his way to Montreal. With a considerable stock of furs to sell, he reached it in the late fall of 1670.

10 ✣ ✣ ✣

LA SALLE's travels in the region south of the Great Lakes had destroyed his last hope of discovering a water passage to the western sea, but they had awakened in him a completely new dream, a dream not only greater than any he had ever known but one which would consume him and direct the course he would follow to the end of his life.

The ideas and desires which burned in him involved a program so vast in scope, so daring in their conception, so promising in their potentialities, and yet so burdened with apparent liabilities, that they astounded and overwhelmed persons who heard of them. The complete proposal was beyond the conception of most of the colonials—common citizens, political incumbents, businessmen, and military officers—who were engaged in routine pursuits and always fearful of incurring the displeasure of either the Quebec or the home government.

It was after he had started back to Montreal from the Ohio that from La Salle's thoughts evolved the genesis of a scheme to build for France an impregnable empire in the interior of North America.

The simplicity of that description, however, does not in any manner indicate the ramifications, the complexities, the intricacies inherent in it, which revealed themselves as he gave it his continued consideration during the long winter of 1670–71. The more he studied its drawbacks and its advantages, its innumerable details and requisite procedures, the more he understood that the desirable state of completeness could never be achieved without further explorations.

The purpose of the new journeys would be to find the most feasible route from the Great Lakes to the Mississippi. The courses he had followed to and from the Ohio would not serve commercial traffic. Information he had obtained from Indians during the past year had convinced him that a much easier and more suitable route existed. Before anything else was done, it had to be located.

As soon as the St. Lawrence was open to boat travel in the spring of 1671, he went down the river to Quebec, and closeted himself with Talon.

In conferring with the astute and practical Intendant, La Salle took the stand that his plan was too big, too comprehensive, to be rushed into, and he made it plain that he had no intention of jeopardizing it with hasty or ill-considered moves. These were arguments that Talon no doubt considered most sensible. Certain projects should be undertaken before any conclusive step should be made, or even proposed to the French government. The first, of course, was an extensive journey to find a route over which canoes, or, better, larger craft, could be taken on commercial voyages. This accomplished, the way would be opened for development of the amazingly lucrative fur trade which could be organized in the interior regions, and which had not yet been thought of by traders. One of the most rewarding aspects of this trade would be in buffalo robes. Their great size and weight made it impossible to transport them in large numbers to the St. Lawrence, but this profitable commerce might be secured by carrying them down the Mississippi to deep-water vessels which would take them to Europe. Obviously, this involved negotiations with the Spanish, but La Salle held the view that this problem could be successfully resolved, possibly by the payment of an export tax.

When he talked of expansion of the French colonial empire and new and greater fur trade in the same breath, La Salle had in Talon an attentive audience. From the time he had taken office in Quebec, Talon had realized that the cornerstone of New France's economy consisted of two main components: fur trade and products manufactured from the skins. The frumpish minister, Colbert, who was never seen without a black bag full of financial statements and state papers, and whose power was surpassed only by that of Louis XIV himself, agreed with him, and had developed the program Talon had devised. The result was that French beaver hats were not only the best but were fashionable throughout the world. Leather made from Canadian deerskins in France was manufactured into shoes. Gowns and coats and other garments were trimmed with fur.

Talon's eyes, like La Salle's, were drawn toward the west for several reasons, all of which had a relationship to the fur trade. The Iroquois, who had always favored the English, had long intruded on the trade which the French conducted with tribes of the northwest. Indians dwelling in the region of Michilimackinac were obtaining English, as well as Dutch, goods from the Iroquois and trading them to tribes farther to the west, which white men had not yet reached. These activities Talon considered intolerable infringements upon French rights, and he wanted them stopped. With the hope of disrupting this traffic between the Iroquois and the northwestern Indians, Talon had sent commercial ambassadors and missionaries to the region.

But Talon understood that these measures, as successful as they had been, were not sufficient to bring domination of the Indian commerce, nor were they a means of securing the territory of French Canada from invasion by rivals. He had willingly approved La Salle's search for the Ohio, thinking then, as had La Salle, that a way might be found to the western sea. Now, like La Salle, he was convinced that such a passage did not exist. He gave him sanction for the additional explorations La Salle proposed, but that was as much as he felt himself in a position to do at the moment. He understood the need for caution on his part, sensing that a drastic policy involving extensive expansion might not meet with the approval of either Colbert or the King. There were indications that Colbert, especially, had begun to believe that French Canada already had been extended as far as was practicable. Too much territory might be annexed, more than France would be able to hold and defend. On the other hand, both Colbert and the King would like to keep the English east of the Appalachians.

Talon's immediate position was difficult, if not precarious. He had clashed seriously with Courcelle. The Governor's extreme conservatism interfered with policies he considered both wise and reasonable. Further, he had no way of anticipating what attitude Colbert would display toward any of the controversial issues.

Talon would have liked to give his unequivocal endorsement to any plan La Salle proposed. He had faith in La Salle's judgment, he admired his ambitions and his enterprise, and he was fully appreciative of what the discovery of an easy water route to the Mississippi would mean to French Canada. But he confined himself to approving another trip of investigation, and he declined, as he had previously done, to advance funds for the project.

La Salle returned to Montreal in the early summer of 1671, eager to start on his journey. Now he began to encounter the red tape, jealousy, resentment, and undisguised enmity that henceforth would plague him. His preparations were interrupted by squabbles with officials, by petty grievances, by the injection of inconsequential matters, by unfounded accusations that he intended to violate trade regulations and conduct business without being properly licensed and without official sanction.

Most of the complaints and the animosity displayed against him could be traced to other traders. They suspected that he had won concessions from Talon that would give him advantages they did not enjoy.

If the merchants and traders had no actual knowledge of La Salle's purpose in setting out for the west in late summer, they were very well aware of his capabilities and his ambitions to rise and prosper as a fur trader. For some time they had been faced with serious difficulties. It had long been their custom to buy furs in the Montreal market. Independent traders, *fermiers* who had opened wilderness posts, and unlicensed *couriers du bois*, had disrupted this system by obtaining furs directly from the Indians, transporting them to the St. Lawrence or the Hudson, and sending them illegally to Europe. Talon's colonization policies, they felt, were responsible for this situation.

La Salle's feats of discovery had impressed the Montreal traders not at all. What concerned them were reports that he had made friends with the Iroquois, and the Iroquois traded largely with the British, obtaining goods from British posts and introducing these into the far western commerce. If Talon was strongly opposed to this traffic, and wanted it halted, he appeared to be acting strangely, for he was sending a known friend of the Iroquois on a second western journey. Some scheme was afoot, and the Montrealers, many of whom had prospered during Talon's tenure, did not like the looks of things. La Salle had traveled with Iroquois trappers. He had brought furs they had taken for him to Montreal. It was not unreasonable to assume that he had sold others, with the aid of his Iroquois *engagés*, to the British.

La Salle himself had been too long away from France and too little in touch with affairs in Quebec to be familiar with the patterns of thinking prevalent in either place, and he was poorly advised about policies advocated by the King or by Colbert having to do with the future of French Canada. Talon was his only reliable source of information. But Talon himself was confused and frustrated to an extent that made vagueness on his part both unavoidable and excusable.

The fields of world politics and European intrigues and diplomacy remained to La Salle strange and remote realms of which he not only had little knowledge but in which, at the moment, he had little interest. Nor did he have the slightest expectation, as he prepared to depart for the wilderness, that before much time had elapsed he would become deeply involved in them. He knew only what he wanted to do, and he sensed that what he did would have a vital bearing not only upon his own career but upon the course of France in America.

La Salle possessed some money, but it was not enough to underwrite the entire cost of his expedition or the plans for trade he had in mind. He was still detained at Montreal in early August, 1671, for on the 6th he signed a note for a quantity of merchandise and other articles obtained on credit. The amount involved was 450 *livres*. The transaction was negotiated through Mignon de Branssac, fiscal attorney for the Seminary of St. Sulpice, "for his need and necessity." The Sulpicians could not have harbored much animosity for La Salle if they would lend him money. This is made all the more apparent by the fact that Dollier de Casson, who had left La Salle on Lake Ontario two years previously, had succeeded de Queylus as head of the seminary.

In August, La Salle, the Shawnee, Nika, and six or eight *couriers du bois* pushed their light canoes up the St. Lawrence. They crossed to Lake Erie, either by the Niagara portage or in the vicinity of it, and pushed steadily westward. La Salle would give the historian, Abbé Renadout, a verbal account of this journey several years later in France:

"I contrived to become acquainted with this gentleman [La Salle]," Renadout would write, "and to hold ten or twelve conferences with him, most of them in the presence of friends whose intelligence and memory were of the highest order." Renaudot maintained that he made notes during these conferences, and jotted down dates and geographical names, so that they would be accurate and not forgotten.

From Lake Erie, said Renadout, La Salle passed through Lake St. Clair, "entered the Soft Water Sea, rounded the strip of land which divides that sea into two portions, proceeding from north to south, left to the west the Baie des Puants, and finally explored another infinitely larger bay, at the western end of which he came upon a very beautiful haven and a river flowing from east to west."

The "Soft Water Sea" was Lake Huron. Renadout applies the name to both Lakes Huron and Michigan, thinking them one, but he speaks of La Salle rounding the "strip of land" which divided "that Sea in two portions." This was the Straits of Mackinac. La Salle had followed the western shore of Lake Huron, passed through the straits, and traveled along the western shore of Lake Michigan, leaving Green Bay to his west. This was water and this was country no white man had ever seen.

The "infinitely larger bay" was not a bay at all. It was the rounded southern end of Lake Michigan. And Renadout's *très-beau havre* was the entrance to the Chicago River. The Chicago then flowed into Lake Michigan. From it the Des Plaines River could be reached by an easy portage. And the water of the Des

[46]

Plaines was contributed to the Illinois River, the river "flowing from east to west."

And, wrote Renadout, La Salle had gone down the Illinois to the thirty-ninth degree of latitude "or thereabouts, when he came upon another stream which, after joining the first, flowed from northwest to southeast."

La Salle had reached the Mississippi River.

II ✤ ✤ ✤

TO THE Mississippi La Salle gave the name Rivière Colbert, not without a design in mind that involved more than an altruistic desire to honor a distinguished statesman.

Abbé Renadout's statement that the Mississippi flowed "from the northwest to the southeast" is important in the recounting of La Salle's achievement. Renaudot had never been to America, and his knowledge of its geography, especially that of the interior, was extremely slight.

Only a person who had actually been to the confluence of the Mississippi and the Illinois could know that at this point in its course the Mississippi did, indeed, make a sweeping turn and flow for a short distance from the northwest to the southeast.

Renadout declared that La Salle told him he had followed the Mississippi downstream to the thirty-sixth degree of latitude, "where he deemed it wise to cease proceeding onwards, satisfied with the well-nigh certain hope of some day reaching the Gulf of Mexico by following the course of that stream and reluctant to imperil an enterprise wherein he might encounter obstacles which would prove insurmountable to the forces at his disposal."

The "obstacles" which La Salle feared were the Spanish. He might, indeed, have imperiled not only himself and his companions by continuing, but also the grand plan that was then taking shape in his mind.

At latitude thirty-six La Salle would have touched the northern border of Tennessee and the easternmost part of the northern border of Arkansas.

La Salle had reached the Mississippi in the winter of 1671–72, about eighteen months before Louis Joliet and Père Marquette pushed their canoes into the Father of Waters from the Wisconsin. Marquette and Joliet found the Mississippi north of where La Salle entered it. They went farther down the river by some three degrees than he had gone. But they were not the discoverers of it, a claim the Jesuits would make in propaganda designed to discredit La Salle.

On his way back to Canada in the spring of 1672, La Salle ascended the Illinois, but he did not take the portage from the Des Plaines to the Chicago. Instead, he turned up the Kankakee—apparently he had learned of this route from Indians—on it crossed northern Indiana, portaged to the St. Joseph River, which he called the River of the Miamis, in the vicinity of South Bend and descended it to Lake Michigan.

This was a longer route than that by way of the Chicago portage, but La Salle found it preferable. He would use it again, and he would erect a fort at the mouth of the St. Joseph. These factors add credence to the statements of Renaudot. In his later journeys La Salle would not have pointed for his River of the Miamis if he had not known from personal observation that the St. Joseph-Kankakee was a more practicable route in traveling from Lake Michigan to the Illinois valley than by way of the Chicago and the Des Plaines. The choice would not have been made simply on the basis of hearsay.

Joliet would credit La Salle with the exploration of the Ohio, but not the discovery of the Mississippi. He would draw two maps of the Great Lakes–Mississippi region, on both delineating the Ohio. On one, over the Ohio's course, he would write: *"Route du sieur de la Salle pour aller dans le Mexique.*" And on the other would be the words: "*Rivière par où déscendit le sieur de la Salle au sortir du lac Erie pour aller dans le Mexique.*"

A third map of the time, however, in the possession of the Jesuits, and drawn a year before the journey of Marquette and Joliet, would trace the Ohio to a point below the falls at Louisville, and would bear an inscription crediting La Salle with descending it. And on this map would be a portion of the Illinois River!

The importance of this bit of cartography is obvious. The location of the Illinois was not known until La Salle found it.

Except in his conversations with Renadout, La Salle would make no public claim to being the discoverer of the Mississippi. He had compelling reasons to hold his tongue in this respect, and they soon become apparent in the light of his subsequent actions. The discovery, had he proclaimed it at the time to the world, would have brought notoriety. It also would have brought unwanted expeditions into the Illinois and Mississippi valleys, and the establishment of trading posts by competitors.

La Salle had his plans, and he reasoned that if he were successful in carrying them out he would receive not only fame and glory as an empire builder but he would acquire immense wealth. He had observed the resources of the interior, and he had found them to be beyond his greatest hopes. He had found deep-water rivers which ran to the sea. Large vessels and barges could travel on them, carrying enormous cargoes of furs and buffalo robes and deerskins and other products. A few forts placed at strategic sites could control this vast network of navigable waterways and hold it for France. But not only for France. For himself.

Settlements would be founded, and agriculture would become an important part of the foundation upon which the greater interior empire would be constructed. Civilization would come to the land, and the Indian peoples as well as the white settlers would benefit and prosper. Above all would fly the flag of his beloved France, and neither the English, the Spanish, nor the Jesuits would conquer one of the richest and loveliest lands on earth. The English would be held east of the Appalachians. The Spanish would be contained in Mexico. The Jesuits would be confined where they were, in the forests of the north. Military installations on the Great Lakes and on the Mississippi, if not at its mouth, would insure the impregnability of France in the vast region.

He would open the gate. He would lead both his country and civilization into this fabulous land.

Yet, he understood that to achieve even a part of his great scheme, to fulfill even a small portion of it, he must travel a difficult road. He could not accomplish anything alone. He must have France behind him, fully in accord with his most extreme ideas, and ready to support them with money, men, and materials.

12 ❧❧❧

AS HE again descended the St. Lawrence in the late fall of 1672, La Salle was filled with misgiving and apprehension. Both Courcelle and Talon had been recalled. A new Governor had taken office in Quebec, a man, it was said, of great administrative ability and social distinction, famed as a soldier, and very much admired by noble personages who held the confidence of Louis XIV.

These reputed qualifications meant little to La Salle. Good manners, a charming personality, and an admirable European military record that might endear him to members of the French Court and win the respect of the King could very well be of no advantage at all in the crude environment of the colonial capital. They might even be detrimental in dealing with fur traders, Indian chiefs, and rough frontier characters, and serve him to no good purpose in meeting the demands and solving the problems of the wilderness colony.

The new Governor was Louis de Baude, Comte de Frontenac,

and La Salle was not long in Quebec before he understood that he need not have been concerned about him.

The physical appearances, characters, motivations, and attitudes toward life of Frontenac and La Salle were in sharp contrast in numerous respects, yet no two men brought together under the same circumstances could have enjoyed greater harmony nor have displayed more equally an unqualified respect and esteem for each other.

Frontenac was fifty-two, La Salle was twenty-nine.

The Governor's hair was gray and thin, and in public appearances he wore a well-curled wig. He was at all times impeccably dressed, favoring scarlet silk linings, figured woolens and linens of various rich shades, plumed hats, military uniforms ablaze with gold and silver decorations, shiny leather boots, and fine leather shoes. He was courtly, gracious, and amiable, but he could in the twinkling of an eye become irascible, cold, and menacing. His years of dissipation were recounted in the lines of his face; he loved fine wines and old brandy, but he was even more devoted to bed-chamber pastimes with women who attracted him, and he was easily aroused by a good figure or a pretty face.

La Salle was swarthy from long exposure to wilderness suns and winds. Physical strength and agility seemed to exude from him. His hair was intensely black and thick against his neck. If he had ever owned a wig, he had long since lost it, and certainly it would have been a hindrance. La Salle's clothes were those of the colonial burgher and the explorer, rough woolens and denims and buck-skins and stout boots or moccasins. He was reserved, calm, quiet-voiced. He had no time for small talk, and if women stirred his passion he confined the matter to his own thoughts. There was no coarseness in either his actions or his manners, but it was apparent that social amenities and the frivolities and pleasant patter of a salon or soirée were not matters to which he gave even casual attention. Talking business, plowing straight to the heart of a question, formulating courses of action, were *divertissements* to him.

Yet, as different as they were in so many ways, Frontenac and La Salle had much in common. Both were bold, willing to take chances, and ambitious to make money. Indeed, both of them badly needed money. Both disliked the Jesuits, not as men of God, but for their trespassing on legal and administrative realms which were properly none of their business, and for their attempts to dictate the policies by which the colony would be governed. Both Frontenac and La Salle held the conviction that the conditions which the Jesuits wished to impose upon New France would result in economic stagnation.

The impecuniousness of the two men had not been caused by events or circumstances of similar nature. Frontenac was ostentatious, spent his money lavishly and foolishly, and had always lived far beyond his means. La Salle had never had money to waste. The little he possessed had come from sales of the furs he had been able to acquire on his journeys. But he was rich in hopes and his confidence that fortune would come to him was without limit.

Frontenac's extravagance had got him into pits of trouble from which he had been able to escape only with the greatest difficulty. His meager salary of eight thousand *livres* a year as Governor was far from sufficient to support him in the manner he desired. He had accepted the post simply because he had had no choice. He was down to his last sou, and he could not keep up the appearances required to maintain his social position and his rank.

If Louis XIV had any fondness or admiration for Frontenac, it was not enough to keep him from being anxious to get the count as far away from Versailles as possible. Both were renowned lovers, and there had been reports that relations between them had become strained because of the attentions each had paid to the same women. With the excuse that Frontenac must make a good first impression on the residents of New France and a proper entrance at Quebec, the King had assisted him with six thousand *livres* for his personal equipage and raiment and had furnished him with a bodyguard of twenty horsemen.

Frontenac had not been long in Quebec before he began to believe that the post would, after all, prove to be lucrative. After he had come to know La Salle he was convinced that this would be the case. No more than a few private conversations on long winter nights in Quebec with the intrepid, shrewd, and dynamic young explorer were necessary to make him feel fully assured that opportunities to get rich in the North American wilderness were open before him. He did not propose to let them escape.

If Frontenac had a number of pronounced attributes, none was the equal of his ability to inspire the common people. He was haughty, arrogant, imperious, and unyielding—qualities that might have been least expected in a man who seemed to have the faculty of looking into the hearts and minds of citizens of any level. He could stubbornly refuse to yield any of his prerogatives, he could criticize and threaten, denounce and condemn the men about him and the policies they advocated, but at the same time he could hold their respect. He seemed to know how far he could safely go in any conflict or argument or debate, as if some signal had flashed to warn him of the proper place to stop.

He was an orator, a showman, a diplomat, and a schemer. To him the grand plan of expansion and economic development which La Salle presented was more than a potential means of getting rich. It contained excitement and drama that he craved. It was a program with which he could serve both the colony and himself. It was empire building, and he believed, as La Salle did, that it would make France impregnable in the New World. Also, it could, if he handled it wisely, bring him greater fame and glory than he had ever enjoyed. His name would stand as the rock of the Fortress Quebec in the annals of France, indestructible and ever-lasting.

Frontenac did not hesitate to enter into an alliance with La

Salle. He admired La Salle's determination, his impatience to proceed, his unwillingness to let any obstacle stand in his way. The spring of 1673 had not arrived before he had formulated with La Salle a drastic course of action on which they would launch themselves as soon as the rivers of the frozen wilderness were again open to travel.

Frontenac accepted La Salle's advice, and agreed to follow the steps he proposed. The first was to build a fort on Lake Ontario. It was La Salle's belief that a strong military establishment in this location would serve to check the trading activities of the Iroquois, and would intercept the fur trade being carried on between the tribes of the Great Lakes and the Dutch and English on the Hudson and in other areas of New York. Force of arms could be used to turn this trade into the St. Lawrence valley, to Montreal and Quebec.

Furs passing through this station also would bring large profits to those who controlled it. Frontenac did not, of course, mention this aspect of the project in revealing his intentions. He spoke glowingly of the plan as a development for the good of the colony, stressing that it would provide badly needed military protection against attacks from either the Iroquois or the English.

The fur merchants of Montreal, however, were not stupid, and some of them were as shrewd as Frontenac. They let it be known to him that they were opposed to the fort, and they did not hesitate in voicing their distrust of his motives.

Frontenac ignored them, and sent La Salle to Onondaga to invite all the chiefs of the Five Nations to a council at the Bay of Quinte on Lake Ontario.

After he had left Quebec, La Salle sent the Governor a map he had prepared. On it he indicated that he thought the mouth of the Cataraqui (Kingston, Ontario) was the most desirable place for the fort. Here the St. Lawrence was born, in the innumerable channels between the Thousand Islands. It was La Salle's opinion that from the site not only the entrance to the St. Lawrence could be easily controlled but the entire eastern end of Lake Ontario. And directly south of the lake was the main route from the west and northwest to the Iroquois country of New York and Albany on the Hudson.

From a military standpoint, Cataraqui was an excellent location. For the purpose of disrupting the fur trade traffic between western Indians and the British and Dutch it was a most practicable site. Studying La Salle's map, Frontenac was quickly aware that a fort at Cataraqui would superbly meet both the main requirements of their grand plan's initial phase. He could propagandize the military establishment as a badly needed defense outpost for the colony. A tribute could be exacted from the commerce passing through the area.

He dispatched a messenger to La Salle with an order directing him to change the site of the council with the Iroquois sachems from the Bay of Quinte to Cataraqui.

La Salle circulated among the Iroquois the invitation to the council. The responses he received were not encouraging. If the new French Governor desired to smoke with them, said the Iroquois chiefs, let him come to their villages. La Salle quickly advised Frontenac of the reaction, and a reply was immediately forthcoming from the Governor.

It was for the father, Frontenac said firmly, to tell the children where to hold council. He would never go to them.

The Iroquois capitulated.

Frontenac had neither the money nor the authority to stage the extravaganza he and La Salle had planned. It was their intention to overwhelm the Iroquois with impressive and frightening displays of colorful pageantry and armed strength.

The course a colonial governor would customarily have followed would have been to request official sanction for such an enterprise from Versailles, and to delay it until the approval had been obtained. It was not because this procedure would have forced postponement of the tour for a year that Frontenac did not follow it. He suspected that neither the ministers at Versailles nor the King himself would approve the idea, but would consider it politically unwise, if not an advance that would be misconstrued by other European nations as an outright act of aggression. Frontenac was taking no chances on having his schemes thwarted. Versailles would learn of the event as a *fait accompli*.

As to paying the costs of his expedition, Frontenac employed force which he euphemistically termed "making use of address." This meant royal authority. He simply ordered the burghers of Quebec, Three Rivers, Montreal, and smaller places to produce the necessary funds, equipment, food, munitions, and canoes, and to supply a sufficient force of armed men to accompany him. The garrison of the Castle of St. Louis was no problem. He could command it to make the trip, but Frontenac, always with an eye to good public relations, also invited all ex-officers who were settled in New France to participate in the affair. It was a clever move, for it brought many of the most prominent citizens of the colony into the picture.

The Jesuits were furious. Opposed to the building of forts and to opening the Great Lakes country to settlements, they sought to block Frontenac with every means at their command. It was their dream to create in the wilderness of North America another Paraguay in which all Indians were converted to the faith, all peaceful and industrious, all commerce and military defenses and civil functions controlled by missionaries, all proceeds to be devoted to the building of churches and schools, all white men who did not wear the cloth or serve the Order to be prevented from entering the sublime and perfect realm of God.

In their efforts to block Frontenac, besides attempting to discredit his motives, they spread a false report that a Dutch fleet of warships had captured Boston, and that a Dutch army was advancing westward for the purpose of conquering New France. Frontenac, they declared, would do better to make preparations to save the colony than to go off gallivanting about the woods to show off his uniforms.

It was Frontenac's retort that the Jesuits wanted to dominate the fur trade only to enrich their own coffers.

Actually, the Jesuits were aiming their fire as much at La Salle as at the Governor. Not only was he a fur trader, but he had accomplished great feats of exploration, and he had designs upon opening the western woodlands and prairies to settlement, building strong defenses, creating a great French interior empire. These dreams and schemes made him truly their greatest rival. If he were successful, they warned, the Indians would be perverted and become slaves of unholy white merchants and unscrupulous traders. The resources that properly belonged to the natives would be stolen from them, and they would be degraded and ruined. Any hope of winning them to the banner of Christianity would be vain.

Riding roughshod over his opposition, Frontenac proceeded with his plan. He departed from Quebec on June 3, 1673, riding in royal splendor in a large canoe, about him other canoes occupied by his staff, a large military escort, and swarms of watermen. At every settlement along the river, he was welcomed with a salute. He advanced leisurely, taking two weeks to reach Montreal.

There the local governor, François Perrot, appointed by the Sulpicians who controlled the island, waited to receive him on the shore with the entire populace and the settlement's garrison. A thunderous salute was fired as Frontenac, splendidly arrayed in his most colorful raiment, emerged from his boat. A procession was formed, and everyone present solemnly marched up the hill to the seminary church, which towered above all. After services, Frontenac was escorted to quarters which had been prepared for him in the fort.

His stay in Montreal was not altogether pleasant. He insisted on arranging himself every detail of his wilderness march, and he ran into dissension, questions of precedence, and matters of protocol.

The old officers, some of whom had served in famous regiments and had been decorated, demanded special favors. Arguments arose between others over who would ride with whom. Jesuits harassed him, and prominent businessmen sought to gain private audiences with him and to be taken into his confidence. Boatmen, Indians, and troops had to be marshalled and organized into companies, assigned their respective duties. Frontenac went at the task in the manner of a commander, which he was, preparing for a military offensive.

Equipment, boats, canoes, supplies, and gifts for the Iroquois were assembled at La Salle's old seigneury, now called "La Chine." It was June 28 before Frontenac was satisfied that all preparations were complete and satisfactory and that a start could be made.

The current and rapids of the St. Lawrence soon made the travelers forget other problems. This great natural force was a formidable leveling power in that it placed everyone on the same footing, and drove complaints and jealousies and conflicts of personalities from the thoughts of the men struggling against it. Citizens, soldiers, Indians, *couriers du bois,* and staff members carried canoes and worked together to drag flatboats over portages and through roaring cold white waters. Wet, numbed, cut and bruised, hungry and wearied to the point of exhaustion, they thought more of staying alive than of engaging in petty quarrels.

Frontenac did not spare himself. He plunged through the frothing swift torrents to lend a hand to boatmen and Indians. When rains fell he rushed from his shelter, ignoring the downpour, to see that food supplies and the gifts for the chiefs were properly protected. He displayed a spirit and a leadership that won the admiration of the redmen, the human beavers, and the soldiers of the ranks.

With the passage of a fortnight, the hardship ended at the beautiful channels of the Thousand Islands, and the immense blue expanse of Lake Ontario soon thereafter spread out before them.

[58]

13 ✤✤✤

NO MORE imposing, colorful, or powerful array of watercraft and men had ever been seen in the northern wilderness than the expedition of Frontenac as it approached Cataraqui on a mid-July day of the year 1673. Every instinct for showmanship which Frontenac possessed was unleashed. This was his day, the day on which he would make his appearance in the leading role of the drama he and La Salle had thoughtfully prepared.

As he approached his destination, Frontenac arranged his forces in divisions. In the lead were four squadrons of canoes carrying *couriers du bois* chanting and singing, inspired to exuberance by extra rations of liquid spirits. Next came two flatbarges mounting cannon and heavily loaded with equipment and tools which had been brought along for a special purpose. These were followed by the large canoes in which rode Frontenac, his guards, and his staff, and the gentlemen and ex-officers who had been invited to participate in the journey. Next came the troops, their guns held in plain view, and at the rear were more noisy woodsmen. From every craft flags and pennants whipped in the brisk breeze coming down the river. Breastplates and swords glistened in the bright sunlight. Plumes waved, and doublets and cloaks and rough woodland garb splashed innumerable colors over the nautical parade.

On the shore, where the city of Kingston would rise, the Iroquois waited in silence, unmistakably awed by the splendor of the spectacle. La Salle had performed his job well. He had brought to Cataraqui some three score of the highest chiefs and headmen of the Mohawks, Oneidas, Onondagas, Cayugas, and Senecas. Surrounded by their own contingents of warrior-guards, their wives and children, they watched in unconcealed astonishment as the Frenchmen, all working as if they had rehearsed many times their respective duties, pitched tents, built fires, stored their supplies and equipment in an orderly manner, posted guards, and prepared a repast.

Frontenac acted as if he were unaware of the presence of the Indians. This attitude was also part of the prearranged plan to stage an unprecedented display which would leave no doubt in the Iroquois of the strength, magnificence, and resources of the French.

The fires of peoples of two worlds burned bright caverns through the summer night. Suddenly in the dawn the quietness was shattered by the roll of drums. The next act of the drama began to unfold, and it was from the beginning sheer magic in the eyes of the Iroquois. Sailcloth was stretched before the Governor's immense tent. The chiefs were invited to assemble upon it. They came, squatting in semicircles, smoking their pipes with an air of gravity. Shortly thereafter, Frontenac, moving slowly and with dignity, sober of mien, impressive and grand in a long scarlet robe, gold cords, fine leather boots, and sparkling decorations, made his entrance, and took the chair which had been placed so that he would look down at the Iroquois leaders sitting on the sailcloth. La Salle and the staff officers took places behind him.

The calumet, the pipe of peace, was passed from hand to hand, and when each of the deputies had drawn smoke from it, a high chief, Garakontie, rose and formally and cordially welcomed to the land of the Five Nations, Onontio, the great Governor of French Canada.

Frontenac replied, startling the Iroquois by addressing them as "my children." Never before had they been called by white men anything but "brothers."

Frontenac could be arrogant without exciting anger, and the resentment which some of the chiefs registered at being greeted as "children" soon disappeared as he continued his opening remarks.

He talked in a straightforward manner which his listeners liked. His words seemed to come from his heart.

"You have done well, my children, to obey the command of your father. Take courage: you will hear his word, which is full of peace and tenderness. For do not think I have come for war. My mind is full of peace."

Before the speeches were concluded a disturbing commotion arose nearby. Men were drawing lines on the earth, cutting trees, stripping logs, digging ditches. Frontenac saw to his satisfaction that the attention of the council members was being attracted to this activity. Abruptly, he terminated the meeting, presenting the chiefs with six packets of tobacco, and again disappeared into his pavilion.

Now the Iroquois had full opportunity to observe what to them was no less than a miracle. As they stared in complete amazement, a fort began to rise before them. Palisades, living quarters, moats, storehouses, bastions took shape under the application of magic tools in the hands of the French workers, each of whom seemed to know exactly what he was to do and lost not a moment in doing it. They had never seen anything like it, and they shook their heads in wonder at the genius of the French.

For three more days the meeting continued. La Salle remained in the background, letting Frontenac do all the talking. And Frontenac demonstrated his astuteness and his ability as a politician. He invited chiefs to his table at each meal. He walked through the Iroquois camp, fondling children and dropping sweetmeats into the hands of women. And one evening he gave all the squaws a special feast and, in turn, they entertained him with a dance.

The fort was almost finished, and riflemen stood at firing positions, when Frontenac held his final meeting with the chiefs. Now there was a tone of warning in his voice, an unmistakable threat in his words. "If your father," he told the chiefs, "can come so far, with so great a force, through such dangerous rapids, merely to make you a visit of pleasure and friendship, what would he do, if you should awaken his anger, and made it necessary to punish his disobedient children? He is the arbiter of peace and war. Beware how you offend him!"

Now Frontenac suavely served the lean meat of the roast he and La Salle had cooked. The fort, he told the Iroquois, had not been built in the expectation that it would be used in armed conflict. Not at all. It was to serve as headquarters of a peaceful commerce which he felt certain would be mutually beneficial to both the French and the Indians. It would be a "great storehouse"—a ridiculous euphemism in the light of his true designs—containing all manner of goods, everything of which they might have need.

As they could well see, the storehouse would stand in a location especially advantageous to the western tribes of the Iroquois alliance, but it also would relieve Iroquois hunters and traders bringing furs from the northwest of the long and arduous journey to the posts of the British on the Hudson.

Bluntly he cautioned the chiefs against listening to the voices of "bad men" who were the enemies of both themselves and the French.

"Give heed," he admonished them, "to men of character, like the Sieur de La Salle."

An aged, half-naked delegate arose and was recognized. "All this is good," he said, "and your plans are welcome news to our ears, but you have neglected an important point. You have not told us what prices will be charged for the goods here, and what prices will be paid for our furs."

Frontenac and La Salle had anticipated the question, and had agreed on an equivocal response to it. Prices, the Governor declared, would be as low as possible. He assured the chiefs that the French had no wish to gouge the Iroquois or anyone else, but it should not be forgotten that the cost of transporting merchandise to Cataraqui was high and the deed time-consuming and accomplishable only under difficult conditions.

The Governor did not disclose that at the time goods to supply the "great storehouse" were being brought up the St. Lawrence in a convoy of cargo canoes in charge of two experienced clerks La Salle had engaged. He and La Salle had seen the possibility of gaining a distinct advantage by withholding the information. Word that the doors of Fort Frontenac had been opened for trade would rapidly spread. Curiosity, if nothing else, would bring Indians to its counters, where they would be happy to learn that prices were competitive with those in the posts of Montreal and on the Hudson. In turn, this good news would be disseminated by pleased customers, with results not unbeneficial to business.

It was unlikely that the Governor was surprised when La Salle proposed Fort Frontenac as a most appropriate name for the establishment. He graciously and appreciatively accepted the honor, and the christening ceremony was held. Nor in all probability was anyone astonished when he announced that La Salle would be in overall command.

A small garrison of soldiers was assigned to protect Fort Frontenac through the winter. The Governor permitted the remainder of his military force and his civilian guests to leave in detachments, seeing nothing to be gained by holding everyone together for a homebound parade. The Iroquois, with friendly signs and cries of farewell, vanished into the wilderness, their canoes low in the water under the burdens of chiefs, warriors, squaws, children, weapons, gifts, household articles, and other baggage.

La Salle and Frontenac, accompanied by the Governor's personal guard, started leisurely down the St. Lawrence. They had not gone far when they met the cargo convoy. After a conference with the clerks, they proceeded onward down the magnificent river in the warm pleasant days of late July.

14 ❧❧❧

IN THE bistros of New France, in the homes of farmers and laborers and clerks, in the small shops, Frontenac received unreserved praise for his successful negotiations with the Iroquois. The workers and inhabitants of these unprepossessing places found indescribable relief in the belief that they could go to bed without the haunting fear that they and their families would be murdered before morning by the vicious and bloodthirsty warriors of the Five Nations.

The same gratefulness was expressed in the large mercantile establishments of Montreal and Quebec, as well as in the fine homes which stood upon the heights that overlooked each city, but in these affluent environments it usually was accompanied by angry denunciation of the characters of both the Governor and his shrewd lieutenant and blasphemous outcry against the underlying motives which had impelled them on their extravagant mission to Cataraqui.

The leading merchants and traders, the men who held government licenses to engage in the fur trade, and who, therefore, were subject to royal decrees applicable to the industry, understood clearly that, by establishing a post on Lake Ontario, Frontenac and La Salle had put themselves in a position not only to secure an immense part of the Iroquois trade but to intercept furs which under normal conditions would have come down the St. Lawrence.

For years the Montreal and Quebec merchants had railed against the illegal trading of *couriers du bois* and *fermiers* in the northwest who, operating without licenses or the most common commercial scruples, sent their furs, either through Iroquois middlemen or directly, to the British posts on the Hudson and elsewhere south of the St. Lawrence Valley. Now their own Governor was supporting the shrewd La Salle in a scheme to gain a monopoly of this illicit traffic as well as the legal traffic upon which they depended for their existence.

They gave voice to their charges in meetings and in appeals made before the colonial counsellors. Some of them, believing that objections brought through these channels were a waste of time, wrote strong letters of protest to Colbert in France. In them they charged that if Frontenac and La Salle controlled the trade, prices in Montreal and Quebec would be forced down until no profit was possible. They accused La Salle of setting up an organization through which he could carry on illegal commerce with the English, with encouraging the Iroquois to increase their trade with western Indians, with inviting the renegade *couriers du bois* to bring their furs to his post, with inciting the Iroquois to war upon tribes which refused to cooperate with them.

If the distressed merchants could have looked into La Salle's mind, they would have known that he had given no thought whatsoever to dealing in any manner with the British. In the light of his plans, it was a ridiculous accusation. Nor was he stupid enough to incite Indians to perform acts of aggression. Tribal warfare to the west of Fort Frontenac would have disrupted the flow of pelts he expected from that direction. Every effort he would make would be undertaken with the hope of preventing conflict and establishing peaceful relationships. To this end, he would, of course, encourage the Iroquois to increase their trade not only with western peoples but also with those to the south, along the Ohio, the Illinois, and the Mississippi. But he, perhaps better than any other man, was aware of the difficulties involved in such a program. War was a way of life to the Iroquois. Conquest was in their blood. And few fighters of other tribes were endowed with the skill, the cunning and intrepidity of the warriors who were united and disciplined by the political and military structure of the Five Nations.

Yet, there was unquestionable legitimacy in the merchants' charge that Frontenac had taken public money to finance his scheme with La Salle. He had made unauthorized use of the colony's credit. He had forced the taxpayers to open their pocketbooks and contribute to the cost of his grand excursion. The fort he had built had turned out to be an ideally located trading post, commanded not by an army officer but by a civilian trader. If augmenting the colonial defenses had been Frontenac's only purpose, a new military installation much closer to Montreal would have been far more practical and efficient than a works on the remote shore of Lake Ontario.

Returning from Cataraqui, Frontenac, actively supported by La Salle, arrogantly defied his accusers. Neither the mounting fury of the businessmen nor the open antagonism of the Jesuits induced him to adopt a more conciliatory attitude.

La Salle had drawn for him a picture portraying conditions adverse to their plans. It was this: François Perrot, who held a royal commission as mayor of Montreal and had been endorsed for the office by the Sulpician hierarchy in France, had proven himself to be a man of little integrity and few moral scruples. He brazenly let it be known that he had come to New France for a single purpose, to gain a fortune, and if he could not acquire it honestly he would adopt illegal methods.

He was prevented by law from engaging in the fur trade, but he circumvented this restriction with little difficulty. A seigneury had been granted to him on an island lying between the Lakes St. Louis and Two Mountains, to which he gave the name Île Perrot. On it he built a trading post and placed in command an ex-officer he had known in France, Antoine de Fresnay, Sieur de Brucey. The place was soon enjoying a brisk business, a large part of it the result of the forceful methods employed. Sieur de Brucey, as unscrupulous as his employer, engaged a number of degraded renegades and army deserters to stop the canoes of Indians who had furs to trade as they descended the St. Lawrence. Alcoholic beverages were freely dispensed to these involuntary customers, and their furs disappeared into the Île Perrot storehouse.

The trading firms of Montreal had sent a deputation to the mayor's office with a demand that the piratical practices be halted. In the group were the prominent and reputable merchants Charles Le Moyne, Jacques Le Ber, Picote de Belestre, and Mignon de Branssac. Perrot recognized his callers only long enough to warn that he knew ways to keep them in their places, and to order them from his office. They departed, and immediately afterward Branssac was arrested on a false charge and held for several days.

The indignant traders appealed to the court, and the judge, Charles d'Ailleboust, had two of the Perrot bandits taken into custody, charging them with engaging in the fur trade without a license. Perrot's aides, led by a henchman named M. Carion, quickly engineered their escape from jail.

Word of this episode was sent by La Salle in an express to Frontenac in Quebec. The Governor responded by dispatching an officer, Lieutenant Jacques Bizard, to Montreal with orders to arrest Carion and a letter to Perrot in which he rebuked the mayor for countenancing the jailbreak. The lieutenant, not an overly brave man, arrested Carion, but he attempted to avoid a meeting with Perrot, whose vicious temper he feared, by giving the Governor's letter to the merchant, Jacques Le Ber, with instructions that it was not to be delivered until after he was well on his way back to Quebec.

The plan failed. Informed by Carion's wife that her husband was in a cell and the lieutenant was with Le Ber, Perrot raced to the merchant's store. Bizard handed him the letter. Raging as if he had gone mad, Perrot threw it back in his face without opening it, and stalked out. Shortly afterward he returned with a deputy sheriff, who took both Bizard and Le Ber into custody. La Salle was present, and when he cautioned Perrot that his acts were both injudicious and dangerous, the mayor cursed him and threatened him with the same treatment. Bizard and Le Ber spent several days behind bars before being released.

La Salle at the time was a guest in the Le Ber home. For

good reasons of his own, Le Ber had not displayed the animosity toward him which other traders had shown. It was his hope that he would be permitted to share in the trade advantages which would result from the building of Fort Frontenac. But La Salle had made no decision in the matter.

In view of the precarious state of affairs in Montreal, La Salle deemed it wise to go to Quebec for a conference with the Governor. Some ideas had come to him which he did not care to commit to writing. Competing now with the well-entrenched espionage staffs of Frontenac and Bishop Laval were the agents of Jacques Duchesneau, who had succeeded Talon as Intendant. Under this condition it had become possible for the contents of reports and correspondence to be improperly transmitted in not one but two directions, even before becoming known to the person to whom they had been sent.

Aware that he was being watched by Perrot's men, La Salle slipped out of the Le Ber home in the middle of the night, climbed over several fences, and followed a circuitous route to the river where a longboat was being held in readiness for him.

From the beginning of their association, Frontenac and Duchesneau had exhibited an intense dislike for each other. The severe clash of personalities had soon spawned a mutual hate which made all but impossible their collaboration.

With the building of Fort Frontenac, Duchesneau, as might have been expected, aligned himself with the unhappy merchants and traders. He took the deposition of anyone who was willing to speak unfavorably of the Governor. These he made public with the assertion that they stood as indisputable evidence of a Frontenac-La Salle conspiracy to plunder the colonial treasury and control the fur trade.

In public appearances, at meetings with the colonial counsellors, and in letters to France, Frontenac furiously charged Duchesneau with perpetrating falsehoods and with seeking to disrupt the progress and undermine the economy of New France. He described

[68]

his own accomplishments in glowing terms, especially his successful negotiations with the Iroquois. Out of his journey to the council at Cataraqui had come a combined diplomatic triumph and military victory achieved without the utterance of a harsh word or the firing in anger of a single shot.

Lest the King and Colbert should be concerned about the money he had spent on the wilderness mission, he could assure them that the cost had been negligible, a mere ten thousand francs. The balance of the expense had been absorbed by towns, villages, and individual citizens. He refrained from explaining, however, that this burden had been assumed by the contributors under duress he had brought to bear on them. It was not necessary to give Versailles every detail.

Frontenac had written nothing to France about his plan with La Salle before it had been put into motion. Now he reversed his strategy. He outlined phases of it which not only had not been undertaken but which had not even been disclosed in Quebec.

He proposed to build a vessel—indeed, construction of it would soon be under way—to sail the waters of Lake Ontario. Armed with cannon and carrying soldiers, it would serve a dual purpose: be useful in keeping the peace with the Iroquois, and aid in cutting the illicit trade with the British. He omitted mention of a third way in which the vessel might be employed, that of transporting furs from the western reaches of Lake Ontario to Fort Frontenac near the mouth of the St. Lawrence.

But he did add that with "another fort at the mouth of the Niagara River, and a second vessel patrolling Lake Erie, we, the French, can command all the Upper Lakes."

In his official correspondence, Frontenac appeared to forget that these extensive plans had originated in the fertile brain of La Salle, but he was not remiss when it came to absolving La Salle of the charges registered against him by either the Jesuits, the Sulpicians or the businessmen, nor did he hesitate to praise him as a patriot and a brilliant son of whom France might be proud.

To this accolade he might well have added a tribute to La Salle as a politician. His shrewdness in this field was never better demonstrated than on his visit to Frontenac in the fall of 1673.

Clearly Frontenac needed to obtain greater control of Montreal affairs, but La Salle persuaded him that more drastic moves would not achieve the desired end. As it was, the situation was not altogether unfavorable to them. The incarceration of Branssac and Le Ber, although of short duration, had caused the merchants to be less volatile in their denunciations of him, for they understood that they must look to him for protection. The Sulpicians disapproved of Perrot's violence and illegal operations, and Dollier de Casson had left a sickbed to call upon Perrot and demand that he stop harassing respectable merchants and desist from his brash and brutal performances. Perrot had ignored him.

It was La Salle's suggestion that Frontenac should resort to a bit of trickery. The Governor might write two letters. One would be an invitation to Perrot to come to Quebec for a friendly chat. Because of Dollier de Casson's illness, the other letter might be sent to the Abbé de Salignac Fenelon, who was temporarily acting in de Casson's place, and whom La Salle knew to be more courageous than prudent. In it Frontenac also might express the belief that a talk between them would be fruitful. And in both letters he might reveal a desire, cautiously phrased, to create an atmosphere of good will and understanding between himself and the authorities of Montreal, which in turn would be beneficial to the entire colony.

True, the Sulpicians were jealous of their prerogative of approving or rejecting royal appointees to civil posts in Montreal. The King had always respected this right, but it should not be forgotten that the King also held the power to override the Sulpicians and to remove summarily an incumbent. It was inconceivable to La Salle that the King would fail to support Frontenac in a crisis with a man of Perrot's disreputable character, even to the extent of defying the wishes of the Sulpicians.

La Salle held the conviction that the flattering letters to

Perrot and Fenelon would bring them to Quebec. When that happened, Frontenac's next moves could be made as his wisdom dictated.

Frontenac penned the letters. La Salle went back to Montreal, arriving only a day or two before the river was made impassable by ice.

His judgment of Perrot and Fenelon and the strategy he had advocated proved to be sound.

So flattered were the Mayor and the abbé by Frontenac's polite suggestion that they confer with him in a private audience, that they eagerly set out for Montreal in the bitter cold of November, traversed most of the distance on snowshoes, and suffered not a little hardship on the journey.

Perrot never got inside the Governor's office. None other than Lieutenant Bizard arrested him at the entrance, and he was clapped into a cell of the Citadel St. Louis.

Abbé Fenelon fared little better. He was permitted to appear before Frontenac, and he registered vehement protests against the demeaning stratagems of the Governor and the disgraceful treatment Perrot had received. Frontenac listened to him only a few minutes, his face a stone mask, and then unceremoniously dismissed the wrathful priest.

On his snowshoes, perhaps kept warmer than he had been on the outward journey by the indignation seething in him, Fenelon went back to Montreal. There the atmosphere was not conducive to calmness.

Fenelon found that he and Perrot had no more than set out for Quebec before Frontenac had installed a new Mayor, an ex-Army officer named M. de la Nouguere. At once, Nouguere had arrested his predecessor's lieutenant, Sieur de Brucey, and had brought him before Judge d'Ailleboust, who had sent him to prison. Next Nouguere had taken into custody the two *couriers du bois* who had been helped to escape from jail by Perrot's ruffians, and had sent them to Quebec to be tried.

Word soon came back to Montreal that one of these renegades had been sentenced to a long term at hard labor, and the other had been executed. Perrot had been forced to watch the hanging from the small window of his cell. Accompanying this news was a warning from the Governor that all other traders and *couriers du bois* who violated fur trade regulations would suffer severe penalties.

From the merchants the announcement brought accusatory cries of hypocrisy. In their opinion, Frontenac himself was a violator of the law by conspiring with La Salle to dominate the fur trade. The Sulpicians held a different view. Their chief concern was that the political and civil control they had enjoyed so long was being taken from them. But, as La Salle had expected, they were more restrained than the merchants in their statements and objections. It was the feeling of Dollier de Casson, the mild and gentle giant, that nothing was to be gained by recriminations or by threatening reprisals, and that the passage of time would bring a solution to the vexing problem. This attitude was not acceptable, however, to the fiery and unforgiving Abbé Fenelon.

La Salle sought to maintain an attitude of cold reserve and to avoid bitter arguments, but not infrequently he was driven into a corner by human hornets. Not the least painful of the stings he suffered was inflicted by his brother. From the time La Salle had sold his seigneury, Jean Cavelier had criticized him openly as a wastrel. He had not ceased his attempts to persuade La Salle to return to a stable and prosaic life, to abandon his desire to explore, an occupation he held to be not only futile but unbecoming to a young man of La Salle's intelligence and social position. He intercepted La Salle's mail. He had La Salle watched on the pretext that he wished to guard him from becoming the prey of some designing and degenerate woman. He hounded La Salle, scolding, spewing reflections on his character, and making dire predictions that his young brother—for whom he professed to have a deep and lasting affection—would know only a ruined life if he continued his association with the diabolical Frontenac. Fanatically religious, intolerant, hypocritical, deceitful, he was a haunting shadow that at times drove La Salle to the point of despair.

15 ⚜ ⚜ ⚜

IT WAS a spring of frustrating confusion, of volatile dissension, of spreading hatred—1674—the thirtieth spring of La Salle's life.

For some men in his situation, it might have been a spring of gratification. Furs were coming down the St. Lawrence to him, packs of beaver and marten and fox and mink and lynx and otter and wolf skins and the hides of deer and bear and panther and even some buffalo robes. Trade at Fort Frontenac was exceeding his most optimistic expectations. The gross business of the post might well amount to more than fifty thousand *livres* in the first full year of its operation, a most satisfactory figure.

But for La Salle it was a spring of dissatisfaction, of consuming restlessness, of foreboding. He did not share Frontenac's confidence that the volume of trade at Fort Frontenac would steadily increase, and that they would be able to withstand successfully the pressures of their opponents. It was his private belief that those pressures would grow in power until they had become too great to be borne, until no means available to him or the Governor in Canada could effectively decrease them. The feuds of Frontenac with Duchesneau, with the Jesuits, with the Sulpicians, with the influential businessmen, were keeping the colony, and especially the Quebec Government, in a constant uproar. The reaction of Colbert and other ministers had not been unfavorable to Frontenac, but to La Salle's way of reasoning that was not a guarantee of continued support for the latter's actions and policies. The wheels of Versailles moved slowly, but they were never still.

The solution could come only through drastic new tactics, and

La Salle devoted himself in long and intense deliberations to devising them.

The prospect of becoming rich as a fur trader had not lost its last shred of appeal for him, not at all. But such ambition continued, as it had been in the past, to be overshadowed by greater, more irrepressible, desires. Yet, paradoxically, money was vital to every plan he hoped to carry out. He had to have it. And there were strong indications that it would not come to him until the adverse situation in which he stood had been relieved, until he had embarked on a more propitious course.

To him the shape of things to come had been forcefully indicated by a single event. He had sent another cargo convoy up the river. The Montreal merchants, understanding that he was obliged to purchase goods from them to prevent a costly hiatus in the trade at Fort Frontenac, had raised their prices considerably above normal levels. The increases would cut sharply into his profits for the coming season, but he had resigned himself to taking losses, if necessary, to maintain a competitive position.

He had effected arrangements by which goods would be shipped directly to him from the factories and wholesalers of Normandy and Brittany, but the first of these could not arrive until summer's end, perhaps too late to be transported to Fort Frontenac before winter had closed the river. Ultimately these direct importations would solve the problem of excessive charges which the Montreal merchants imposed, but they would not countervene the attempts to destroy the trade advantages he and Frontenac enjoyed, they would not decrease the forces aligned against them.

Yet, La Salle's discontent stemmed not as much from pecuniary troubles as from the distressing realization that he had made little or no progress toward the supreme goal he had long before set for himself. His situation was not the same, however, as it had been before he had found the Ohio. Then his restlessness and his impatience had their source in the inordinate zeal and blind confidence of an untested and inexperienced young man. Now they arose out of fact and knowledge, out of what he had seen with his own eyes, out of what he knew to be true.

The time had come for him to make a new and forceful attempt to achieve some measure of progress. The time had come for him to return to France.

He was not unaware that in pursuing such a course he would have to travel much of the way alone, dependent upon his own intellectual resources and his own abilities to secure the subsidies he required. Neither the legal authority nor the political influence of Frontenac was limitless. And here was another paradox. He might incur Frontenac's displeasure by going over his head, yet Frontenac's acquiescence in the move was necessary.

He saw no alternative but to take Frontenac into his confidence, to explain with complete candor his intentions, obtain his approval of the plan, and thereafter let the chips fall as they may.

Midsummer had arrived when La Salle went down the St. Lawrence to Quebec. With him was the faithful Shawnee, Nika, whose devotion to him since the day they had set out from Otinawatawa to find the Ohio had been unfailing, and who had stubbornly refused to be left behind in Montreal. He would go with La Salle to France, or to the moon, but he would never leave him.

In the autumn they were aboard a vessel destined for St.-Malo.

Once again Frontenac had heeded La Salle's advice. It was his conviction that he could have no more able emissary to Versailles. Without hesitation, he prepared a series of letters of recommendation for La Salle to carry with him which would open the doors to Colbert, to members of the Court, and, hopefully, to the King.

16 ⚜ ⚜ ⚜

FOR LA SALLE, his mission to France was both highly rewarding and a profound disappointment. What he sought the most, what he wanted more than anything else, he did not get.

Before going to Paris, he visited his mother in the old family home at Rouen, and enjoyed a reunion with his brother and sister and their children.

His feats of exploration and his discoveries in the American wilderness had brought him not a little distinction. He was warmly received by Colbert, and he was entertained by members of the court. His wealthy cousins in Paris, the Plets, who had shown no great concern about his welfare before he emigrated to Canada, appeared to have undergone a change of heart. They displayed a gracious hospitality toward him, and seemed to be sincerely interested in his future plans.

Those plans he sought to keep secret as much as possible. They involved aggressive actions that could well lead to diplomatic controversies with other nations. The disclosure that France was contemplating territorial acquisitions in North America would not have been passively disregarded by either England or Spain.

Before Colbert, however, La Salle presented detailed and exhaustive arguments in favor of the projects he advocated. If they could be enumerated with relative simplicity, they were not to be accomplished before the passage of years and the expenditure of enormous sums of money. The building of an empire in the heart of a wilderness almost completely unexplored, the size of which remained a mystery, was not to be accomplished by wishing for it. The first necessary move was, of course, to take possession of the valleys of the Ohio, the Illinois, and the Mississippi. That might be done by a comparatively small expedition, but following immediately must be provided larger forces to establish military installations that would assure security for the areas acquired and safeguard the commerce that would be developed and which would ultimately repay the costs of the conquest.

The time to move was in the coming year. Any further delay might be disastrous. The English would not remain much longer east of the Appalachians, nor would the Spanish be content to confine themselves to Mexico and the Gulf coast of New Spain. Between these two perimeters lay a fabulously rich land, rich in furs, rich in timber, rich in good soil, bisected by navigable rivers on which large ships and barges could sail.

La Salle knew these things because he had traveled through much of that land. But these things were not yet known to the civilized world. Continued exploration, however, would reveal them, bring them to the knowledge of the British and the Spanish courts, and the enterprising businessmen of those countries would waste no time in demanding that definitive measures be launched to exploit them. France, by virtue of its strong position in Canada and the explorations already accomplished—not exclusively by himself, but by missionaries and other *voyageurs*—possessed an incomparable opportunity to acquire without organized opposition a gigantic new colony of incalculable resources, virtually the entire interior of the North American Continent.

Colbert presented La Salle's plea to the King and his counsellors. The decision, with which Colbert thoroughly agreed, was negative.

"Wait," Colbert told La Salle. France had only recently emerged from an expensive war with the Dutch. English assistance in the conflict had been secured only by the payment of immense sums to Charles II. The French treasury was not in a position to undertake conquest on the scale La Salle proposed. Delay was advisable until it could be ascertained that France could hold such an enormous new colony. Moreover, all the furs needed at the time could be obtained from already existing sources. French industry could not consume greater amounts. It was most desirable, of course, to develop markets for other products—metals, timber and fish, for example—and to prevent any expansion by England and Spain. But, perhaps, these things could be accomplished to a great extent by means other than the annexing of immense territories, and the building and maintaining of costly military installations.

Both Colbert and the King were appreciative of La Salle's unqualified loyalty to his country and his eagerness to see it prosper through the development of French Canada, but caution and careful observance of the trend of European events—which might take a turn for the worse at any moment—was deemed by them to be the wisest course to be followed, at least for the present.

Louis, however—and Colbert once more was in agreement with him—thought it befitting that La Salle be rewarded in some manner for his discoveries. Perhaps there was something else that La Salle desired.

There was.

La Salle's disappointment had not destroyed his astuteness as a trader nor his determination to execute his plans to the greatest extent possible without royal approval and financial support from the public treasury.

He needed rank that would give him political advantages. And, under the present conditions, the future of Fort Frontenac was extremely precarious.

In the spring of 1675, La Salle presented two petitions to the French court. Both were granted and signed by the King in May.

The first awarded him the rank of an untitled nobleman. The second petition, granted by Louis XIV the following day, awarded to La Salle "the fort called Frontenac, situated in New France, with four leagues of adjacent country and the adjoining islands and circumjacent Rivers, the whole by the title of Fief, Seigniory and Justice. . . . For the erection and establishment there of settlements. . . . said de la Salle offers to reimburse the sum of ten thousand *livres*, the amount expended for the construction of said

Fort Frontenac, to keep in good order the said Fort, and the garrison necessary for the defense thereof, which cannot be less than the Fort of Montreal . . . to maintain twenty men during nine years for clearing the land . . . and until he shall have a church built, to keep a Priest or Friar to perform Divine Service and administer the sacraments . . . which expenses the said de la Salle will defray at his sole cost. . . ."

Colbert had found a way to recover the money Frontenac had expended without authority to build Fort Frontenac.

La Salle thus could claim a new seigneury on which stood the most valuable trading post in the Canadian wilderness. The merchants of Montreal had been routed. The way was open for him to control legally and permanently the immense fur traffic of the Great Lakes. He had been placed by a stroke of the King's quill, and the impression of the royal seal, in an almost invulnerable position to become the most powerful and perhaps the richest fur trader in all of French Canada.

And he had no money to execute the functions he had sworn to perform. But this problem was quickly solved.

The enthusiasm of the Plets was without bounds. They willingly underwrote a loan to him that was more than large enough to offset the stipulations in the King's decree awarding him Fort Frontenac. His brother and sister dug into the Cavelier family coffers, previously closed to him, to advance him money for equipment and to pay the wages of the soldiers and *engagés* he would have to employ. Several thousand *livres* were pledged by manufacturers and merchants anxious to share his good fortune with him.

Altogether, as La Salle sailed for Quebec, he had been favored with credits amounting to some fifty thousand *livres*.

17 ⚜ ⚜ ⚜

CONDITIONS IN the colony had changed, but only for the worse.

The intensity of the storm about Frontenac had grown. He was delighted with La Salle's accomplishments in France, smelling the sweet perfume of greater profits. Expansion would have been desirable, and he acquiesced in La Salle's view that delays might prove harmful, but obviously Colbert and the King were adamant, and pressing them further would be unwise. In time they might be prevailed upon to reconsider the matter. La Salle must not abandon all hope.

A philosophical attitude brought little comfort to La Salle. Anger lived in him which could not be quelled by soothing words. At times it mounted until he had difficulty in controlling it. He would not be stopped by the shortsightedness and stupidity of men who could not see beyond their own noses, who were incapable of recognizing the opportunities he had opened for them to make France the most powerful nation in the New World.

His wrath was not alleviated by receipt of information that his financial supporters in France had appointed his brother, Jean, at the Seminary of St. Sulpice, to manage the disbursement of their loans in Canada. Jean, who had disapproved of almost every ambition La Salle possessed, almost every plan he had made, who had sought to dictate the course of his private life, was now the master of his pocketbook. It was apparent that, although his cousin, François Plet, had been eager to share in his advantages, he was unwilling to trust him to handle the money.

The situation was almost more than La Salle could bear, and he experienced a strong urge to abandon the entire project, return Fort Frontenac to the crown, and go his own way without the assistance of persons who obviously had no faith in him.

Frontenac cautioned him not to permit emotion to destroy his own opportunities. The advice was unnecessary, for La Salle was not addicted to rashness. Beneath his raging persisted a strong and increasing current of cold reasoning that in the end invariably succeeded in cooling his hot-headedness.

He responded to Frontenac's admonishments with icy calmness. He had no intention of injuring himself by imprudence. On the contrary, he was determined to fulfill every obligation he had accepted, to give his undivided attention to gaining for himself an impregnable position in the fur trade. He would, if necessary, be totally unscrupulous. If he could not legally take possession of the interior in the name of Louis XIV, there was nothing to stop him from extending his fur trade into it.

That was not quite the truth. There were several forces that might raise barriers in La Salle's path. But Frontenac saw nothing to be achieved by debating the question with a man whose blood was permeated with so great a fury. And it was not, after all, an attitude with which Frontenac could find fault. He would share in whatever successes La Salle enjoyed, and about that he need have no concern, for La Salle owed him much, and he himself had ways of disrupting La Salle's progress if proper considerations were not forthcoming.

With the awarding of Fort Frontenac to La Salle by royal patent the tempers of the fur traders burst into flames. It had been built with public money and had been handed to a private individual. This was proof of their contention that it had never been considered as an adjunct of the colony's defenses. Frontenac's sole purpose in constructing it had been to use it as a trading post. Even if La Salle repaid the ten thousand francs, the brand of corruption could never be removed from the Governor. Now, making matters all the worse, both Colbert and the King had condoned the malfeasance and had made themselves part of the unconscionable conspiracy of Frontenac and La Salle.

If the protests of the Jesuits were less noisy than those of the traders, they were far more diabolical and degrading. La Salle's proposals to Colbert and the King aroused strong new fears in them, for they had their own plans to take possession of the interior, not for France but for God. La Salle's bold assertions that he was determined to extend his fur trade into the western wilderness aroused in them the vision of hordes of unruly and debased *couriers du bois,* carrying more liquor than trade goods, invading the homelands of tribes who had not yet become victims of the white man's evils.

Leaving no stone unturned in their efforts to infiltrate the innermost official sanctums of the colonial government and to gain information that might be used against Frontenac, the Jesuits had created an association of women spies called "La Sainte Famille." These snoopers in skirts, many of whom were the wives of government officers and merchants, met each Thursday in the Quebec Cathedral behind locked doors. By vow they were bound to relate all intelligence they had gathered for transmission to Bishop La Val. Much of it was nothing more than malicious gossip, and some members were not above using the meetings to launch venal attacks on the characters of persons they disliked or of whom they were envious.

It was not surprising that soon after his return from France in the autumn of 1675 La Salle became a victim of this female inquisition. Prompted by La Val, the leaders condemned him as an immoral ingrate and planted the seeds of a plot to bring him into the spotlight of a public scandal.

The duty of perpetrating La Salle's entrapment was assigned to one Madame Vazire, the wife of a government tax collector who had once entertained the hope that he would be favored by Frontenac with a fur trade concession such as the Governor had made to La Salle. M. Charles Vazire also operated a mercantile establishment and maintained a fine house with several servants. It was suspected that his affluence was derived less from the sale of cooking utensils, bed covers and chamber pots than from the careless manner in which he kept the tax records of the colony, but if that were true, his defalcations had not been discovered. However, having been disappointed by Frontenac and jealous of La Salle, Vazire readily agreed to cooperate with his wife in her chicanery.

La Salle made the mistake of accepting an invitation to be a house guest of the Vazires. After an evening of sumptuous dining and pleasant chatter, his host showed him to his room. A few minutes later, Madame Vazire, wearing only a negligée, entered without knocking. She advanced upon the astounded La Salle with outstretched arms, the gown falling open to expose her charms.

Pushing her roughly aside, La Salle, who was fully clothed, rushed to the door and threw it open. He found himself facing Vazire and several other guests. Without hesitating La Salle continued on, ran from the house, and sought refuge for the night under the safer roof of Frontenac.

Madame Vazire was obliged to report at the next gathering of "La Sainte Famille" that her scheme had failed.

The Jesuits were disappointed, but not discouraged. La Val directed a new attack on La Salle from another quarter. He charged that La Salle was encouraging the use of alcoholic spirits by *couriers du bois* in the fur trade with western Indians. In a controversy of this nature, which involved no bedroom scenes or amorous advances by a misguided female, La Salle felt more sure of himself and showed no reticence to stand his ground or to retaliate in kind.

The issue was as old as New France. Samuel de Champlain had been one of the first officials to attempt to prevent the sale of liquor to Indians. He and the early Jesuits achieved a moderate success in their fight against the traffic, but neither they nor their successors in New France could prevent English and Dutch traders from supplying the Indians with unlimited quantities of rum.

Through the years the controversy had continued to rage, with kings, governors, and leading merchants advocating stringent enforcement of laws forbidding it, and liquor continuing to flow

[83]

into the Indian countries. Always in the forefront of the fight were the Jesuits, and Laval had taken up the battle where his predecessors had left it.

In 1675, he brought the liquor question into his bitter controversy with Frontenac and La Salle over their scheme to expand the fur trade to tribes which had not been debauched. Both the Governor and his protégé promptly instigated violent counter-attacks.

Laval and the Jesuits, La Salle charged, were guilty of unworthy motives. The Jesuits were engaged in the fur trade in the far west and were attempting to stifle competition. Money was pouring into the Jesuit coffers from this commerce. The missionary, Father Albanel, was directing an immense trade for the order.

Claiming that he had seen Jesuits themselves give brandy to Indians, La Salle told of having heard an Indian leader testify in Quebec that "he had prayed and been a Christian as long as the Jesuits would stay and teach him, but since no more beaver were left in his country, the missionaries were gone also."

Frontenac supported La Salle with similar accusations, declaring that the Jesuits worked more "for the conversion of beavers than of souls."

There was some truth in the arguments of both sides. Frontenac and La Salle did not propose to lose the French fur trade to the English by preventing *couriers du bois* from taking liquor to the Indians. The Jesuits were in the fur trade, and in places were enjoying handsome profits from it. Some missions employed *couriers du bois* to conduct the trade for them.

For years the Jesuits had been as powerful in Canada as the colonial government. In some respects they had wielded a greater authority than the Governor-General. That was no longer the case. The temporal influence of the Society of Jesus had been steadily decreasing, especially in the cities and the settled areas adjacent to the St. Lawrence Valley. Making matters worse for them, religious contributions had declined in Europe, and in New France Laval and his missionaries were badly in need of funds to carry on the work of establishing new missions.

The Jesuits had turned to the fur trade to supplement their income, and had looked to the great untouched region of the far west as a land of promise and hope. They had explored it, and it was their fanatic prayer that they would be able to carry the Faith into it before some other order undertook the task, and before the unscrupulous fur traders had perverted the minds and the bodies of Indians with irreligious teachings and kegs of firewater.

La Salle had become the greatest enemy of their program, their strongest rival for control of the west, and he had to be stopped. If he succeeded in his enterprises, the banner of God would not wave there.

La Salle, in the fall of 1675, weary of the disorder and intrigue of Quebec, disgusted by the contemptible schemes to discredit and disgrace him, gathered equipment and employed *engagés* in preparation for his return to Fort Frontenac. He longed for the solitude of the great forests, longed to hear the roaring of white water, to gaze across the blue reaches of the inland seas, to know and to feel and to see and to smell once more the world of the unspoiled wilderness, the world that was closest to his heart.

18 ✤ ✤ ✤

BY THE summer of 1677, a new Fort Frontenac had risen on the shore of Lake Ontario. The last vestige of the first fort, erected in a few days by Frontenac to awe the Iroquois, had disappeared. The old palisades and blockhouses, built of green timber and hurriedly thrown together, had been supplanted on the land side by stone bastions, and facing the water were strong ramparts of heavy logs. Much larger in every dimension than its predecessor, it contained barracks for soldiers and *engagés*, a cellhouse, quarters for officers, a forge, a well, a gristmill, a bakery, and central cooking facilities from which the entire garrison could be served.

Nearby were two villages. In the neat log houses of one dwelt several French families whom La Salle had induced to come there with an offer of free farms and employment. In the other, in somewhat less tidy bark and wooden huts surrounded by corn patches and poorly tended gardens, lived a small band of Iroquois, its male members useful to La Salle as canoemen and hunters, and their squaws available to dress pelts and perform other duties customarily considered women's work.

Adjacent to the villages were the house and the chapel of two Recollect friars, Father Luc Buisset and Father Louis Hennepin, who had been sent soon after the seigneury had been granted to La Salle to serve the religious needs of the men at the fort and to preach the gospel to the Indians who came to it to trade.

Hennepin, who would become famous for his wilderness journeys and notorious as a liar and a plagiarist, was enthusiastic about both his assignment and the station. Seldom overlooking an opportunity to slap at the Jesuits, he expressed the fear that the "fine progress Sieur de la Salle has made on his fort aroused jealousy among certain people who feared what he might accomplish with the assistance of our Recollect missionaries. . . . These envious ones persuaded Sieur Joliet to forestall Sieur de la Salle in his project of discovery." Referring to Joliet's journey [with Father Marquette] down the Mississippi, Hennepin criticized him for having "made no attempt to start settlements, nor has he added to the information possessed by the court." La Salle had preceded Joliet and Marquette in discovering the Mississippi, and was planning to return, en route building forts and trading houses and establishing settlements, all of which in Hennepin's belief, would be of great benefit to France.

Iroquois traveled great distances from the east, south, and west to see Fort Frontenac. If they had been impressed by the speed and efficiency with which the original structure had been built, they were more than astounded by its successor. La Salle's industry and ingenuity were almost inconceivable to them. He had brought stonemasons and carpenters and shipbuilders from Montreal and Quebec. *Engagés* had struggled around the great rapids bearing cases of chickens, staggering under loads of squealing swine. Cattle had been driven overland on the narrow rough forest trails, and grazed peacefully in fine meadows. The friars conducted a school which, as Hennepin said, "created friendly feeling because we are teaching the Iroquois children to read along with our French children. As a result, the pupils learn one another's language."

Nor did the Iroquois who came to stretch their necks and trade fail to take careful note of nine cannon frowning upon them from the impregnable stone walls, and the fact that a score of soldiers and officers, resplendent in uniform, stood guard in the parapets and marched on sentry duty before the gates. Altogether, it was a wondrous thing to behold.

The structure of the system under which furs were sent from Canada to France—they could not be sold to any other nation—had, within a century, undergone numerous changes. At times, monopolies holding royal patents had controlled all colonial exports and imports. Most of these had brought political and financial controversies and had proved to be commercially unsatisfactory to both the home government and the St. Lawrence traders. Several charters had been revoked before they expired, and the merchants had been allowed to sell their stocks and order goods through licensed commission houses or through other marketing channels, but never without paying a percentage tax to the government.

In 1664, a year before La Salle emigrated to Canada, Louis XIV, upon the advice of Colbert, had granted a monopoly of both imports and exports to a newly formed organization called the Company of the West Indies, more popularly known as the Company of the West. Besides New France, its territory included the French West Indies and the French colonies on the west coast of Africa. Head of the company's New World operations was the soldier-statesman-businessman, Marquis de Tracy, who had forced the Iroquois to sue for peace shortly after he reached Quebec in his new post.

While this victorious campaign had removed, at least temporarily, the danger of Indian attacks, it had not brought the increase in trade from regions south of the St. Lawrence which Montreal and Quebec had expected. The Iroquois had realized the futility of warring against the French, but they would not abandon the trade they maintained with western tribes, and they continued to compete with *couriers du bois* in this field. The Iroquois could obtain large quantities of arms and ammunition from the English and Dutch, and they exchanged these for furs with western Indians they had conquered, by this means holding a powerful advantage over French traders.

La Salle had not been long in Canada before he recognized that only through western expansion could New France disrupt the trade of the Iroquois, the larger part of which went to the English. His shrewd observation that the future of the colony lay in country not yet explored, and which caused him to be labeled a visionary, had been in line with Intendant Talon's thinking. Indeed, Talon had given consideration to building a line of forts westward from the head of the St. Lawrence, but had been recalled before the project could be undertaken.

La Salle had made two journeys to the west, discovering the Ohio, the Illinois and the Mississippi, and then had presented his plan for expansion to Frontenac, who had acted in accord with it. In effect, La Salle's plan had been an endorsement of Talon's policy to encourage independent trading, a policy the Company of the West, insisting on its exclusive right to export furs, had strongly opposed.

Talon had charged that the Company of the West was not importing goods suitable for the Indian trade, that it was making excessive profits, and would impoverish the colony if it were allowed to continue many years. Frontenac, following the reasoning of La

Salle, was taking the same stand. Talon had claimed that the Company was stifling enterprise. Frontenac and his young protégé were making the same claim.

In 1666, Talon had succeeded in persuading Colbert to destroy the Company's monopoly, and to throw the fur trade open to Montreal and Quebec traders. However, the Company's members, possessing significant political powers, were able to salvage something from the wreckage. Although the traders were free to buy and sell where and when they pleased, they were still obliged to pay the Company a heavy tax on every beaver and deerskin they marketed. On this issue, Frontenac and La Salle shared the view of the merchants, by whom they were opposed on virtually every other question, that the tax was unfair. The tax did not go to the government. It went into the pockets of the officers of the Company of the West.

In 1674, the King had been persuaded to revoke the charter of the Company. It went out of business with a bookkeeping debt of three million *livres*. The fur trade was placed under the control of officials appointed by the crown.

La Salle had been the first trader to urge that prices for all furs should be fixed by the industry, subject to the King's approval. Louis XIV adopted this system, but included provisions which allowed him to keep full control of it and which brought money into his own coffers. The merchants could recommend prices, year by year, but he retained the power to approve or disapprove of them. Further, a royal tax of one-fourth the beaver skins and one-tenth the deerskins exported was imposed. Furs could be sold only through his appointed agents, who were obliged to take all offered to them at the fixed prices.

It was not good business, but it was better than a monopoly, and La Salle had strongly urged that it be supported. A majority of the St. Lawrence traders saw no better alternative, and adopted a similar attitude. The system was, at least, a step toward the freedom they desired, the tax money was going to the King and not to grafters, and they could be assured of receiving certain prices for their pelts.

La Salle, out of whose shrewd brain had come the price-fixing idea, received no credit for it from the men who profited the most from it. Outwardly, the traders, almost to a man, appeared as his enemies, but had most of them been willing to admit their true feelings, it would have been seen that they had no wish to silence his voice nor exclude him from their ranks. They feared his astuteness, and even under a strained relationship it might be possible to learn something of new schemes he and the Governor had up their respective sleeves.

La Salle had consistently advocated the fixing of prices higher than those paid to *couriers du bois* and Indians by the English. Although he had not been able to attend the meetings of 1674 and 1675, he made certain that his views were known to the participants. In the summer of 1676, however, he had interrupted his work of rebuilding Fort Frontenac long enough to journey to Montreal to attend the conference which would submit prices for the coming year to the King.

He found himself surrounded by men who had made every effort to smash his alliance with Frontenac and his operations in the Iroquois country, and who had blackened his name at every opportunity. The Governor was not present, but the Intendant Duchesneau was on hand to represent the Government. In the audience were the famed *voyageurs* and traders, Jean Baptiste des Groseilliers and Pierre Esprit Radisson, who had explored the region beyond Lake Superior and the rivers running to Hudson's Bay. There, too, were the wealthy and influential merchants Le Moyne and La Chesnaye. Louis Joliet, who claimed that he had preceded La Salle in reaching the Mississippi, was present, but La Salle disdained to argue with him. In La Salle's opinion, the discovery of the Mississippi was not as important as building forts on it and taking possession of its great valley for France.

Also in attendance was Charles Vazire—whose wife had so

brazenly attempted to involve La Salle in an intimate scene—now bearing the additional duty of collecting the King's tax on furs. La Salle ignored him, and Vazire had no wish to engage La Salle in even polite chitchat.

La Salle again proposed prices for all types of furs bought from *couriers du bois* and Indians that were higher than those paid by the English on the Mohawk and the Hudson. It was his argument that unless the traders of French Canada paid more for pelts of all grades than their rivals in New York, both the *couriers du bois* and the Iroquois would refuse to send their catches down the St. Lawrence.

He was overruled. The conference fixed prices for poor grades of furs that were higher than English prices, and set prices for fine pelts that were lower than those paid at posts on the Hudson. To La Salle the decision was not only stupid but inconceivable. He returned to Fort Frontenac completely discouraged by the lack of business acumen in his countrymen.

As La Salle had predicted, the result was almost disastrous for the merchants of Montreal and Quebec. The fine skins went to the British, the poor ones to Montreal and Quebec. The best furs were taken between the late fall and the early spring, but the attractive prices for low grades at the posts of the lower St. Lawrence brought indiscriminate trapping the year round. Some areas were denuded of the most desirable animals—beaver, mink, otter and marten. French warehouses became jammed with useless and worthless furs. Nothing could be done with them, for French laws prohibited the export of raw furs to hatters and clothiers in other nations. The King ordered a sharp decrease in prices his agents were paying in Canada, and, as the poor grades continued to pile up, the prices were lowered still more, until no profit was possible for the Canadian exporters.

Adjustments eventually would bring relief, but La Salle did not wait for them. He bought only the finest pelts at Fort Frontenac, and sent them to the English through Iroquois emissaries.

This brought new charges that he was disloyal to his country and was undermining the colony's economy.

There was, however, nothing wrong with La Salle's patriotism. Indeed, everything he had proposed, everything he had tried to accomplish, had been first for the glory of France and second for himself. At every step he had taken, the traders of the St. Lawrence had sought to block his path. They might succeed in thwarting his plans for expansion, but he did not propose to let them ruin him as a trader by their senseless acts.

In their struggle to defeat the plans of La Salle the Jesuits did much more than explore the west and build missions. As the stone bastions of Fort Frontenac took shape, they sent missionaries to the south of Lake Ontario to spread the falsehood among the Iroquois that La Salle was strengthening his defenses only for the purpose of making war on them. The Jesuits would have fomented a conflict in which hundreds of men, both red and white, would have been wounded, maimed and killed, in which villages and settlements would have been laid waste, which would have brought hunger and pestilence to the land and to all the people, warriors, women, and children, in it.

No man understood better the moods and the ways of the Iroquois than La Salle. No white man was closer to them, and none had more friends among them. When he heard of the activities of the Jesuit propagandists, he had gone among the tribes to make a personal investigation of the situation, and he had learned that many warriors, "in consequence of the Jesuits' intrigues, were in an excited state." At once he had sent an urgent message to Frontenac to come to Fort Frontenac.

The Governor quickly set out, escorted by forty canoes carrying troops. By the time he reached Fort Frontenac, La Salle had assembled the leading Iroquois chiefs and headmen. Once more in a solemn council Frontenac gravely warned them against opening their ears to men who would injure them. Once more he warned them of the immense power and resources of the French.

And once more he won their confidence and their pledges of loyalty to the fleur-de-lis.

Renadout would attribute to La Salle the belief that the "object of the intrigue was [not only] to make the Iroquois jealous of him, [but to] engage Frontenac in expenses which would offend the King. After La Salle and the Governor had lost credit by the rupture, the Jesuits would come forward as pacificators, in the full assurance that they could restore quiet, and appear in the attitude of saviors of the colony."

Quiet had been restored by Frontenac. The fears of the Iroquois had been quelled. And, before the summer had ended, a letter would come to the Governor from the King.

"I cannot but approve," Louis XIV would write, "of what you have done, in your voyage to Fort Frontenac, to reconcile the minds of the Five Iroquois Nations, and to clear yourself from the suspicions they had entertained, and from the motives that might induce them to make war."

If Frontenac had had any reason to be apprehensive about the attitude of the home government toward the activities in which he and La Salle were engaged, the royal missive dispelled them. Not only had the Jesuits failed in their scheme to arouse the Iroquois, but they had lost face at Versailles. Had they been anything but a religious order they undoubtedly would have suffered severe penalties for their traitorous scheme to embroil France in a costly and unreasonable conflict.

But the setback did not prevent the Jesuits from playing the next card in their hand.

To Fort Frontenac came the noted *voyageur* and interpreter, Nicholas Perrot, known by *couriers du bois* and Indians from the St. Lawrence to Michilimackinac as Jolycoeur. It was he who had reported seeing La Salle in the summer of 1670 hunting with Iroquois on the Ottawa River. La Salle made him welcome, and discussed the possibility of engaging him as a trader.

Shortly afterward, La Salle was taken violently ill. An examination of a salad which had been served to him revealed the presence of hemlock and verdigris, a mixture poisonous enough to have taken the life of anyone but a man of exceptional stamina. Jolycoeur's previous association with Jesuit missionaries in the Great Lakes region was well known, and suspicion turned toward him. To the astonishment of everyone, he not only confessed the crime, but charged that the Jesuits had hired him to commit it.

The attempt on his life revealed a mystifying side of La Salle's character. Instead of arresting Perrot and sending him under guard to Montreal for trial, a course he might have been expected to take, he banished him from Fort Frontenac and announced that he had no wish to see him punished. La Salle's reaction would never be satisfactorily explained, although he would attempt to give his reasons for it in a letter to the Prince de Conti in Paris.

"I am bound to render them [the Jesuits] the justice to say that the poison which was given me was not at all of their instigation," he told Conti. "The person who was conscious of the guilt, believing that I was their enemy because he saw that our sentiments were opposed, thought to exculpate himself by accusing them, and I confess that at the time I was not sorry to have this indication of their ill-will; but having afterwards carefully examined the affair, I clearly discovered the falsity of the accusation which this rascal had made against them. I nevertheless pardoned him, in order not to give notoriety to the affair; as the mere suspicion might sully their reputation, to which I should scrupulously avoid doing the slightest injury unless I thought it necessary to the good of the public, and unless the fact were fully proved. Therefore, Monsieur, if anybody shared the suspicion which I felt, oblige me by undeceiving him."

This was a strange statement for a man to make who had not hesitated to "sully the reputation" of the Jesuits on numerous previous occasions. The honorableness it seems to suggest falls of its own weight.

Yet, an ensuing event appears to indicate that La Salle was

attempting to effect at least a partial reconciliation between himself and the Jesuits in the belief that continued open warfare could result only in injury to both factions. If that were true, his efforts proved to be futile, and the event itself, although insignificant, disclosed a naïveté he seldom displayed.

A *voyageur* who gave the name of Deslauriers arrived at Fort Frontenac asking employment. He presented letters signed by two Jesuit missionaries whom La Salle knew and for whom he had no dislike. The letters recommended Deslauriers as a man of good character and extensive experience in the fur trade. La Salle engaged him.

A few days later Deslauriers vanished into the forest, and with him went a canoe loaded with powder and weapons and six *engagés* with whom La Salle had contracts and to whom he had advanced half a year's wages that had not been repaid. La Salle sent men in pursuit of the deserters, but they were not overtaken. In time, he learned that they had fled to the mission which the Jesuits maintained among the Mohawks near Albany and had been employed by English traders.

From a canoe at the gate of Fort Frontenac on a summer day in the year 1677 stepped a familiar figure in the grey robe of a Sulpician. It was Jean Cavelier.

The Jesuits had struck on a new salient.

Their strategy was clever. Not only did they know that the money La Salle spent must pass through the hands of Father Cavelier, but they were fully aware of the strained relations of the two brothers. Perhaps even more important, they knew that the bigoted and fanatical Sulpician disapproved of what La Salle was doing and would have liked to find a means of thwarting him. Jean Cavelier was a man admirably suited to carry out the opprobrious scheme they had concocted.

In Montreal and Quebec, the Jesuits spread the rumor that La Salle had kidnapped a comely young French girl in her teens, had raped her, and then had carried her off as his mistress to Fort

Frontenac, much against her will. They made sure that the sordid details of the brutal act reached the ears of Jean Cavelier. The immediate result was all that they could have desired.

Father Cavelier, escorted by several *engagés*, lost no time in setting out for Fort Frontenac. There, without waiting to ascertain the truth or falsity of the accusation, he excoriated his younger brother, condemning him for blackening the family name with an abominable scandal.

When Father Cavelier took the trouble to investigate affairs there, however, he found, to his dismay, that he had been tricked. There was no kidnapped, raped, and imprisoned young French girl. La Salle, lacking a mistress of any age or nationality, presided "with edifying propriety over a most exemplary household." Father Cavelier returned to Montreal chagrined and angered at his religious brethren, if not a little disappointed.

The plot backfired on the Jesuits, for it was a factor in La Salle's decision that the time had come for him to make another supreme effort to advance the great plan which had never ceased to dominate his thoughts during the two years he had been at Fort Frontenac. All he could attain there was a measure of security and a good income. It was not enough. Even without the constant harassments, without the pressure brought against him by other traders, without the unrelenting efforts of the Jesuits to discredit him and to destroy his trade—not to mention their attempt to murder him—without having to ask his brother for money and account to him for all expenditures, his situation would have been insupportable, more than he could continue to bear. Adding its weight to this intolerable state was his inherent restlessness which, although it had been temporarily quieted by his preoccupation with the rebuilding of Fort Frontenac and the development of a stable trade, had risen anew in him to burn with a heat that destroyed any possibility of his enjoying personal peace or contentment.

As the first frosts of the fall of 1677 painted the trees enclosing Lake Ontario, he left Fort Frontenac in the command of his chief lieutenant, William de la Forest, and started down the lovely channels of the Thousand Islands, on his way to France. Nika was with him.

19 ✤ ✤ ✤

WHEN THEY learned that La Salle was en route to Quebec and would sail for France, the unrelenting Jesuits hurriedly sent word to the Superior of the order in Paris to make every effort to discredit him and to oppose strenuously any plan he might propose to Colbert. Emissaries of the Jesuits responded to the appeal with calls upon both Colbert and his son, the Marquis de Seignelay, who, under the excellent tutelage of his brilliant father, was rising fast toward a high government post.

The Paris agents, representing the hierarchy of the Society of Jesus, echoed the cries of their Canadian colleagues. La Salle was a visionary, a grasping, dishonest trader. La Salle's "head was turned" to the extent that he was "fit for nothing but a mad-house." If the King desired to establish settlements and forts beyond the Great Lakes, Louis Joliet should command the projects, not an insane man.

Colbert already had declined to grant Joliet permission to build a fort in the Mississippi Valley, and he was not persuaded to change his mind. He and Seignelay, however, listened respectfully to the appeals of the high-ranked Jesuits, but promised them nothing except that they would give the matter further consideration.

Not all men of the cloth, however, approved of the Jesuits' attacks on La Salle or their attempts to defeat his plans. Two venerable, brilliant, and influential ecclesiastics who believed that he, and not missionaries, should be authorized to open the western wilderness for France rose to his defense. They were Abbé Renadout, a member of the French Academy, and Abbé Bernou, a

[97]

gifted author whose writings affected the trend of both spiritual and temporal affairs in the latter half of the seventeenth century. Both contributed regularly to the *Gazette* and kept in close touch with current events.

Renadout enlisted the support of his close friend, the powerful Louis-Armand de Bourbon, Prince de Conti, and arranged "ten or a dozen" meetings at which other prominent persons could meet La Salle and judge "his sanity" for themselves.

Bernou willingly assisted La Salle in preparing a petition to be presented to Colbert. It bore the marks of a talented writer and the thoroughness of a brief prepared by an astute and capable trial lawyer. Prince de Conti endorsed it, and saw that it was given immediate consideration by the minister.

In countering the contention of the Jesuits that La Salle gave first thought to enriching himself, his friends stressed that he had not established Fort Frontenac as the hub of a commercial empire he hoped to build but as a first step in plans that were directed toward gaining advantages for France in the New World. Now, they maintained, the time had come to launch those plans.

The memorial laid before Colbert repeated accounts of his discoveries in the western wilderness, for which he had been rewarded by the King with the Fort Frontenac seigneury, and then presented a description of the unknown regions he had penetrated that would have put to shame the most inspired copywriter of a modern-day chamber of commerce.

The country south and west of the Great Lakes, it proclaimed, was "nearly all so beautiful and so fertile; so free from forests, and so full of meadows, brooks, and rivers; so abounding in fish, game, and venison, that one can find there in plenty, and with little troubles, all that is needful for the support of flourishing colonies."

The soil "will produce everything that is raised in France," continued the memorial. "Flocks and herds can be left out at pasture all winter; and there are even native wild cattle, which, instead of hair, have a fine wool that may answer for making cloth and hats. Their hides are better than those [the cattle] of France, as appears by the sample which the Sieur de la Salle has brought with him. Hemp and cotton grow here naturally, and may be manufactured with good results; so there can be no doubt that colonies planted here would become very prosperous."

Ecstatic and exaggerative, the memorial, nevertheless, confirmed La Salle's extraordinary capabilities as an observer and his remarkable perspicacity—if that confirmation was needed. He was speaking of the region that would comprise the middle west of the future United States, one of the richest agricultural lands on earth, and a land that would, indeed, support through every form of commerce and industry not prosperous colonies but immense cities and countless towns. One must wonder at his intuitive cognition, his incredible discernment, and the immensity of the visions he held, visions that rose before him as he gazed on a land that was as it had been created, an utter wilderness.

The settlements which La Salle hoped to establish, he told Colbert, "would be increased by a great number of western Indians, who are in the main of a tractable and social disposition; and as they have the use neither of our weapons nor of our goods, and are not in intercourse with other Europeans, they will readily adapt themselves to us and imitate our way of life as soon as they taste the advantages of our friendship and of the commodities we bring them, insomuch that these countries will infallibly furnish, within a few years, a great many new subjects to the Church and the King."

French Canada as it existed was an impoverished country, a land of impenetrable forests, of barren soil, of harsh climate. The country south and west of the Great Lakes was open, blessed with rich earth, and enjoyed comparatively mild winters. Conquering and colonizing it, however, would not be easy. Distances were vast, there was great danger from the Iroquois, a people that would always be intractable, who were instilled by a love of conquest and fighting. There would also have to be reckoned with the rivalry of the English, who coveted the western country, but as yet had not made any strong moves to conquer and control it.

It was the anticipated rivalry of the English, said the memorial, a rivalry that assuredly would be launched, that "only animates the Sieur de la Salle the more, and impels him to precede them by the promptness of his action."

La Salle proposed as the first project to be undertaken the building of a fort and the establishment of a settlement at the outlet of Lake Erie, an area of "which the English, if not prevented, might easily take possession." Next, another fort should be constructed at a strategic location, to be selected by him, farther to the west.

These installations were to be built at his own expense. To enable him to finance them, he asked for seignorial rights over any lands he would open to development for a period of twenty years, and a monopoly of the trade in buffalo hides, which he proposed to carry on by means of ships sailing down the Mississippi River to the Gulf of Mexico.

Colbert did not exercise his right to reject or approve any of La Salle's propositions. His only promise was that he would place the entire matter and the memorial before the King and his other counsellors at an expedient time.

Meanwhile, La Salle waited. He had taken lodgings in a comfortable but unpretentious hotel in the Rue de la Traunderie. His money was limited. His wardrobe was small and unsuitable in several respects for a social life. He avoided soirées and meetings which he judged it would not be to his advantage to attend. The gay and glamorous aspects of Paris life had little appeal for him. The narrow streets and walls seemed to press upon him, the clamor and confusion pained him, and he longed for the vastness and the stillness of the wilderness, knowing that he could never be content to live away from it.

The Prince de Conti and Renadout were tireless in their efforts to aid La Salle, and pressed the court for a decision. Conti, convinced that when it came it would be favorable, sent to La Salle a man named Henry de Tonty whom he believed would be useful in the great venture in America.

Tonty and La Salle liked each other at once, and as the weeks of the winter and spring dragged away they spent a great deal of time together. Often with them was an ex-soldier, La Motte de Lussiere, who had appeared with letters of recommendation from La Salle's supporters, and who was eager to join his enterprise.

In this way began an association that would comprise a significant and dramatic chapter in the history of American exploration. It would be said that Tonty was the only true friend La Salle ever possessed, but, if that is not quite accurate, the assertion that he was La Salle's most devoted and trustworthy friend is undeniable.

Tonty, an Italian by birth, was the son of Lorenzo de Tonty, a Neapolitan banker who was forced to flee to France by political enemies. There he was welcomed by a fellow countryman, Cardinal Mazarin, an expert in obtaining money, ostensibly for the church, by extortion and blackmail. Putting their rascally heads together, Tonty and Mazarin came up with a scheme called the "Tontine Royal." They termed it a form of insurance to which people of all ages might subscribe and build an estate for their heirs. It was in fact nothing more than an ingenious swindle, but Mazarin was able to persuade Louis XIV that it would benefit the state. The money raised would be handed over to the government, and the subscribers would receive interest on their so-called loans. The King advanced money to promote the idea, but, when the parliament refused to authorize the scheme, he asked that it be returned to him. It was then discovered that the royal contribution had vanished into the pockets of the Cardinal and the refugee banker. Mazarin's red cap and influential position saved him from punishment, but Lorenzo de Tonty went to the Bastille. He remained there during the time of his son's youth.

At the age of seventeen, Henry de Tonty enlisted as a cadet

in the French Navy. Later he transferred to the Army and rose rapidly to the rank of captain. Highly intelligent and skillful as a leader, he was also a young officer of great courage and bravery. When his left hand was shot off in Sicily no medical attention was immediately available to him. He cut away the jagged flesh and bones with a knife, bandaged the stump, and continued to lead his company in an assault. The injury ended his military career, but it marked the beginning of a life that would secure for him a permanent place in history. He had a hand fashioned from metal, covered it with a glove, and went to Paris to seek employment.

Tonty looked like his father. He was tall, handsome, and somewhat of a dandy in his dress. But he had inherited none of his father's uncommendable qualities. He was scrupulously honest, completely unselfish, and unqualifiedly honorable.

The decision for which La Salle had unhappily and impatiently waited came in the spring. It was, as Prince Conti had predicted, favorable. Indeed, La Salle was granted more concessions than he had requested. The door was completely opened to him to carry out his plans by the letters patent signed at St.-Germain-en-Laye on May 12, 1678, by Louis XIV. The document was addressed "To Our dear and well-beloved Robert Cavelier, Sieur de la Salle," a salutation that did nothing to calm the fury seething in the Jesuits.

Nor were the apprehensions of the Spanish alleviated in any way by the contents of the order. Not only did the King permit La Salle "to endeavor to discover the western part of New France," but, in the second paragraph, he wrote that "We have consented to this proposal the more willingly, because there is nothing We have more at heart than the discovery of this country, *through which it is probable a road may be found to penetrate to Mexico. . . .*" (author's italics).

The italicized words appear as incontrovertible evidence that La Salle was looking far beyond his proposed conquest of the lower Mississippi Valley. They suggest, if they do not prove, that he had confided in Colbert ideas and plans that were not included in the memorial presented to the minister and to the King. And they indicate as well that both Colbert and the King looked with favor on the proposals, whatever they might have been, that La Salle had not reduced to writing.

For La Salle was given "full powers" to carry out the immense development, but not in the twenty years he had requested. He was to accomplish it "within five years." The imposition of this limit may only be taken as further proof that Louis XIV had in mind in the spring of 1678 an invasion of the Spanish colonies of America, and that he was looking to La Salle to prepare the ground and to open the way for it.

La Salle was not restricted to building the two or three forts he had proposed, but was given the privilege of constructing as many forts as he wished "wherever you shall deem it necessary."

He was awarded the exclusive right to trade in buffalo skins, but he was no longer to conduct trade with Indians north of the Great Lakes "and others who bring their beaver skins and other peltries to Montreal." This was a concession to the merchants of the St. Lawrence who had so vehemently opposed La Salle, but it was a sacrifice he was willing to make without protest. It did not preclude him from shipping furs down the St. Lawrence from Fort Frontenac, as long as they had not originated north of the Great Lakes. And he held seignorial and trade rights in regions south of the Great Lakes which fur traders had not touched. Moreover, the traffic in buffalo skins would, in his estimation, be of far greater value than any trade he might have enjoyed in northern regions.

As they had done when he had received his seigneury at Fort Frontenac, friends, relatives, and even total strangers, sought to share in the good fortune which had come to him. His cousin, François Plet, was one of the first to congratulate him with money in hand. Plet's loan was small in comparison with some of the others made to him, a mere eleven thousand *livres*, but Plet assured him that much more would be forthcoming if he needed it. Of course, in view of the poor state of the nation's commerce and an unpromising business outlook, Plet regrettably was obliged to charge an interest rate of forty per cent. Plet would claim that he and his family had advanced La Salle more than five hundred thousand *livres*, and had spared no effort to enable La Salle "to respond worthily to the royal goodness."

La Salle had deposited to his credit some hundred and fifty thousand *livres* before May had ended. He spent a part of it for iron, cordage, anchors, and other equipment for two vessels to be built on Lake Erie and on the Illinois.

In June, with Tonty, whom he had appointed his chief lieutenant for the expedition of discovery, La Motte, and a company of thirty men composed of ship carpenters and other craftsmen he had engaged, he went to Rochelle to take ship for Quebec. There he encountered a prime example of the corruption which permeated numerous bureaus of the French government.

Papers and passports were found not to be in order. Export permits had not been correctly issued. The straightening out of one tangle seemed only to result in creating others. Days and weeks passed in hopeless arguing. Still the vexatious delays mounted. Always there was another regulation with which La Salle had failed to comply.

Then, suddenly, all the problems were resolved when La Salle appealed directly to M. Bellinzani, the director of commerce and trade. Before achieving his government station, Bellinzani had served on the staff of Cardinal Mazarin and had received a thorough education in the black art of extortion. Bluntly he informed La Salle that all his difficulties could be terminated by the payment of a bribe of twelve thousand *livres*.

La Salle, realizing that he was caught in a net from which there was no other means of escape, signed a promissory note for the amount.

The red tape which had entangled him vanished as if by

magic, and on July 14, he and his company sailed. As La Salle watched the shores of France vanish over the stern he swore to himself that at some future time he would expose Bellinzani and force him to repay the money. He would be successful in reclaiming the money, but other debtors would take it.

The voyage took two months. As La Salle stepped ashore at Quebec, with Nika beside him, Father Hennepin was waiting for him, having journeyed down the St. Lawrence from Fort Frontenac to meet him. Also on the wharf were aides of the Governor who had come to escort him to the Chateau.

20 ❧ ❧ ❧

COLD AND SNOW were in the offing. Ice would soon begin to form on the river. La Salle pushed the loading of cargo boats with all possible speed. Tonty busied himself recruiting rivermen and aiding in the purchase of additional equipment, food supplies, and goods for the Indian trade.

Frontenac urged upon La Salle a plan which would increase his funds and decrease the enmity of the leading merchants. It involved selling shares in the great enterprise and mortgaging his holdings at Fort Frontenac. The idea did not appeal to La Salle. He saw danger in an association with his enemies. But Frontenac persuaded him to accept it, arguing that it would be to his advantage—and to the advantage of himself—to have friends among the important traders of the St. Lawrence.

Frontenac selected half a dozen subscribers. Their identities were not immediately revealed, but no doubt they were wealthy men with whom he desired to establish better relationships than had existed in the past. Nor do the records make clear the financial arrangements they had with La Salle or the amount of money they invested. Unquestionably, part of it was given in the form of credit. The amount of the mortgage on Fort Frontenac is known. It was some fourteen thousand francs.

Hennepin was too impatient to wait until the preparations of the company for the voyage up the river had been completed. He was eager to return to his mission at Fort Frontenac, and he left Quebec early in October in a small canoe with two rivermen. He was garbed in his customary manner: a coarse grey capote with a peaked hood, heavy woolen socks and underwear, and deerskin sandals. About his thick waist was the cord of St. Francis, and at his side hung a rosary and crucifix. His baggage consisted mainly of a portable altar, constructed so that it might be contained in a skin pack and carried on his back. In a small knapsack among spare undergarments was a treasured document which La Salle had delivered into his hands. It was a "written order" to accompany La Salle on his western explorations from Father Hyacinthe Le Fevre, Provincial of the Recollect Order in France.

In Quebec, Bishop Laval had given Hennepin his blessing and had sanctioned his journey in the name of the Jesuits. Apparently, this act of courtesy was not known in Montreal, for when Hennepin reached there a Jesuit succeeded in inducing his canoemen to desert him. After some delay, he obtained replacements and continued his trip. He reached Fort Frontenac at eleven o'clock on the night of November 2, and received "a very warm welcome at the mission house from the missionaries, Father Gabriel de la Ribourde and Father Luc Buisset."

The cargo convoy and the craftsmen, led by La Motte, arrived a week later. La Salle was still detained in Quebec and he had kept Tonty, whose counsel he had come to value greatly, with him, but had not permitted his inability to start to delay the launching of the western expedition. With La Motte he sent orders to get it under way by sending fifteen men in canoes to Lake Erie. The party was to proceed as far as possible before ice closed the waters, en route trading for furs. In the spring, they were to go on to Lake Michigan and by way of the Miami [St. Joseph] to the Kankakee and the Illinois, where they were to continue their trading and gather provisions for the parties to follow.

La Salle gave further instructions to La Motte. As soon as preparations could be made, La Motte and Father Hennepin, with sixteen men, were to sail in one of the small ships from Fort Frontenac for the Niagara River at the head of Lake Ontario. There they were to begin construction of a fort on the most favorable site while awaiting the arrival of himself, Tonty, and the remainder of the company.

These orders were duly executed before La Salle was able to leave Quebec. One of the matters which detained him, in addition to the completion of financial and other business affairs, was a request by Frontenac that he attend a meeting of traders and officials which had been called for the purpose of preparing new regulations governing the use of alcoholic spirits in the fur trade.

The conference would come to be known as the "Brandy Parliament of 1678." Bishop Laval, supported by Intendant Duchesneau and a number of leading traders, had protested so vehemently and noisily in a campaign to prevent *couriers du bois* from taking brandy to the Indians, that the question had been brought to the attention of the King. He had directed Colbert to instruct the Canadian merchants to meet and formulate a policy to which would be given the force of law.

The "Brandy Parliament" convened at Quebec late in October. Present were the Governor and the colony's sovereign council, some twenty of the leading merchants, the noted *voyageur* Joliet, and Bishop Laval. Several delegates maintained that liquor had destroyed the enterprise of the Indians and decreased their physical powers to the extent that they hunted only enough to keep themselves supplied with alcohol. Numerous instances were cited in which Indians who had obtained goods on credit did not pay their debts but took their furs to other posts where they traded them for new supplies of liquor.

[107]

La Salle was the leading speaker opposed to discontinuing the use of spirits. He argued that it was impossible to keep liquor from the Indians, that if licensed *couriers du bois* were not allowed to sell it, unscrupulous individuals would smuggle it into the Indian country, and he insisted that most of the Indians would not trade with those who did not furnish them with drinks. In this contention he had support from the writings of a prominent Jesuit who had maintained that "it is useless to forbid the trade in wine and brandy with the Savages. There is always found some base person who, to gain a little beaver fur, introduces by moonlight some bottle into their Cabins."

La Salle bolstered his stand with a case in point with which he was familiar: three hundred Iroquois were en route to Montreal with furs, but when deceived into thinking they could not obtain any liquor there, they turned about and went to Albany, where traders willingly supplied them all the drink they desired. If the French, declared La Salle, were to forbid the use of liquor in the trade, the English and Dutch would continue to hold not only the alliance but the love of the Iroquois and they would secure the loyalty of the western tribes.

La Salle's position was endorsed by a delegate who advanced the theory that brandy was helpful in saving the Indians' souls. If the English and Dutch were permitted to hold the Indians through drink, they might also convert them to heresies which would send their souls to perdition.

Another trader contended that the Indians could not purchase enough alcohol to hurt them. The French trade in beaver amounted to some eighty thousand pelts a season from twenty thousand Indians, an average of only four skins per person. Four beaver pelts would not pay for enough brandy to harm anyone. He did not trouble to add that the larger percentage of the twenty thousand Indians were squaws and children who did not hunt beaver. It was his belief that more was to be gained by teaching Indians to use alcohol in moderation than by imposing unenforceable restrictions.

Joliet rose in support of strict prohibition, pointing out that Indians became violent and uncontrollable when intoxicated. To obtain drink they went into debt, neglected themselves and their families, deteriorated physically, and became poor hunters and people of degraded character. So extreme were Joliet's views on the issue that he urged the death penalty for *couriers du bois* who used liquor in the fur trade.

Laval, Joliet, and their supporters lost. The "Brandy Parliament" voted to continue the traffic in liquor.

La Salle had become profoundly worried about the safety of a ship which was bringing him a large quantity of stores he had purchased in France. He had expected it to arrive in Quebec early in October, and had hoped that he would be able to transport the goods to Fort Frontenac before the river was closed. No word of the vessel had been received when, in mid-November, he, Tonty and several *couriers du bois* left Quebec. Because of ice they were forced to abandon their canoes near Montreal and to travel on foot, much of the way through thick snow. It was the second week of December when they reached Fort Frontenac.

Drawing to a close was the year of great change, 1678—the thirty-fifth year of La Salle's life.

It was the change which lifted him from the level of prominence to that high elevation achieved only by men whose innate ingenuity, perspicacity and courage had served in concert to bring them undying fame.

21 ❧❧❧

LA SALLE AND Tonty, with men and supplies, sailed from Fort Frontenac in mid-December to join La Motte and Hennepin at Niagara. La Salle had left a letter to be sent to Prince Conti which revealed his attitude of the moment. "I hope to give myself the honor of sending you a more particular account of this enterprise when it shall have had the success which I hope for it; but I have need of a strong protection for its support. It traverses the commercial operations of certain persons, who will find it hard to endure it. They [the Jesuits] intended to make a new Paraguay in these parts, and the route which I chose against them gave them facilities for an advantageous correspondence with Mexico. This check will infallibly be a mortification to them; and you know how they deal with whatever opposes them."

Here La Salle was charging the Jesuits with informing the Mexican colonial government, if not the government of Spain, of the French plans to advance to the Gulf of Mexico. This was done, of course, only for the purpose of enlisting the aid of the Spanish in defeating La Salle. They might have spared themselves the trouble. As subsequent events demonstrated, the Spanish were already alarmed and were preparing to prevent the incursion of French forces into their territories.

It should be noted that Tonty suffered little from his handicap. He had no difficulty with weapons and performed arduous labor as well as other men. His iron hand, as it was called, although it was made of alloyed metal to give it lightness, was used with telling effect in times of trouble, which not infrequently occurred. With it he knocked unconscious a towering, powerful *courier du bois* who attacked him. On other occasions he broke the heads of rebellious Indians and *engagés* who defied his commands, often leaving them with bleeding mouths containing shattered teeth. Word that his gloved hand was "bad medicine" to be avoided soon spread among the western tribes.

La Motte and Hennepin had already reached Niagara when La Salle left Fort Frontenac. As the dedicated Recollect diarist recorded, they had started on November 18, and the "men were afraid of sailing in so small a vessel, about ten tons, because it was bitterly cold and the autumn winds were very strong. Consequently, La Motte, who was in command, had to hug the north shore of Lake Ontario. . . . We had a dangerous night on the twenty-sixth. Our little ship was tossed so badly that we had to lie at anchor all night at sixty fathoms of cable. Finally the wind changed. . . . We went on to the head of the lake . . . where on the north shore was an Iroquois village."

They fought their way around the western end of the lake, several times forced to chop the vessel out of an ice floe, and on the sixth of December, "St. Nicholas Day, we entered the beautiful Niagara River." Senecas living there "caught more than three hundred whitefish in one seining and gave them all to us."

Hennepin's early writings were largely truthful, but his pen later went astray, perhaps directed by the excessive vanity and spitefulness with which he was afflicted. When his contemporaries expressed doubts about the veracity of his tales, he replied with a note to readers: "I here protest to you, before God, that my narrative is faithful and sincere, and that you may believe everything related in it." Yet, despite their mendacity and the enormity of their fabrications, his accounts have historical value. La Salle would write few letters, and many of the records he kept would be lost. Were it not for the narratives and correspondence of Hennepin, some other priests, and Tonty, knowledge of both the events of La Salle's life and his great explorations would, indeed, be sparse. But those men were with him, they shared his fortunes, both good and bad, and inaccuracies and even outright prevarications become inconsequential in the light of their contributions to history.

The friendliness shown at first by the Senecas living in the area quickly vanished when they learned that the white men had come to build a fort, and their ensuing sullenness and inhospitality caused profound concern in the French camp. No mystery was attached to the change of attitude. The reasons for it were clearly discernible. Niagara was the gateway to the four Great Lakes to the west. Whoever held possession of it could control the fur trade of the interior. And at the time this advantageous position was held by the Iroquois.

The fort, said Hennepin, also "could have put an end to their very extensive fur trade with the English and Dutch. To get furs the Iroquois must go to the western country and in going and coming must pass Niagara, where they could have been stopped amicably in peacetime and forcibly in wartime."

La Motte, whom La Salle had instructed to make every effort to maintain good relations with the Senecas residing along the shores of Lake Ontario, found himself in a menacing situation. He decided that further attempts to conciliate the residents of the immediate vicinity would be futile, and he determined to make a journey to the great town of the Senecas. It stood five or six days' march to the east, beyond the Genesee River. With seven heavily armed men and Hennepin, he set out from Niagara on the twenty-sixth of December.

It was a forced march through snowy forests. Each man carried a heavy pack of goods to be used as gifts. No game was encountered, and hunger threatened, and when "we had only a few sacks of roasted corn left, we fortunately met Iroquois hunters who gave us venison and fifteen or sixteen black squirrels," which Hennepin thought "are very good to eat." It was the last day of the year 1678 when they reached the town, and, surrounded by a staring crowd of women, and children, they were escorted to the lodge of the head chief.

They were not encouraged by the appearance of two Jesuit missionaries. Their interpreter, Antoine Brassart, soon learned that the priests had been stirring up the Iroquois with reports that La Salle was building a fort to make war on them and to steal their trade with western tribes. La Motte cursed the priests to their faces and ordered that they be kept out of his sight.

On the first day of 1679, after Hennepin had said mass and preached a New Year sermon, for which the Indians displayed no enthusiasm, La Motte and his men were invited to a council. When they appeared they found forty-two elderly Senecas arrayed against the walls of a bark house, "almost all of them large men," wrapped in robes of beaver, wolf, and black squirrel skins, and puffing on calumets.

Brassart, translating La Motte's words into Iroquois, delivered an eloquent harangue, pausing frequently to place before the elders valuable gifts such as woolen coats, strips of scarlet cloth, hatchets, knives, and bright beads. La Salle, the interpreter told them, was their true friend and he represented Onontio, the great Father in Quebec, whom they knew well, having sat with him in council at Fort Frontenac. Instead of war, La Salle wanted only peace and to make them prosperous. He would build a post at Niagara and "big wooden canoes" on the Great Lakes so that he could bring "European goods to them more conveniently. . . . Consequently, he would be able to offer goods at lower prices."

The smoke continued for three days, during which the Senecas gratefully accepted every gift proffered, but gave no sign that they were impressed by La Motte's pleas. Their replies were evasive, and consisted mainly of meaningless generalities.

On the last night of the meeting, the Senecas insisted on entertaining their visitors with the burning of a prisoner. "Never, I believe, did Nero or Maximinus contrive greater torture to try the patience of martyrs," Hennepin thought, "than the torments the Iroquois made their enemies undergo. After the captive had been killed with unheard-of cruelty, the children each cut a chunk of meat from his body. These little cannibals ate his flesh in our presence. . . . We did not want to eat there anymore."

The mission had failed, and in the dawn, still sickened by the terrible scene they had witnessed, La Motte and his men started back to Niagara.

Two days later, the small vessel carrying La Salle and Tonty anchored in the mouth of the Genesee. They had had a bad trip from Fort Frontenac, and twice had come close to being wrecked by storms. La Salle, bearing suitable gifts, proceeded by land to the main town of the Senecas, unaware until he had reached it that La Motte's group had been there. The head chief willingly consented to hold another full-dress council, and graciously thanked him for his generous contributions.

La Salle was more fortunate than La Motte. "I told them my plan," he said, "and gave the best pretexts I could, and I succeeded in my attempt." It was his claim that he won from the Senecas their consent to transport arms and ammunition through the Niagara portage, to establish a fortified warehouse—not a fort—at the mouth of the Niagara River, and to construct a large vessel on Lake Erie.

A few days after leaving the Genesee, La Salle's brigantine reached the mouth of the Niagara. La Motte had erected a building surrounded by a palisade near the site of Lewiston. La Salle ordered his pilot to hold the vessel in a safe anchorage off shore, and set out to cross the portage and locate a suitable site for a shipyard above the falls. When he returned he was staggered by the news that through the carelessness of the crew his vessel had been dashed upon the rocky shore and destroyed. It had been heavily laden with provisions, trade goods, tools, and equipment valued at more than fifteen thousand *livres*. Some articles were recovered, among them anchors and cables to be used on the new ship, but it was an appalling reverse. Hennepin thought it great enough to have made anybody but La Salle "abandon the enterprise."

Indeed, a number of the men in the company urged La Salle to turn back. They appeared to have lost all interest in boat building or in going farther into the wilderness. La Salle became convinced that he had mistakenly engaged men who were loyal to the Jesuits and who had joined him as spies and saboteurs. His wrath turned on La Motte, whom he suspected of being the ringleader of the faction seeking to defeat him.

There were, however, mitigating circumstances in La Motte's actions and attitude. The winter ordeals, and especially the journey to the Seneca village, had been more than his body could endure. He was ill, and at last La Salle acceded to his request to return to

Fort Frontenac. La Motte departed, carrying only blankets and some corn to sustain him on the winter journey. He reached his destination almost blinded by inflammation of his eyes.

In the first weeks of 1679, strange events, unlike any ever before seen in the western wilderness, took place on the high forested ridges surrounding the great falls of the Niagara River.

The little vessel which had brought La Motte and Hennepin, and the goods and equipment salvaged from the wrecked ship, had been hauled with the use of capstans to the foot of the rapids. From that point, day after day, up the steep slopes, some thirty men toiled under burdens of tools, forges, ironware, cables, ropes, rolls of sail canvas, fittings and rigging and anchors, saws, axes, sledges, caulking, merchandise such as bolts of cloth, beads, hatchets, knives, guns, ammunition, seven cannon, tin plates and cooking pots and kettles, beads and bright braids and buckles, and supplies of flour and corn and beans and molasses and tea and kegs of brandy and other spirits. It was back-breaking, exhausting work, a carry of more than ten miles. After the ridges came thick forests, deep in snow. At all times the temperature was near zero, and frequently biting winds swept in from Lake Erie.

The site La Salle had chosen for his shipyard was near the mouth of a creek which discharged from the east into an arm of the Niagara River that lay behind a protective island. The stream would come to be known as Cayuga Creek, and a settlement that would grow there would be called La Salle.

Ground was cleared and cabins were erected. Ways were built and timbers felled for the ship under the direction of the master carpenter, Moïse Hillaret. Most of the Senecas of the area were away on a hunt, but others loitered nearby as the shipbuilders worked, with dark scowls and unpleasant gestures making known their disapproval of the project. From a squaw it was learned that the angry Senecas were scheming to burn the unfinished ship on the stocks, and it was heavily guarded at all times. Large fires were kept burning throughout each night, and the weary men slept uneasily beside their guns in their little bark huts.

Augmenting the tension was the continuing dissension. Not all of the troubles that arose, however, could be attributed to disloyalty to La Salle. The workers feared they would be murdered in their beds. The Senecas had refused to sell any of their corn and to supply the company with either fish or meat. Because of Indian threats, the camp hunters hesitated to journey very far into the forest without the company of guards. Some game was obtained, but most animals were driven away from the vicinity by the noise of the hammering and sawing. Meals were not always adequate, and seldom appetizing.

Despite the apparent danger to the shipbuilders, in early February La Salle took several men back to the mouth of the Niagara and set them to work on two blockhouses—Fort Conti. Then with two *engagés* he started for Fort Frontenac. It was his intention to bring out more supplies as soon as the lake opened. With their robes and a bag of corn on a small sled pulled by an Indian dog, the three men completed the journey of some two hundred and fifty miles in less than a fortnight, at all times traveling on snow and lake ice. On the last two days of the trip they had no food at all.

At Fort Frontenac, La Salle received dismal news. The Jesuits, aided by Intendant Duchesneau, had been hard at work against him. Even though his expedition was under way, and some of his men were far in the west, they did not relax their efforts to defeat him.

All manner of false reports had been circulated in Montreal and Quebec, some of them attributed to the sick La Motte. Indians had attacked and killed most of La Salle's men to stop him from stealing their trade. No vessel could be built because all the materials to go into it had been lost. La Salle had failed miserably, and would be forced to abandon his harebrained venture. The furs he had acquired had been stolen by Senecas. La Salle himself was planning to flee to Mexico. The few men of his company who were still alive were convinced he had gone mad. All the money loaned to him had been lost and could not possibly be recovered.

Alarmed by these stories, the merchants who had bought shares in his enterprise at the instigation of Frontenac had taken legal action against him. Now their identities, at first publicly unknown, were revealed. Frontenac had favored traders named Migeon, Charon, Giton, and Peloquin. They seized a large number of furs owned by La Salle which had been stored in Montreal to await shipment to France, hoping in this way to recover at least a small part of their investments. Frontenac's political machinations had delivered La Salle into the hands of men who had always been his enemies.

Perhaps the bitterest blow La Salle received was delivered by his brother. The Abbé Cavelier, purportedly to protect the interests of the family members, had obtained a court order which allowed him to confiscate all furs stored at Fort Frontenac and to sell them at auction in Quebec. La Salle then learned that even before he had left Quebec the previous fall, his brother had sent a letter to France urging François Plet to come to Canada, take charge of Fort Frontenac, and protect the family's fortune. It seems unlikely that the meddlesome Abbé was unaware that the value of La Salle's seigneury and the income from the immense trade at the fort would have more than repaid all debts to the Cavelier family which La Salle had incurred had he permitted his younger brother to continue the western enterprises as they had been planned. (François Plet would come to Canada and take charge of the trading at Fort Frontenac. He would cheat the Indians whose confidence and trust La Salle had won. Before that happened, La Salle would discover that a large quantity of cloth he had purchased from the Plet mercantile company at an exorbitant price, for use in the Indian trade, was of low grade, so shoddy, indeed, that it became known as

"La Salle Iroquois cloth." La Salle had spared no effort to dispense only merchandise of good quality in his trading, and the dishonesty of his cousin caused him no little embarrassment.)

Thoroughly disheartened, La Salle considered going to Quebec to protest the gross injustices he had suffered and to fight the suits which had been filed against him. He chose instead to attempt to have them quashed and to regain the confidence of his creditors through correspondence.

Summer had come before he became convinced that all efforts toward this end were futile.

A man of less courage would have thrown up his hands and have waved a white flag of surrender.

La Salle harbored no such thought.

22 ✣ ✣ ✣

NEVER AVERSE to blowing his own horn, Hennepin immodestly took credit for keeping the work progressing smoothly at the ship-building camp during La Salle's absence. His rebukes forced contumacious Indians to "withdraw quietly." Hennepin represented the enterprise to the workmen "as concerned solely with the Glory of God, the good of the French colony, and their honor. In this way I encouraged them to work more diligently so as to get rid of their anxiety. Likewise, they took heart when they saw me give orders to the Indians . . . to supply us with venison. The men applied themselves more earnestly and in a short time our ship, though still unfinished, was in proper condition for launching."

A more dependable record of events taking place while La Salle was absent shows that it was Tonty who inspired the men to complete the ship. Perhaps La Salle himself could not have done as well as his lieutenant. Certainly he could have accomplished no more. Tonty's calmness in the face of the most dangerous situation, his unfailing courage and determination, his fairness and unselfishness, won the confidence of most men in the camp. They were reassured, as well, by the respect with which the Indians obviously regarded him.

Tonty gave the forty-five–ton ship its name. It was derived from a remark of La Salle: "I will make the griffon fly above the crows." The fabulous animal, half eagle and half lion, embellished the armor of Frontenac. The crows were the black-gowned Jesuits.

On a bright day in the spring of 1679, the company gathered about the hull of the *Griffon*. Hennepin pronounced a blessing on her, and the voices of the workers rang out against the greening forest in the Te Deum. Brandy was passed about, a generous ration being distributed to the watching Senecas. Cannon thundered. Blocks were driven from place with sledges. To the wild cheers of the white men and the wilder yelps of the Indians, the *Griffon* glided smoothly into the water of Cayuga Creek.

Tonty ordered the ship towed upstream where the current was moderate, and there it was securely anchored. He then directed the entire company to live on board, and "there," said Hennepin, "we slept in peace, safe from attack by Indians."

By early summer the *Griffon* had been fully completed. Each day men watched from the mouth of the Niagara for La Salle, their concern for his safety steadily growing. But their fears were ended on a day early in August when they saw a brigantine gliding toward them over the silvery blue waters of Lake Ontario.

With La Salle had come three more Recollect missionaries, all Flemings. Father Nelithon Watteau would establish a mission at Fort Conti. Fathers Zenobe Membre and Gabriel Ribourde had been assigned to join their countryman, Hennepin, and accompany La Salle to the west.

By bringing the Recollects out with him, La Salle had drastically increased the competition of the Jesuits. Ribourde was a man of remarkable strength, good health, and cheerful disposition, although he was sixty-four years of age. Membre, perhaps thirty years younger, was exultant at the opportunity to go into the western wilderness.

In view of the disastrous turn of events on the St. Lawrence, La Salle had begun to fear that the fifteen men he had sent out the preceding fall from Fort Frontenac might prove to be either tools of the Jesuits or more loyal to rival traders than to him. Upon his arrival at Niagara he at once sent Tonty and two men to endeavor to learn something of their progress. Tonty was to proceed "to the extremity of Lake Erie," questioning Indians en route, and was to wait for La Salle "at a place called Detroit."

The builders of the *Griffon* had not attempted to move her onto Lake Erie, fearing the strong current of the Niagara River. La Salle undertook the task. Full sails were raised and tow ropes were lashed to trees along the shore. Slowly the ship was forced forward, and at the end of a day of struggling, the calm waters of the lake were reached.

By the seventh of August, 1679, the *Griffon*, anchored in a bay near the head of the river, had been loaded. Some thirty men went aboard. Cannons were fired. The sails swelled in a fresh breeze. With La Salle standing beside the helmsman, the first sailing ship to plow the waters of the Great Lakes above Niagara Falls left its wake on the sparkling waters of Lake Erie, the course "west by south."

Good weather prevailed, and on the third day after sailing, Tonty and his two men were overtaken. They had seen few Indians and had learned nothing of the advance company. On August 10, the *Griffon* stood into the Strait of Detroit. All marveled at the beauty and richness of the country that reached away on each side of the passage. Groves of black walnut and wild plum trees and oaks festooned with grapevines stood like islands on the fine prairies.

Lake Huron spread out before them, and the stout little vessel moved steadily ahead, with the men enjoying the leisure, their stomachs full of good meat washed down by "a little wine" which had been squeezed from the wild grapes hunters brought aboard.

Then, suddenly, they encountered the typical inconstancy of Great Lakes weather. The wind died, and they lay becalmed. Then a gale rose, and soon became a raging tempest. Short waves smashed furiously against the *Griffon*, as if to devour her, and several times she was in danger of being capsized. The night of August 26 was an unceasing terror. La Salle, no less than the others believing they would go down, called on the men to commend themselves to Heaven. All complied "except the Godless pilot, who could never be persuaded to pray." He cursed La Salle for having brought him, an honored sailor of oceans, to drown ignominiously in a fresh water lake. Crowded together in the cabin, the men were led by Hennepin in prayer, and "La Salle joined us in asking St. Anthony of Padua to protect our enterprise." All swore to God that if they lived they would erect a chapel in the wilderness that "would be dedicated to that great saint."

The winds soon began to die. Under a moderate southeast breeze they coasted the islands of Georgian Bay. In the distance they saw the forested shores of the Manitoulins. On August 28, the *Griffon* was at anchor in the tranquil cove behind the point of St. Ignace of Michilimackinac, "where crystal waters cover but cannot hide the pebbly depths beneath."

Beyond a narrow beach stood the palisaded mission of the Jesuits, the headquarters for all their activities in the western regions. Nearby was a Huron village of bark houses surrounded by tall pickets. Some distance along the shore were the trading houses, and beyond them rows of wigwams inhabited by Ottawas. Several scores of canoes bearing Indians came out to surround the *Griffon*. La Salle ordered a cannon fired as a salute, and the noise so terrified the Indians that some of them plunged into the water in their haste to escape "the formidable floating fort."

No man could have appeared at Michilimackinac who was more hated and feared by the traders, priests, and Indians living there than was La Salle. The traders hated him, because of his alliance with Frontenac, because he was in a position to control the trade passing Niagara, because he had been given the exclusive right to trade in buffalo hides south and west of the Great Lakes, and they feared him because they believed he had come to violate the royal edict which forbade him to trade with the northern tribes. The Jesuits hated him because he had defeated their own plans, and had been chosen by the King to open the western country from which they would have liked to exclude all commercial developments. The Ottawas and the Hurons hated him because he was a friend of the Iroquois, and they feared he would plot with the latter to make war on them.

All these things La Salle fully understood, but he was undeterred by them and exhibited no apprehension. Leaving only a few guards on the ship, he led his company ashore with the attitude of a man on his way to a summer garden affair. He wore a mantle of scarlet bordered in gold and a plumed hat, the silvery scabbard of a sword glinting in the sunlight. Two Jesuits came forward from a crowd of *couriers du bois*, traders, and Indians to extend him a cordial welcome that he knew very well was sheer pretense. Yet, he attempted to make them think he was deceived by the show of hospitality. Graciously he accepted their invitation to attend mass, and marched solemnly with them at the head of a motley parade to the chapel.

It was not difficult for La Salle to learn the fate of his advance party. Those of whom he inquired appeared only too willing to inform him that all his men had deserted and had sold the trade goods he had entrusted to them. Further investigation disclosed that four members of the party were still at Michilimackinac. La Salle quickly tracked them down and had them arrested. Informed that two more of the deserters were then at Sault Ste. Marie, La Salle dispatched Tonty with six men to take them into custody. No one seemed to know the whereabouts of the others.

Hennepin thought that La Salle was "all the more displeased at the conduct of his men because he had treated them well and had advanced money to all of them. For example, at Montreal he had paid twelve hundred *livres* that one of them owed to various people." The arrested men "were given no other punishment."

September had come. La Salle had given thought to returning himself to Montreal by way of Georgian Bay and the Ottawa River, and leaving Tonty to take the company on to the Illinois. He decided against this course for several reasons. Reports had come to him that the Jesuits were encouraging the Iroquois to attack the Illinois Indians who inhabited the region to which he was going. Tonty was away on the mission to Sault Ste. Marie, and the time of his return was undeterminable. There was no one else whom he felt he could trust with the command of the expedition.

In the first week of September, he set sail for Lake Michigan. Thirteen men were left at Michilimackinac to await the return of Tonty and the six *couriers du bois* who had gone with him to Sault Ste. Marie. The combined groups were then to travel down the eastern shore of Lake Michigan and rejoin La Salle on the St. Joseph River.

The *Griffon* soon dropped anchor at the entrance to Green Bay. There near the village of a friendly Potawatomi chief, Onanghisse, La Salle found the nine missing men of his advance party. They had remained unwaveringly loyal to him and had collected an immense quantity of beaver and other valuable furs worth some ten to twelve thousand *livres*.

It was a happy reunion, made all the pleasanter by the unrestrained hospitality of Onanghisse. The chief, said Hennepin, "had the highest regard for Count Frontenac, having been entertained by him at Montreal . . . and had his warriors dance the calumet for Sieur de la Salle.

Now La Salle once more changed his plans. The stock of furs would be most useful in appeasing the creditors hounding him, and he determined to send them back to Niagara on the *Griffon*. There the ship would take on supplies which he had ordered brought out to Fort Conti from Fort Frontenac, and return immediately to the lower end of Lake Michigan.

Membre, Hennepin, and others protested that the decision was unwise. The vessel would be under the command of the "godless pilot," and such a disbeliever could well turn out to be a thief. His temptation would be great, for he would have to pass Michilimackinac with a fortune in furs. "Would to God," Membre would say, "that the sieur de la Salle had continued his route in the vessel. His wisdom could not forsee the misfortunes which awaited him." Hennepin was more blunt in his comment that La Salle would accept "advice from no one. . . . Having only four canoes, he was forced to leave in the ship some of his goods, including many implements and tools. He directed the pilot to unload these things at Missilimackinac, where he could pick them up on his return."

On the eighteenth of September, a single cannon shot was fired from the *Griffon*. La Salle and the fourteen men who remained with him watched from the shore until the sails had vanished into the vastness of the great water.

Then, in four heavily laden canoes, they paddled southward along the dark forested shores of Lake Michigan.

23 ✣ ✣ ✣

FORTY-THREE DAYS were spent in reaching the Miami River [St. Joseph] from Green Bay.

Fall storms swept the southern end of Lake Michigan, and on several occasions La Salle and a number of his men came close to losing their lives. The small stock of food with which they had left Green Bay was soon consumed, and on many days they had nothing at all to eat. Game seemed to have vanished from the country, and hunters, one of whom was Saget, an expert Mohegan tracker, returned on most days empty-handed. The men ravenously devoured haws and wild berries, which made several of them weak and ill.

On October 1 they sighted a village of Potawatamis. The Indians ran to the shore making signs of friendship. Although the height of the waves was steadily increasing and the sky darkening with another storm, La Salle refused to land. He feared, said Hennepin, that his starving men "might desert or waste his goods, [and] he proceeded three leagues beyond the Indian village, and we were obliged to follow him in spite of the obvious danger." To gain the beach, the men had "no alternative but to leap into the water . . . lift the canoe and its contents to the shore, and drag it to safety, although the waves sometimes broke over their heads."

Having thrown up a breastworks of logs and brush, La Salle sent three men back to the village of the Potawatamis to barter for food. They took with them a calumet which had been given to him by the friendly chief at Green Bay, and which he thought might be accepted as a sign that they came in peace. The village was deserted, the Potawatamis having become frightened when the white men had not stopped and vanished into the forest. The emissaries confiscated several parfleches filled with maize, and returned to the camp. Later the Potawatamis reappeared. When they saw the calumet their fears vanished, and they gratefully accepted presents from La Salle and brought the visitors more food.

The rough weather continued, but the company pressed ahead, their hunger again becoming almost unbearable. When they sighted a congregation of crows and turkey buzzards ahead, they paddled "with redoubled effort toward these carnivorous birds," and found "half of a very fat deer which wolves had killed and partly consumed."

From this point onward—between the present cities of Milwaukee and Chicago—game became plentiful, and Saget kept the group well supplied with venison and fat turkeys. Wild grapes "as large as damson plums" were plentiful.

On October 28 high winds forced them upon the southern shore of Lake Michigan. They camped in a driving rain. During the night Indians stole unseen among the canoes and made off with a number of garments, one a coat belonging to Nika. La Salle understood that if the thefts were allowed to go unpunished, the Indians would return to steal more goods, believing the white men were afraid of them. He moved the camp to a woody peninsula, posted guards, and set out alone to find the culprits.

He had not gone far when he came upon a young Fox brave, who, confronted by a gun aimed at his chest, surrendered. La Salle marched him back to the camp, where he was manacled.

La Salle then set out again, taking with him Saget, who not only could talk in the language of signs but spoke several Indian tongues. They soon came upon a Fox village and were taken before the chief. Bluntly La Salle informed him that unless the stolen goods were returned, the prisoner would be killed.

The chief replied that he would be glad to make restitution, but unfortunately the stolen garments had been cut up and the cloth and attractive buttons had been distributed among numerous warriors. La Salle abruptly left.

The Foxes decided to solve the dilemma by a forceful recovery of the prisoner. Three Recollects armed with rosaries and twelve men with flintlocks at the ready soon faced some hundred and twenty-five Indians crouched behind trees a few yards from them.

Once again the calumet proved effective. When it was displayed, Hennepin, after "saying his office," advanced toward the Fox chief, "who, noticing that I was unarmed, rightly concluded that I was approaching in order to stop the fight and act as mediator. . . ."

The Indians were not eager to fight. Although they greatly outnumbered the white men, they had among them only seven guns and little ammunition, and they had learned from sad experience in clashes with the Iroquois that bows and arrows were ineffective against firearms. The chief presented La Salle with a number of beaver pelts, in payment for the stolen goods, the calumet was smoked, and violence was averted.

When the chief learned that La Salle and his men were on their way to the Illinois, he displayed great concern, and imparted news that confirmed the reports, which La Salle had heard in Michilimackinac, that rival traders and Jesuits were inciting the Iroquois to make war on the Illinois tribe.

Deeply perturbed, La Salle inquired how the Fox chief had received this intelligence. It had come, replied the chief, from a captured Iroquois, whom the Illinois later tortured to death.

"Do not go," the chief begged La Salle, "because we know the Illinois want to massacre all the French."

Several men urged La Salle to heed the chief's advice and to turn back, but he refused, telling the chief that he was "grateful for the warning but that Frenchmen were not afraid of the Illinois and would manage to bring them to reason either by friendship or by force."

The Foxes were left behind, and on November 1 the mouth of the Miami River was reached. Neither Tonty nor the *Griffon* had arrived. The rendezvous was deserted, and there was no sign that men, either red or white, had recently been there.

Now a few of the more timid men again urged La Salle to turn back. There was still time to reach Michilimackinac by way of the eastern shore before the lake was closed by ice. The majority, however, pleaded with La Salle to waste no time in going on to the Illinois. He himself had previously visited that tribe, and he had said they were well supplied with food, that their land was inhabited by the buffalo, and that they had been friendly to him.

La Salle closed his ears. He would go neither back nor ahead until Tonty and his twenty men or the *Griffon* had arrived. Even if the others deserted him, he and Nika and Saget would remain at the appointed meeting place.

No one deserted. La Salle, his own fears mounting, ordered that a fort be erected so that the grumbling men might be "diverted by some useful occupation." The fort, he proclaimed with a confidence he did not feel, would be useful for storing the goods that would come in the ship and would serve them all as a refuge.

Each day men went out to hunt and to reconnoitre the country. They managed to procure enough meat to keep the garrison from suffering great hunger. Each day anxious eyes watched the horizon of the lake for a sight of a canoe or a sail. But nearly three weeks passed before several black specks were sighted under the lowering wintry skies.

Tonty and ten men reached Fort Miami on the twentieth of November. He had lost two men by desertion, but the others were hunting a few miles to the north. They would soon arrive.

Tonty had heard no word of the *Griffon*.

La Salle ordered two experienced *couriers du bois* to return to Michilimackinac and make further inquiries. If the *Griffon* was found, they were to direct her to the St. Joseph. The cargo was to be unloaded and stored in the fort, and the ship was to be made safe for the winter.

He could delay no longer his departure for the Illinois country, for thirty-three men could not be sustained at Fort Miami without additional supplies of food.

His heart heavy with concern, he led his company up the St. Joseph on December 3, 1679, on the way to the Kankakee portage and the waters of the Illinois River. The bare limbs of the forest reached toward an overcast sky, the surrounding marshes were gray and devoid of birds, the weedy banks of the St. Joseph were glazed with ice.

24 ✤✤✤

NEAR THE present site of South Bend, Indiana, a few days later they portaged their canoes and baggage to a little stream that twisted its way through endless swamps. It was the Kankakee, and on it they floated along between the high dead grasses like men traveling by no discernible means across the land. But the little stream soon widened to become a river, and the swamps gave way to great prairies dotted by islands of barren oaks. And the prairies gave way to ranges of hills and bluffs, and, at last, before them lay the valley of the Illinois.

For the remainder of the month they traveled on the river that grew ever deeper and wider, passed wooded islands, passed sites where one day towns would rise—Morris, Seneca, Marseilles, Ottawa. Much of the country had been burned by Indians in their hunts. They saw the bones and skulls of innumerable buffalo. They came upon a great bull mired in mud, and they killed him and enjoyed a feast, but they found little other game. The animals had been driven away by the fires.

December was almost gone when they reached a great Indian village (near Utica, Illinois, on the north side of the river). They counted nearly five hundred lodges "shaped like long barrel vaults and covered with double mats of flat rushes." The mats were "so well sewn that no wind, snow, or rain ever penetrates them." Each cabin "had four or five fires" and all were deserted. More than six thousand Illinois men, women and children who resided there had gone, leaving not a dog to guard the empty settlement.

It was presumed that in accord with their custom they had scattered in bands to the south and west on winter hunts. The situation was awkward for La Salle and his men. They were badly in need of provisions, and La Salle hesitated to take them without permission. Yet, his men must have food, and at last he sent a party to locate the storehouses of the great village. Several pits containing corn were found, and La Salle authorized them to take thirty *minots* of the grain. At the first opportunity he would repay the Indians with appropriate gifts.

Their bellies filled with boiled corn and wild turkey, they embarked once more. The year 1680 began for them in a lonely woodland camp beside the river. Hennepin said mass, and then he and Ribourde and Membre embraced each man "very tenderly, encouraging them in the pursuit of so important a discovery."

Four days later the eight canoes moved across Peoria Lake and a camp was made where the city of Peoria would stand. They had passed out of the lake and had reentered the river the next morning when smoke was seen rising from the bleak forest ahead. As they floated around a point a village containing eighty to a hundred wigwams came suddenly into view.

La Salle again illustrated his thorough understanding of the ways of Indians. He commanded that the eight canoes be brought abreast. Paddles were stored and the men displayed their guns. Held together, the canoes drifted down the stream, presenting a formidable show of armed might. La Salle knew that signs of peace might be misconstrued as signs that the Frenchmen were afraid, and none were given.

This Illinois village was thrown into wild confusion. Warriors howled as they took up bows and arrows. Squaws screamed and fled with the children to the trees. Several elderly men advanced to the bank and called out to the strangers to identify themselves. "They replied that they were French," said Membre, "still keeping their arms ready, and letting the current bear them down in order, because there was no landing place till below the camp. The Indians alarmed and intimidated by this bold conduct . . . although there were several thousand against a handful . . . immediately presented three calumets." The milling Indians may have appeared to number thousands to the priest. Actually, there were less than five hundred, including squaws and children.

Hennepin recorded that La Salle "cried out, according to the custom of these tribes, to ask whether they wanted peace or war; it was very important to show courage at the outset."

The canoes landed a short distance below the village, the men leaping ashore and arranging themselves in a battle line. Hennepin judged that because "of their confusion, the Indians could have been overcome." A fight was the last thing La Salle wanted. He had demonstrated that he and his men had no fear, and he was relieved to find that his strategy had been successful. Two "principal men" shortly advanced toward him, holding aloft calumets. Thereupon, La Salle displayed his own calumet.

In Membre's words, the Indians' "terror changed to joy, they conducted our party to their cabins, showed us a thousand civilities, and sent to call back those who had fled. They were told that we came only to give them a knowledge of the true God, to defend them against their enemies, to bring them arms, and other conveniences of life. Besides presents made them, they were paid for the Indian corn at their village; a close alliance was made with them, the rest of the day being spent in feasts and mutual greetings."

This was the first white trade mission to reach the Illinois in their own country. Only La Salle and the expedition of Marquette and Joliet had previously passed through their land on the river, but these journeys had been made for the purpose of exploring, not trading.

However, if the Illinois had seen no more white men than could be counted on the fingers of two hands, they knew much about them. French traders had been among their friends and enemies in Wisconsin and Michigan. They knew some of the wonders of European goods, they knew of ironware and firearms and bright cloth and knives and hatchets and swords and such beautiful and desirable articles as buckles and buttons and braid the color of gold. Some of these valuable things they had obtained from Indian traders. They knew, too, that Spaniards had invaded countries to the south. News traveled far and swiftly across the illimitable reaches of the interior wilderness. And they knew of the missions and trading posts of the upper Great Lakes. They knew of the white man's God. Indeed, they had heard of Him from the lips of Marquette, who had preached to them in the summer of 1673.

When he addressed the council, La Salle wasted no time on salutations or other preliminaries. He drove at once to the core of the matter he considered most essential, the establishment of good relations between the French and the powerful Illinois, the forging of an indestructible commercial bond between them.

If the Illinois believed that the French wished for anything else, they were deceiving themselves, and they were believing untruths spread by the black robes and other traders who not only wished to injure him but their great father, the king of the French, and who wished to keep from the Illinois the goods they so sorely needed and which would bring them prosperity. If the Illinois persisted in believing these falsehoods, he would go on to their enemies, the Osages, and he would take to them all the benefits to be derived through trade with him.

This blunt assertion delivered, La Salle turned his attention to the Iroquois. His enemies and the evil men who would harm the great Onontio had been urging the Iroquois to invade the country of the Illinois and destroy them. They had made it very difficult for Onontio, for he was also the Great Father of the Iroquois and the French had for many years lived in peace with them.

Yet, if such a catastrophe occurred, if the Iroquois were persuaded to launch such a war, the French would not hesitate to aid the Illinois as much as possible in defending themselves. He, himself, would furnish the Illinois with guns, and he and his men would fight on their side. That was his solemn pledge, made to the Illinois with his hand on his heart, and he would never violate it.

In return for this allegiance he asked permission of the Illinois to do two things: to build a strong fort in their country and to construct a vessel. The fort would be garrisoned by soldiers whose duty would be to protect them from invaders. The great wooden canoe would sail down the Mississippi to the Gulf of Mexico. There it would meet cargo ships which had come across the ocean from France, and it would return laden with all manner of goods to be exchanged for the furs and buffalo hides of the Illinois. This trade would make them far more prosperous than their enemies, who already had access to French goods from the north.

If they rejected his plans, La Salle warned, the Illinois would be left at the mercy of the Iroquois.

His threats had the desired effect. His appeals were successful. The chiefs of the Illinois unqualifiedly accepted his proposals, granted him his requests, and promised to enter the alliance he proposed.

In responding to La Salle's address, one Illinois leader imparted to him intelligence that greatly encouraged him. The Mississippi, declared the chief, was wide, beautiful, and open to navigation. He named four tribes living upon its banks which had been mentioned more than a century earlier in the accounts of the De Soto expedition, which La Salle had read. The Illinois were familiar with the river. They knew of the Tulas, Casquins, and the Daminoias who lived on the west bank of the Mississippi and of the Cicacas who dwelt on the east side of it. In their wars against enemies who lived far to the south, declared the chief, the Illinois had "taken captives who told them they had seen ships on the open water that fired shots resembling thunder."

But even more significant to La Salle was the chief's statement that there were "no European settlements on the [Gulf] coast; for if there had been, they [the Illinois] would certainly have gone to trade there, as the sea was only twenty days' journey in their pirogues."

La Salle went wearily to his bed convinced that he had been victorious in his negotiations with the Illinois.

By morning he knew the erroneousness of this conviction, and he knew that his enemies had caught up with him.

25 ✤ ✤ ✤

IN THE AUTUMN of 1669, the Jesuit Claude Allouez, an intrepid and fanatical religious, had been sent to Green Bay to establish a mission. He explored much of the Wisconsin country alone, and visited the important town on the Fox River, above Lake Winnebago, in which lived some three thousand Algonquians of the Miami and Mascoutin tribes. Allouez returned the next year to the town in the company of Father Claude Dablon. They were well received and made numerous friends there. In the ensuing years, Allouez traveled widely west of the Great Lakes.

From the time of La Salle's ascendancy as an explorer and the disclosure of his plans to open the west to French commerce and settlement, Allouez was a leader in the schemes of the Jesuits to stop him. When La Salle led his expedition westward in the winter of 1679–80, Allouez contrived a plot to discredit him in the eyes of the Illinois, and called on his old friends, the Mascoutins and Miamis, for assistance.

As La Salle rested that January night of 1680 in his camp, following a day of feasting and powwowing with the Illinois, he was unaware that in the nearby village a nocturnal council was being held.

After dark a Mascoutin chief, whom La Salle called Monso, and six Miami warriors had arrived at the village. They brought with them a small fortune in kettles, hatchets, knives, and other goods, which they presented to an Illinois leader named Nicanope. Announcing that he had news of great importance to the Illinois, Monso asked that the headmen be summoned to an immediate council. This was done, and the conference had continued through the remainder of the night.

La Salle, Monso told the Illinois, was not their friend and

was a spy for the Iroquois. It was La Salle's intention to throw the Illinois off guard while he armed their enemies on the west side of the Mississippi. A two-pronged war would follow. Attacked by the Iroquois from the east and their enemies from the west, the Illinois would be destroyed. The French were already arming the Iroquois in preparation for the invasion.

It was Monso's contention that the Illinois would be caught in a vise from which they could not escape unless they took forceful steps at once to halt La Salle and frighten his men into deserting him. La Salle's promise of support was false. Any agreement the Illinois made with him would lead to their undoing.

As the light of dawn appeared, Monso and his companions stealthily vanished.

La Salle first learned of the attempt to discredit him in the morning, when an Illinois chief, Omawaha, whose favor he had won with gifts, appeared at his camp and recounted Monso's accusations. Hennepin would claim that he had been present when Omawaha and La Salle talked, and that La Salle had thanked Omawaha, and with an additional present had put Omawaha "under obligation to warn us of all that was happening. . . . It was easy to imagine that Monso had been sent and instructed by other Frenchmen jealous of our success, because this Monso did not know us and had not been within even four hundred leagues of Fort Frontenac. In speaking of our affairs, however, he referred to details and circumstances as if he had been familiar with us all his life."

La Salle needed no imagination to tell him who had sent the embassy to thwart him. His apprehension mounting, he went among the elders of the village, and he found them "cold, sullen, and suspicious."

In the afternoon, La Salle and his men received an invitation to a feast in the lodge of Nicanope. It was accepted.

The guests had no more than been seated when Nicanope, who was a brother of Chassagoac, head chief of the Illinois, arose and launched an emotional speech. His words were translated by Saget, but two veteran *couriers du bois* present also understood the Illinois dialect of the Algonquian tongue and they confirmed Saget's interpretations.

He had not, Nicanope declared frankly, invited the white men to partake of his food as much as to induce them to abandon their foolish plan to build a boat and descend the Mississippi. They could not hope to return from such a hazardous journey. The Mississippi's banks were inhabited by savage people "who by their numbers alone would overpower the Frenchmen, however well armed and brave they might be." Also, the river "was full of monsters; alligators and serpents." Even if their great wooden canoe would protect them, "there was another danger that was inevitable: the lower part of the river was full of falls and precipices above which the water was so undisturbed that one came upon them without warning. All these falls . . . ended in an abyss where the river disappeared underground; no one knew what became of it."

As he responded to Nicanope, La Salle could see that some of his men were profoundly disturbed. With a calm manner that concealed the anger seething within him, he thanked Nicanope for warning him of the perils of voyaging on the Mississippi, but expressed the doubt that any very serious dangers existed. However, if the dangers were, in fact, real, Frenchmen would not flinch before them.

Then in a voice touched by the fury he could no longer entirely suppress, he declared:

"You are being deluded by lies.

"We were not asleep, my brother, when Monso talked to you secretly in the night, and told you we were spies of the Iroquois. The presents he gave you to make you believe his lies are still hidden in the earth under this lodge. If he told the truth, why did he skulk away in the dark? Why did he not appear by day, if he had nothing but the truth to tell you?

[136]

"Have you forgotten that when we arrived your camp was in such confusion that we could easily have killed many of you? We would have needed no help from the Iroquois, nor from anyone else. Yet Monso wants you to believe that after we have settled here and built a fort we will ask the aid of the Iroquois to do what we could have done without them.

"If we, the French, meant to make war on you, we would need no help from the Iroquois, who have so often felt the force of our arms, and who fear us and have fled before us. Look at what we have brought with us. Not weapons to destroy you, but to help you protect yourselves. We have brought tools and goods that are useful to you.

"If you wish to prove to yourselves that this Monso is an impostor, pursue him and bring him back. We will not run. We will wait here to confront him and call him a liar to his face. He will be silenced. For he does not know us. He never saw us or the Iroquois. He knows of no plots that he claims we have made with the Iroquois. He speaks with poison and falsehoods fed to him by others who would harm you."

Nicanope had nothing more to say. He signaled to squaws to begin serving the meal, and bowls of buffalo meat and corn boiled in bear fat were brought into the lodge. After they had eaten, La Salle and his men quietly departed, leaving Nicanope sitting by a fire with a dark and brooding face.

Fearing that some treacherous act might be committed during the night by Monso and the Miamis, or by some excited Illinois, La Salle assigned several sentinels to patrol the camp. When he arose the next morning, none was on duty.

Six men had deserted, and had disappeared into the woods on foot, taking with them their guns, a quantity of powder and shot, and a sack of maize that had been purchased from the Indians.

Sick at heart, La Salle assembled his company. Before him stood three gray-robed Flemings, Hennepin, Ribourde, and Membre; an Italian, Tonty; the Shawnee, Nika; the Mohegan hunter and interpreter, Saget; his personal French-Canadian servant, L'Espérance; and nineteen *engagés* and craftsmen from France.

Fires of defiance illuminated the sadness in his eyes. He excoriated the deserters as cowards and timid souls who had swallowed the fictions of Nicanope and swore that they would be punished, if they did not first perish in the wilderness. He would make no attempt to pursue them, for he wanted the Indians to believe that he had dispatched them on a mission. This was the story that was to be told in the village. It would not be wise to let the Illinois know that Frenchmen had faint hearts and would run from perils that did not exist.

"If there are more of you who would run away, contain yourself until spring," he said. "I give you my word that then I will let you go freely, by canoe, and you can arrive in Canada as honorable men and not as traitors."

Few men of his time were more successful than La Salle in dealing with Indians. And few were plagued and injured more by desertions than was he. The situation suggests that while he was a wilderness ambassador of exceptional ability and astuteness, he was a poor leader, unable to inspire confidence or loyalty in those under him. But such an assumption would be without foundation.

The craftsmen he engaged in France—and this was the case on his later expeditions—knew nothing whatsoever of the wilderness or of Indians. The stability they possessed was dissipated by fears they had never known. The ordeals they encountered, the sufferings they underwent, killed initiative, broke them in spirit and made it impossible for them to demonstrate a willingness to make sacrifices and a devotion to duty they might have shown under less harrowing conditions. They had only one thought: to stay alive until they could get back to the safe harbors of civilization. And they sought to save themselves by any means available. Honor was not a quality that influenced them in their fight against death.

The French Canadians, the *couriers du bois,* were another

breed. They were inured to the hardships of a life in the forest. They were skillful as hunters and as watermen. They were as unpredictable as the wind, as suspicious and as superstitious as the red people with whom they were at home. Their predominating instincts were those of animals, to feed and fornicate and protect themselves. Few of them had normal ambitions, fewer any moral scruples. They were outlaws, submitting only under duress to authority, free, inherently gay, unrestrained, easily corrupted.

Hennepin, who fancied that he could look into the minds of all persons, wrote that La Salle "decided to prevent further desertion[s] by getting them [his men] away from the Indians. To make them consent without grumbling, he told them they were not safe with the Illinois and besides, staying there exposed them to the Iroquois forces that might perhaps come during the winter to attack the village. The Illinois, he explained, were incapable of resisting the Iroquois and probably would flee at the first encounter. . . . The Iroquois would be unable to overtake them and would vent their fury on the Frenchmen, who, being few in number, would be unable to cope with these Indians . . . there was one remedy: to fortify themselves in some easily defended position."

The statement reflected Hennepin's own thinking more than La Salle's.

La Salle had come to the Illinois country with definite plans in mind, and one of them was to build a fort on the Illinois River. He considered this project an essential part of his great design to make France supreme in the western wilderness.

Hennepin would soon learn that nothing, and certainly not desertions and the scheming of his enemies, could influence La Salle to deviate from the course on which he had embarked. Only death could do that.

26 ✣ ✣ ✣

IN A search along the river, La Salle had found a site, several miles below the Illinois town, that was suitable for the fort. It was on a hill that rose behind a marsh some two hundred yards in width on the south bank of the river. Ravines which would serve as protective declivities lay on the other three sides of the height and could be flooded by means of ditches draining from the river. Adjacent was level ground for ways from which a ship could easily be launched.

There in the early weeks of the year 1680 the first permanent habitation of white men in the region that would become the state of Illinois took shape. Within a palisade twenty-five feet in height were living quarters, a blacksmith shop, a magazine and storage house, and a combined dwelling and chapel for the Recollects.

The name La Salle gave to the installation reflected upon the reverses he had suffered and indicated not at all the determination and defiance that were unwavering and indestructible in him.

He called it Fort Crèvecoeur.

The men labored with diligence—they were, after all, providing themselves with a measure of protection—but their fears went unabated. They worked with an eye on the surrounding forest, as if expecting every moment to see a howling horde of bloodthirsty Iroquois sweep upon them. Nicanope persisted in his attempts to terrorize them, sending warriors to repeat tales of the dreadful monsters swarming in the Mississippi. These fabrications were effective in keeping alive, if not augmenting, their dread of essaying the voyage down the river.

Someone put poison in the pot in which La Salle's food was customarily cooked by L'Espérance. He was made very ill. Tonty wrote that he "was saved by an antidote a friend had given him in France." Ever since he had been poisoned at Fort Frontenac, La Salle had carried with him an unidentified antidote, fully expecting that another attempt would be made to kill him in the same manner. The perpetrator of the vicious act at Fort Crèvecoeur was not discovered. No suspicion was attached to his servant, who had demonstrated his loyalty on numerous occasions, and in whom La Salle had implicit trust. As a precaution, La Salle thereafter took his food from the vessels in which the meals of the other men were prepared.

A singular event aided La Salle in calming his men to some extent. On a February morning, a lookout shouted that a lone Indian in a canoe was ascending the river and approaching the fort landing. La Salle and Saget went down the hill to meet him.

Nosing his small craft into the bank, the Indian, a powerful young warrior, stared in astonishment at the palisade and the newly cut ribs of the ship on the ways. The Mohegan soon learned that he had been absent with a small party of Illinois raiders for several months. In that period, he and his companions, whom he said were not far behind him, had traveled a long distance down the Mississippi. La Salle, with the hope that he might acquire information of the country, invited him into the fort, had a meal placed before him, and presented him with a hunting knife and sheath.

In response to casual questioning, the young Indian talked freely, describing in detail the river and the peoples living along it. He spoke of their modes of dress, their customs, their dwellings. Taking up a piece of charcoal, he drew on a sawn timber a map of the river's course, delineating its major curves and highest banks, and showing its entrance into the sea. He appeared highly amused when questioned about monsters and great falls. The river was smooth and without troublesome rapids along its entire length. The only monsters were alligators who inhabited the swamps of southern reaches. The people of the Mississippi would welcome the

Frenchmen. Many years before they had seen white men, but no one alive could remember them. The people would be eager to receive the miraculous goods of the French, for they had nothing of the kind. La Salle and his men would be joyously welcomed everywhere along the great highway of water.

By the gift of a hatchet, La Salle extracted from the young Indian a promise to say nothing of their talk. Then, accompanied by several of his men, he went to the Illinois village. According to Hennepin, who was in the party, they found the Illinois elders "assembled in the wigwam of one of the most important Indians. He was feasting them on bear meat, a food of which they are very fond. They made room for us in the center on a fine rush mat. . . ."

Saget was instructed to inform the gathering "that the Maker of all things . . . takes particular care of Frenchmen." With that opening remark, La Salle accused them of gross deceptions regarding the Mississippi. He then repeated all the information given to him by the young warrior. The accuracy with which he described the river dumbfounded his listeners. They clapped their hands to their mouths to signify their astonishment. La Salle, they proclaimed, had received his great knowledge through some powerful "medicine." Nicanope confessed his dishonesty, and attempted to defend himself with a false contention. He declared that his stories of serpents and savage peoples and great falls and waters disappearing in bottomless pits had been manufactured with the hope that La Salle and the gray-robes would be persuaded to remain with the Illinois. Admittedly, the Illinois were greedy. They wanted to prevent other tribes from enjoying trade with the French.

The men appeared to be relieved of some of their tension by Nicanope's confession. La Salle was grateful, but he did not permit himself to be deluded into believing that more than a partial appeasement of their fright was possible. As long as they were in the wilderness they would be ready to flee in panic. If he could manage to hold them until the vessel was launched, he would consider himself fortunate. The construction would take longer than he had expected, for two of the deserters had been expert pit-sawyers and two others had been master carpenters. Men who had taken over their jobs were inexperienced in the work, and struggled with tools with which they were unfamiliar, with the result that progress was extremely slow.

On a day toward the end of February, La Salle summoned nine men to his quarters in Fort Crèvecoeur. They were Tonty, Hennepin, Saget, and six *couriers du bois*—Accau, Auguelle, (nick-named Le Picard), Hunaut, La Violette, Collin, and Dautray.

Gravely he told them that his concern for the *Griffon* had grown to the extent where he could contain himself no longer. Aboard it were cables, rigging, and other equipment without which the half-completed boat on the stocks could not sail. Although the rivers might still be frozen, forcing him to travel on foot, he would go back to learn what had become of the vessel. If he found that the *Griffon* had not arrived at Fort Miami, he would go on until he got some word of her whereabouts, on to Niagara, if necessary. He would take with him Saget, Hunaut, La Violette, Collin, and Dautray.

During his absence, Tonty would be in command at Fort Crèvecoeur, and he wanted Accau, Le Picard, and Hennepin to make a journey of exploration for him. He wanted them to go down the Illinois and turn up the Mississippi—up, not down. They would be his emissaries, and he expressed his confidence that they could be fully trusted to carry out his instructions.

Accau, who spoke several Indian tongues, would be their leader. Le Picard had been selected because he had become an able hunter. Hennepin might find it feasible to establish a mission, per-haps at the mouth of the Wisconsin. It was a well-known con-fluence. Marquette and Joliet had entered the Mississippi from the Wisconsin. The place would be designated as a rendezvous, and if he had returned by midsummer from his search for the *Griffon*, he would send men to meet them there. Above the Wisconsin the river was unknown to white men. Hennepin would have the honor of being the first Recollect among countless red people who knew nothing at all of the true Faith. Not only would he have an opportunity to save innumerable souls but he would win renown and glory for himself. It is not a matter of dependable record whether La Salle added that he believed Hennepin would be more useful to him in such a capacity than preaching dull sermons to the disgruntled and sad men at Fort Crèvecoeur. Yet, if he did not voice the thought, it seems reasonable to assume that he had it. The Jesuits would not be pleased to learn that a Recollect was established on the upper Mississippi.

La Salle explained why the mission was extremely important to him. Traders who were his rivals and who were involved in the schemes to defeat him were pushing toward the upper Mississippi. Perhaps some of them were already there. If that were true, Jesuits would be there, too. It was vital that the Indians of the region know of his plan to bring them goods from the Gulf of Mexico, which he would obtain in the French West Indies, if not in France. He wanted it known in this area, as well, that he had successfully overcome the intrigues of the Jesuits, and that any reports to the contrary were false. He wanted it to be known to the Indians there that he had not failed, that he held the exclusive right to trade with them, a right given him by the King of France, and that they would soon enjoy the benefits of the goods he would bring and which would be exchanged at prices advantageous to them.

Hennepin did not want to go. He protested that for more than a year he had suffered with an abscess in his mouth from which matter continually drained. He should return to Canada to have it treated instead of going farther into wild and unknown countries. Membre or Ribourde were in better condition to undertake such a hazardous journey.

Membre declined to accept the assignment. He had been spending most of his time in the Illinois town, and although he was discouraged in his labors for the faith, he preferred to continue them. Ribourde, although hale, had reached the age of sixty-five, and feared he could not endure excessive hardships. He urged Hennepin to go, telling him that God would be glorified by his apostolic labors.

Thereupon, said Hennepin, "I offered to undertake this voyage to make the acquaintance of the people with whom I soon hoped to settle in order to preach the faith."

On the morning of the last day of February, Accau, Le Picard, and Hennepin prepared to depart. Father Ribourde spread his knotted hands over them in benediction. "Be of good courage and let your hearts be comforted," he told them.

In a large canoe heavily laden with trade goods, gifts, weapons, corn flour and their personal baggage, the three men pushed off. La Salle stood on the bank watching in silence until they had vanished around a bend in the river.*

* Here Father Louis Hennepin passed out of the life of La Salle, but not out of history. In mid-April, he, Accau, and Le Picard were taken prisoners by the Sioux. Their goods, valued at a thousand *livres*, were stolen. They were taken far north into Minnesota, and for a time were badly treated. They were the first white men known to have entered the country between the Wisconsin and the Falls of St. Anthony, which Hennepin named in honor of St. Anthony of Padua (St. Paul-Minneapolis). In the late summer they were rescued by the famed explorer Daniel Greysolon du Lhut and four other Frenchmen. During the autumn, the eight men traveled by way of the Wisconsin and Fox Rivers and reached the Jesuit mission at Green Bay. They went on to Michilimackinac, where they spent the winter. In the spring, Hennepin, Accau, and Le Picard went by canoe to Niagara, crossed the portage to Lake Ontario, and continued on down the St. Lawrence to Montreal. Hennepin soon embarked for Europe, where he wrote his first book, *Description de la Louisiane*. It was published in Paris in 1683, received wide acclaim, and was translated into several languages. Hennepin was not content to bask in the glory and honors accorded him. In 1697, he published a second book, *Nouvelle Découverte d'un très grand Pays situé dans l'Amérique*. In it he claimed that

27 ✣ ✣ ✣

THE JOURNEY of La Salle and his companions from Fort Crèvecoeur to Fort Frontenac in the early spring of 1680 ranks with the most daring, courageous, and arduous exploits in the annals of American exploration. For La Salle it was the most heart-breaking period of his career. It brought him to the brink of utter disaster, every dream he had held verging on complete destruction, every plan he had made seemingly blocked by insurmountable barriers.

The start was made on March 1, the day after Hennepin had departed. The forests were still leafless. Sheet ice in the rivers made canoe travel impossible most of the way. Snows, sleet and cold rains fell almost incessantly. The prairies were alternately frozen and vast tracts of half-thawed earth and bogs of slush. When the ice of streams was broken open, they became raging yellow torrents, forcing the men to detour until a place might be found where they could cross by holding on to logs or on hastily constructed rafts. On most of the journey the thermometer hovered at the freezing point, at times falling several degrees below it, and rising above it only on the few days when the sun broke through the gray overcast for a short period.

---

before ascending the Mississippi from the Illinois, he and his two companions had gone down the river to the Gulf of Mexico, had returned and traveled upstream to the country of the Sioux, where in mid-April they had been made prisoners. This great journey had been accomplished in less than a month. In his second book, Hennepin stole from the accounts, reports, and correspondence of several other explorers, notably Fathers Le Clercq and Membre and La Salle, often quoting verbatim from them. Discredited and disgraced, he died in well-deserved obscurity.

It was a journey of desperation. "I felt," La Salle would write to one of his creditors, M. Thouret, "there was no one else I could trust to go." If the equipment that was to be sent out in the *Griffon* were not obtained, his entire expedition would have been set back a year, while more was being brought out from Montreal.

They passed over the frozen Des Plaines River near the site of Joliet on March 18, and struck eastward. On the 23rd, after crossing the flooding Calumet River on a raft, they touched the southern shore of Lake Michigan. As dark was falling on the 24th, they came in sight of Fort Miami. A thin column of smoke rose from one of the cabins. The *Griffon* was not there.

The smoke came from the cooking fire of the two *couriers du bois* whom La Salle had sent to Michilimackinac the previous fall to seek word of the ship, Chapelle and Leblanc. They had made a complete circle of Lake Michigan, and had looked into innumerable harbors and river mouths, but had found nothing to indicate that the *Griffon* had returned. Nor had the residents of Michilimackinac or the Indians they questioned on their long search heard any word of the ship.

La Salle resigned himself to the belief that the *Griffon* had foundered. The conviction made it all the more imperative that he push on to get more supplies. By the light of the fire he wrote a letter to Tonty, directing Chapelle and Leblanc to take it to him at Fort Crèvecoeur.

In the letter he instructed Tonty to fortify the cliff, Starved Rock, which rose above the river a short distance upstream from the great Illinois town at Utica. He held no doubt that the Iroquois would strike before he could return to Fort Crèvecoeur. Starved Rock could be defended by a few men against a multitude, he told Tonty, and in the event he was delayed in returning with an additional force and with new supplies and ammunition, Tonty and the others would be able to protect themselves for an indefinite period. They could not survive a long siege at Fort Crèvecoeur.

On March 25, the day after his arrival at Fort Miami, Chapelle and Leblanc started for the Illinois, and La Salle and his five companions set out across the wilderness of Southern Michigan.

The woods, recorded La Salle, were "so interlaced with thorns and brambles that in two days and a half our clothes were all torn, and our faces so covered with blood that we hardly knew each other."

But on March 28, they "found the woods more open, and began to fare better, meeting a good deal of game, which after this rarely failed us."

There was a good reason for the abundance of game. Few Indians hunted in the region, for it was "debatable ground between five or six nations who are at war, and, being afraid of each other, do not venture into these parts except to surprise each other, and always with the greatest precaution and all possible secrecy."

The reports of their guns were heard by a war party, and one evening, "having made our fire by the edge of the prairie, we were surrounded by them; but as the man on guard waked us, and we posted ourselves behind trees with our guns, these savages, who are called Wapoos (Potawatamies), took us for Iroquois, and thinking that there must be a great many of us because we did not travel secretly, as they do when in small bands, they ran off. . . . We were two days without meeting anybody."

In the belief that the Wapoos would return in a stronger party, La Salle adopted tactics to scare them. He stripped pieces of bark from trees as they went ahead, on the smooth surfaces drawing with charcoal Iroquois signs for *war-party*, *prisoners* and *scalps*. He also set fire to the dry grass along the trails he and his men took to destroy their footprints.

The ruses "answered very well so long as we were passing over an open country; but on the thirtieth we got into great marshes, flooded by the thaws. . . . Our tracks betrayed us."

For three days they were closely pursued by a band of Mascoutins, "who were out after Iroquois. . . . We made no fire at night, contenting ourselves with taking off our wet clothes and wrapping ourselves in our blankets on some dry knoll. . . ."

On the 2nd of April, however, "there came a hard frost, and our clothes, which were drenched when we took them off, froze stiff as sticks; so that we could not put them on in the morning without making a fire to thaw them."

The Mascoutins, attracted by the smoke, soon surrounded them. Half-dressed, the cold white men went out to face the Indians, and "whether our fire-arms frightened them, or whether they thought us more numerous than they were, or whether they really meant us no harm, they called out in the Illinois [Algonquian] language that they had taken us for Iroquois, but now saw that we were friends. . . ."

For two more days the men went forward. Then Hunaut and Collin were stricken with dysentery and cramps and could not travel. La Salle pushed on in search of a stream flowing toward Lake Erie. He reached the Huron River. It was open. There he, Saget, La Violette and Dautray constructed a canoe of elm bark which they removed from the trees with hot water. The two sick men were carried to the river, and all embarked. Two days later they were stopped by impassable jams composed of fallen, rotted trees. Hunaut and Collin had recovered enough to walk, and all set out once more on foot, and soon reached the Detroit River.

A slight hope that the *Griffon* had not been lost still lingered in La Salle, and he directed Hunaut and La Violette to construct a canoe and search Lake Huron for the ship until they had reached Michilimackinac. He, Saget, Collin and Dautray crossed the Detroit on a raft, traveled through the thick forests of southern Ontario and reached Lake Erie near Point Pelee in a driving snowstorm. Here on the bitterly cold white shore of the lake, the Mohegan and Collin were stricken with fever and began to spit blood.

La Salle and Dautray, nearing exhaustion themselves, built another canoe. The invalids were placed aboard, and La Salle and

Dautray paddled the craft eastward along the northern shore of the lake.

On Easter Monday, the four enfeebled men landed at the site near the mouth of the Niagara where the *Griffon* had been launched. Three of the craftsmen who had worked on the vessel the year before were still encamped there, loyally waiting for orders which they had begun to believe would never come.

During the long months they had been in touch with *couriers du bois* traversing the Niagara portage, and they had sad tidings for La Salle.

The *Griffon*, which had been loaded with merchandise worth ten thousand crowns, had vanished en route back to Michilimackinac. Worse news was to come. A ship carrying goods valued at more than twenty-two thousand *livres* had gone down in the lower St. Lawrence. None of the cargo had been recovered.

And there was still another sorrowful report. Twenty expert craftsmen who had been sent from Europe to join La Salle had been detained in Quebec by the Intendant Duchesneau, who told them La Salle was dead. All but four of them had gone back to France.

But, once more, La Salle concealed his burning sorrow and wasted no time in lamentations. He crossed the portage. The garrison at Niagara had collected a valuable supply of furs. He ordered four men to join Dautray, who had been left to recover his strength at the shipyard on Lake Erie, and go back with him to Tonty. With them they were to take all supplies that could be spared. Foodstuffs and ammunition to replace these would be sent out to them.

With the three men, La Salle started for Fort Frontenac. They reached it on the sixth of May. François Plet, armed with legal authority, was directing the trading, not without regard for the forty per cent interest on his investment. La Salle did not clash with him. Indeed, he appeared to be no more than casually interested in the business affairs at the post. Matters of far greater importance weighed on him.

The journey from Fort Crèvecoeur had consumed sixty-five days, during which time La Salle had traveled some thirteen hundred miles, beset, as he said himself, by every possible form of peril and obstruction.

And now he was faced with the terrible task of rebuilding the whole structure of the great venture he had begun with such confidence and high hopes on the day the *Griffon* had started across Lake Erie to the cheers of its builders, the wild yelps of Indians, and the prayers of the fathers.

He continued almost immediately down the St. Lawrence.

The fate of the *Griffon* would never be determined. Innumerable reports about her would circulate through the wilderness, but all would be without foundation. She had been burned by Ottawas and all aboard had been scalped. She had been destroyed by Potawatamies. She had been scuttled by her godless pilot. Traders had stolen her cargo and had wrecked her. Some of the goods had been taken as far as the upper Mississippi and had been lost to the Sioux. The Jesuits had hired saboteurs to sink her.

No evidence was uncovered to support any of these stories. La Salle, however, would always hold the conviction that inasmuch as none of the six members of the crew was ever found she must have gone down in a storm. But he would never learn the truth. Only one fact would remain indisputable: the *Griffon* was gone.

28 ✿ ✿ ✿

LA SALLE'S SUDDEN and unexpected return caused excitement in Montreal and Quebec.

The Jesuits had spread the word that he had been killed on

the Illinois. If this propaganda stemmed from wishful thinking, it also had roots in their confidence that the agents they had sent to destroy him would meet with success.

The Abbé Cavelier had publicly shown himself to be profoundly grieved by La Salle's demise, and he had not overlooked the opportunity to remind his colleagues and friends of his prediction that his wild young brother would come to no good end. Now La Salle stood before him in robust health, giving every appearance of being completely undaunted by the adversities he had suffered and obviously fired with no less zeal and determination than he had previously displayed.

Yet, Jean Cavelier could derive a certain measure of private satisfaction from the knowledge that La Salle's future seemed less propitious than it had in the past. His losses had been great and apparently were not recoverable, even in part. His creditors had control of his property, his trade, and, therefore, his personal income. The abbé had reason to believe that his dire prophecy might come true after all—La Salle, even though he continued to survive, could hardly avoid being ruined.

The imbalance which the books of La Salle's career showed, however, were deceptive. Either the Abbé Cavelier was blind, or he refused to recognize facts set forth before him, facts which the Jesuits, and even some merchants, being less influenced by personal emotions, did not fail to perceive.

La Salle still possessed at least three powerful assets: He still held royal patents to build posts wherever he chose south and west of the Great Lakes, to continue his explorations, and to trade exclusively in the furs and buffalo hides in those vast regions.

La Salle had another asset, perhaps even more significant, which might not have been understood by more than a few of his opponents. The Jesuits and the Recollects were locked in a death struggle in the court of Louis XIV. It had by necessity to be waged covertly, but feelings ran deep and the tentacles of the conflicting bodies might be traced in every decision and action of the government.

There were, as well, in Paris two opposing factions on the question of French conquest in North America. One group advocated curtailment of expansion, holding the view that the colony had already become larger than could be adequately supported and protected. They rejected La Salle's warning that unless France moved into the interior, the British and Spanish would take control of regions that would make them impregnable and prosperous powers in the New World.

Their rivals, who included such influential persons as Eusebe Renadout, Prince Conti, Claude Bernou, François de Callières, the Marquis de Seignelay, Cabart de Villermont, and, in Canada, Frontenac, were dedicated to military conquest and the development of trade in the American interior, and their combined hands were on the tiller of the French ship of state. They held the confidence of the King, and, for the most part, he had reacted favorably toward them.

They were in the ascendancy, and their preferred explorer was La Salle. They had secured for him his letters patent. They prepared reports of his discoveries, but these they kept secret, only for themselves and the King and his closest advisers. They made certain that neither La Salle's letters nor accounts of his explorations appeared in any book available to the public.

This latter group had private ambitions: to control both the government and the trade of the empire they wished to build in the American wilderness, an empire that would absorb the Spanish dominions, including Mexico and the southwest, and all for their own private gain.

La Salle, they believed, was the man to open the gates, and they had endorsed him. Adversities had been encountered, but these were not considered insurmountable or totally disastrous to their great scheme—La Salle's great scheme. The expansionists had not lost confidence in La Salle. Frontenac assured him of that. (Frontenac would be recalled in 1682, but the expansionists would have him restored as Governor-General of Canada seven years later.) Nor had La Salle lost faith in himself.

La Salle got the credit which would enable him to purchase the supplies and equipment in Quebec and Montreal he must have to continue. He got what he requested—men and the money to pay them, guns, ammunition, powder, foodstuffs, and trade goods.

By mid-July, 1680, he had returned to Fort Frontenac with a cargo convoy. As he prepared to leave for the West, he received news that sickened him and almost destroyed the last vestige of his courage.

On July 22, two *couriers du bois* arrived in a small canoe. They brought a letter from Tonty. The two men, Chapelle and Leblanc, whom La Salle had sent from Fort Miami with instructions to Tonty to fortify Starved Rock, had arrived safely at Fort Crèvecoeur. They had done more than deliver La Salle's orders. They had told the men at the fort that the *Griffon* was lost, that Fort Frontenac had been seized by La Salle's creditors, that La Salle was without funds and unable to obtain more, and that no money would be forthcoming to pay them their wages, which were nearly two years overdue.

Tonty, after making an effort to convince them that the situation was not as serious as it appeared, and that La Salle would find a way to continue the venture, had set out at once with three *couriers du bois* for Starved Rock. It was his plan to examine the place and then move the garrison there from Fort Crèvecoeur and construct a bastion in which they would be secure from attack.

He was gone only a few days, but during this time Fort Crèvecoeur had been burned. Nine men, believing that La Salle had abandoned them, had deserted. All goods and stores they could not carry on their backs had been thrown into the river. On a plank of the unfinished bark someone had scrawled the words: *Nous sommes tous sauvages.*

Tonty had immediately sent four men, by two different routes, to inform La Salle of the catastrophe. Only Chapelle and Leblanc had reached Fort Frontenac. It was later learned that the other two messengers also had deserted.

Remaining with Tonty were only Fathers Membre and Ribourde, L'Espérance, Nika, a *courier du bois*, Boisrondet, and a Parisian youth, Etienne Renault. The Illinois were returning to the empty dwellings in the great town above the mouth of the Vermilion, and Tonty and the others had taken refuge among them. They would, he told La Salle, wait there for him. He had managed to save the forge from the wreckage of Fort Crèvecoeur. Almost all the other tools had been sunk in the river or destroyed. Fervently he hoped that La Salle would not be long detained, for he and his five companions had little ammunition, and the attitude of the Illinois was not favorable to them. If they were obliged to leave, they would have difficulty sustaining themselves until they could reach safety.

Almost on the heels of La Chapelle and Leblanc had come two *habitants* of Fort Frontenac who had been trading with Indians at the western end of Lake Ontario. There they had come upon the camp of the Fort Crèvecoeur deserters, who had been joined by several men from Michilimackinac and Fort Conti. The fugitives also had burned Fort Miami, had stolen furs stored there and others being held for La Salle in St. Ignace, and had taken guns and ammunition from the magazine at Niagara. At that place they had separated. Eight of them were traveling along the south shore of Lake Ontario with the intention of fleeing to Albany. Twelve others in three canoes had elected to follow the north coast of the lake. They could not be far away, and they had sworn that if they encountered La Salle they would shoot him in cold blood. The two *habitants* had paddled night and day to reach Fort Frontenac ahead of them.

Three canoes, containing La Salle and eight men, and bristling with weapons, pushed westward along the northern shore of Lake

Ontario. They traveled fast, and near the Bay of Quinte took up stations in the beach foliage.

The fight which occurred early the next morning was brief, but deadly. As the canoes of the renegades approached, La Salle and his men burst from their places of concealment. Two of the deserters were killed in an exchange of gunfire. The other ten surrendered and were taken to Fort Frontenac as prisoners. La Salle left the matter of punishing them in the hands of Frontenac, who was expected to make a trip to the fort later in the summer. He would later learn that Intendant Duchesneau had arranged to have murder charges filed against him, and that the ten deserters had been allowed to escape. Some of his creditors objected to the cost of maintaining them in idleness at Fort Frontenac.

News traveled with amazing swiftness through the wilderness. During the first weeks of August, Indians and *couriers du bois* came into Fort Frontenac with the intelligence that the drums of war were sounding in the Iroquois camps. La Salle understood that the reports could mean only one thing, an invasion of the west. Nothing could stop it.

It was on August 10 that he started back to the Illinois. With him he took La Forest, the aide who had striven to serve him well at Fort Frontenac, and twenty-four other men, among them a surgeon, ship carpenters, experienced *couriers du bois,* and several common laborers.

He had concluded that in view of the ominous conditions it would be well to avoid the Niagara portage, and the heavily laden canoes were paddled steadily westward along the north shore of Lake Ontario, their destination the Humber River. (Toronto.)

29 ⚜ ⚜ ⚜

IN THE last decades of the sixteenth century and the first half of the seventeenth—that is, after the French had established themselves on the St. Lawrence and the Dutch and English had settled in New York and New England—the main causes of the wars which the Iroquois launched could still be traced to their innate characteristics, to such forces as an unquenchable love for conquest, to an unshakable belief that they were the masters of their race, and to a fiendish passion for conquering and killing.

The warriors of the Iroquois confederacy, created in the 1570's and known to history as the Five Nations, destroyed the Hurons, virtually exterminated the Eries, the Atirhagenrats (whom the French called Le Nation Neutre), and the Andastes, and desolated the country of the Algonquians in Canada. From the Hudson to the Great Lakes, from the St. Lawrence to the Ohio, they were supreme.

By the time of La Salle's explorations of the Illinois and the Mississippi, however, another cause had been added to those which had for so long impelled them in their bloody aggressions. It was economics.

European traders in the region of the Hudson had long been their main source of the firearms with which they could overcome peoples who had none, and, in exchange for their furs, had provided them with the utensils, trade goods, and alcoholic spirits which had become indispensable to their economy. The reign of terror they had for years maintained in the valley of the St. Lawrence had been brought to a halt by French arms. French *couriers du bois* were monopolizing the trade with tribes north of the Great Lakes. On the south, the Cherokees and the Catawbas stood as a powerful barrier against them. Conquering these tribes, however, might have satisfied temporarily the Iroquois' lust for blood, but it would have been unprofitable otherwise, for furs from the south were comparatively few, generally poor, and were not wanted by the traders.

A most important factor in the situation in which the Iroquois found themselves was the growing scarcity of game in their own country. Years of intensive hunting had depleted the streams of beaver, and had destroyed natural supplies of other valuable animals, such as marten, sable, silver foxes, and otter.

The eyes of the Iroquois turned toward the west, and there they saw La Salle embarked on his great venture of opening that region. Not only would he obtain the trade of western Indians, but this new commerce would flow not to and from the east, not to and from the St. Lawrence, but up and down the Mississippi. The Iroquois saw themselves in the center of a great noose that was steadily being drawn closer around them. The French would soon control the fur trade of the north and west. If the Iroquois could not supply furs to the Hudson traders they would lose their main source of goods. But not only would they suffer economic strangulation. The power which they had so long enjoyed would steadily diminish until their supremacy had been irretrievably lost.

The conquering of new lands and the subjugation of more tribes was their only alternative. In the Hudson traders they found ready allies. Large quantities of guns and powder were given them at the Albany posts. But the Iroquois also found other supporters, sympathizers whom they might reasonably have expected would oppose their conquests. These were the enemies of La Salle, the French merchants who were jealous of the rights given him by the King and the Jesuits who wanted to make of the west a heaven on earth.

As astute, shrewd, and intelligent as the Iroquois leaders were they could not have been aware of either the religious conflict or the struggle between the conservatives and the expansionists in the court of Versailles, but had they been aware of these deep-rooted controversies they would have given them little consideration. They would not have understood their significance in the French political structure. It was enough for them to know that France's Canadian house was divided, and that two of the major factions it contained stood beside the Hudson Valley traders in support of them.

Only La Salle, a few Recollects who would not bear arms, and a handful of men stood to challenge the Iroquois in the west.

From the Hudson to Lake Erie, along the Mohawk and the Genesee and the Niagara and the Cuyahoga and the Sandusky, the drums sounded, songs of war and dancing and weird cries shattered the stillness of the wilderness nights.

It was a select Iroquois army that moved in scores of canoes westward along the south shore of Lake Erie in the hot month of August, 1680. From the western end of the lake, more than five hundred carefully chosen young warriors, their naked bodies greasy with war colors, carrying British muskets, their parfleches heavy with powder and lead, moved in long files through the summery forests and meadows and swamps of the land that would be called Indiana.

At an appointed rendezvous south of Lake Michigan they were joined by a hundred Miamis. The Miamis had long been their enemies, but no longer. For as long the Miamis also had been enemies of the Illinois. Instead of attacking the Miamis, the crafty Iroquois had sent emissaries among them to induce them to join in the war against the Illinois. The success of this strategy had prevented fighting that might have made their presence in the country known to their ultimate victims. The Miamis could be destroyed later.

During the summer, more than seven thousand Illinois men, women, and children had assembled at the great village that stood between the mouth of the Vermilion and Starved Rock on the north bank of the Illinois. It was the time of year in which the Illinois lived quietly, lazing through the hot days, fishing in the cool dawns, singing and dancing in the evening, a time for courtship and love-making and conducting rituals for the dead who lay on scaffolds in the adjacent cemetery, a time for remembering past feats and for dreaming of glories to be achieved while waiting for the maize to ripen in the broad fields that reached away to the hills.

In a mat house were Tonty, L'Espérance, Nika, Boisrondet, and Renault. Throughout each day they anxiously gazed up the river, hoping to see La Salle's canoes approaching. In another mat house some distance away were Fathers Ribourde and Membre, busy each day in preaching and striving to open the hearts of the heathens to the faith of Christ.

Throughout the summer Tonty and his men endured an unpleasant atmosphere and lived under a constant strain, for, as Iron Hand would write, "The desertion of our men, and the journey of M. de la Salle to Fort Frontenac, made the savages suspect that we intended to betray them."

Early in September, a Shawnee who had been visiting in the village started home. Two days later he was seen paddling back furiously across the river. He had not gone far on his journey when from a height he had seen a great number of Iroquois traveling down the valley of the Illinois.

Panic swept with the speed of a tornado through the great town. Scouts grabbed their weapons and set out to confirm the report. They were soon back with word that it was true.

Hundreds of women and children, with sixty men to protect them, were herded toward wooden canoes and embarked down the river. An angry mob surrounded Tonty and his companions, threw into the river the forge and some other equipment they had salvaged from the fire at Fort Crèvecoeur, and demanded that they be scalped, but calmer heads were able to restore order.

Great fires were built, and hordes of naked warriors, painted

[160]

and befeathered and brandishing their hatchets and bows and arrows to show their courage, danced and howled about them through the night.

In the morning more scouts came in to report that the Iroquois were heavily armed. One declared he had seen a "black robe" (Jesuit) among them. Another swore that La Salle was in one of their camps.

Once again Tonty was surrounded by a crowd of angry warriors who demanded he be killed. He faced them defiantly, and Membre praised him as a man "full of intelligence and courage." Tonty, declared the priest, retorted that the report was untrue, that La Salle would not side with the Iroquois against the Illinois, and for the scout's claim "there was no foundation, except that an Iroquois had a hat and a kind of vest." Although the furious Illinois "talked of tomahawking us . . . Tonty undeceived them and, to show the falsity of the report, offered to go with the few men he had to fight the Iroquois with them."

Tonty's offer changed their attitude and they raced away with wild howls, encouraged by the knowledge that they would have the guns of the Frenchmen on their side.

The Iroquois, no longer quiet but screaming their war cries, appeared on the plain above the bluffs and began to fire into the village. The Illinois raced out to meet them, returning the fire. The two forces, dancing wildly, moved slowly toward each other.

Now Tonty exhibited the incomparable bravery that had won him honors on the battlefields of Europe. As Membre would tell the story, ". . . Tonty, having grounds to fear for the Illinois who had almost no firearms, offered to put matters into negotiation, and to go to the Iroquois as a man of peace, bearing the calumet. . . . The Iroquois received without any demur a man who came with a calumet of peace, telling them that the Illinois were his brothers, friends of the French, and under the protection of Onontio, their common father."

Membre said that he had followed Tonty, and that Tonty's "proposals for peace did not please some young men whose hands itched for a fight; suddenly a volley of balls and arrows came whizzing around us, and a young Onondaga ran up with a drawn knife and struck M. de Tonty near the heart, the knife fortunately glancing off a rib."

Tonty sank to the ground. Several warriors had started to carry him away to be tortured when an Iroquois leader ran forward and called out that Tonty's ears were not pierced and that he was a Frenchman and must be spared. A plaster was made to stop the bleeding of Tonty's wound, but "a mad young Iroquois hoisted Tonty's hat on a gun" with the intention of deceiving the Illinois into believing that he was dead.

Both armies had halted and were milling about, although skirmishing continued on the perimeter of the battlefield. As Tonty himself recounted the scene, ". . . a young [Iroquois] came to give notice that their left wing was giving way, and that they had recognized some Frenchmen among the Illinois, who shot at them. On this they were greatly irritated against me, and held a council on what they should do with me. There was a man behind me with a knife in his hand, who every now and then lifted up my hair. They were divided in opinion."

Believing his last moments of life had come, Tonty desperately sought to save himself by lying. Sternly he told the Iroquois that the Illinois had twelve hundred well-armed warriors waiting to attack, and with them were sixty Frenchmen ready to support them. A Seneca chief still "desired to have me burnt," but an Onondaga chief, who proclaimed himself a friend of La Salle, "wished to have me set at liberty, and he carried his point."

The Iroquois counsellors at last agreed on a scheme to deceive the Illinois into believing they desired a treaty and would withdraw. They gave to Tonty "a necklace of porcelain beads to prove that they were also children of the Governor, and ought to unite and make a good peace. They sent me to deliver this message to the Illinois. I had much difficulty in reaching them, on account of the blood I had lost, both from my wound and from my mouth." As he staggered toward the Illinois lines, Tonty met "Fathers Ribourde and Membre, who were coming to look after me."

Tonty had seen the guns of the Iroquois, and he knew that the Illinois would have no chance against them. He advised the Illinois to retreat, but his counsel was not heeded. For several days negotiations were continued, during which time the Iroquois built a strong fort of logs and brush.

The Iroquois sent a message that they wished to consult again with Tonty. Accompanied by Membre, he went to the fort. There he found the Iroquois chiefs awaiting him. Six packets were placed before him. An Iroquois interpreter who spoke French explained their significance. Two packets, which contained beaver skins, "were to inform M. de Frontenac that they would not eat his children [the Illinois] and that he should not be angry at what they had done." The third packet was medicine for his wound. The fourth was oil to soothe his limbs. The fifth and the sixth also contained beaver pelts. One was to show "that the sun was bright" for the Illinois. The other was a plea to the Frenchmen to return to Fort Frontenac.

Tonty thanked them for the gifts, and then demanded that they show their sincerity by leaving the country of the Illinois. Angry shouts "arose, and some of them said they would eat some of the Illinois before they went away."

Immediately Tonty stood and kicked away the gifts, announcing that he "would have none of them, since they desired to eat the children of the Governor." He and Membre were roughly pushed from the council.

They returned to the Illinois, and once more Tonty warned them that the Iroquois would not honor a treaty. Throughout the night, the five Frenchmen lay sleepless in a mat house, expecting to be attacked, but "resolved to kill some of them before they should kill us. . . ." In the dawn, thankful to be still alive, they slipped away, embarked in a canoe and pushed upstream with all possible speed.

They stopped in the afternoon to repair leaks in their frail craft. Father Ribourde, breviary in hand, strolled across a sunny meadow to meditate and to pray.

Tonty found his body. The gray head of the elderly priest had been smashed with a hatchet and he had been scalped.

Weighted with sadness and filled with the fear that they also would be set upon and killed, Tonty, Father Membre, L'Espérance, Boisrondet, and Renault pushed on up the river. Two days later their canoe sprang leaks they were unable to repair, and they were forced to abandon it and continue on foot.

They crossed the Chicago portage and turned north along the western shore of Lake Michigan. In southern Wisconsin, Tonty collapsed with fever and a swelling of the legs. For several days he lay virtually helpless in camp. When at last he was able to hobble slowly, they started on. No big game was seen, and they sustained themselves on herbs and an occasional turkey or rabbit.

They were near starvation when they reached an arm of Green Bay, and would have succumbed had they not come upon a deserted Indian village where they found a small quantity of corn and some frozen squash. A blizzard swept down from the northwest, and for five days they huddled about a fire in a small hut. When the storm abated, they followed Sturgeon Creek for a time, maddened by hunger. Renault fell desperately ill from swallowing pieces of leather torn from an old Indian shield he had found.

On a bitterly cold day in early November they were grouped about a fire eating some wild onions when two Ottawas appeared out of the forest, and "we gave them such a welcome as was never seen before."

The Ottawas guided them to a Potawatami village "only two leagues off." It was the village of Onanghisse, the Potawatami chief who had shown great hospitality to La Salle when he arrived in the *Griffon* the previous year. The starved and sick wanderers enjoyed the same kindness. Five *couriers du bois* were spending the winter there, and they "received us kindly, and all the Indians seemed to take pleasure in sending us food. . . . Our famine turned to abundance."

During the winter an Indian arrived in the village with a message for Tonty: La Salle was dead. The Indian had come from the Green Bay mission of the Jesuits.

30 ⚜ ⚜ ⚜

IN THE autumn of 1680, as they made their way from the Humber to Lake Simcoe and down the Severn to Georgian Bay, the men knew a grim La Salle. They knew a La Salle who talked little, whose face was dark with brooding, who often seemed to be dwelling in a private world of his own creation, and in whose eyes was to be seen at times a cold and menacing light. He frequently was occupied in the chill evenings with writing letters that in all probability could not reach civilization until the spring, but he applied himself diligently to the task, as if a post box would be found the next day. On other occasions he would leave the camp, go to stand alone on a wilderness shore, and appear to be gazing at the brittle stars, as if he were struggling to see beyond them.

September was almost gone when they passed along the coast of the Manitoulins and reached Michilimackinac. La Salle was inhospitably received. Traders refused to sell him supplies. The Jesuits sought to avoid him. A Huron named Scortus appeared at his camp with a story that Tonty had been slain by the Illinois. With a curse, La Salle sent the Indian away, and accused Father Allouez, who was believed to have gone to the Illinois country, with spreading a falsehood.

Making no effort to conceal his own aggravation with the

attitude of the traders, La Salle assigned the task of obtaining the foodstuffs needed to La Forest, and pushed ahead with twelve men in three canoes. They traveled down the east shore of Lake Michigan. On the fourth of November they came in sight of the ruined Fort Miami on the St. Joseph.

Displaying an impatience unusual in him, La Salle started on the next day. He took with him seven men, one of them Saget, ordering the others to begin at once the construction of cabins and to wait until La Forest had arrived.

As they traveled up the St. Joseph and portaged to the Kankakee, which would take them to the Illinois, they constantly watched for some sign that would tell them white men had recently passed over the route. They found none. A number of Indians were encountered, wandering and homeless Abnakis, Mohegans and Shawnees banded together for their mutual protection, but they had neither seen a trail made by white men nor had they heard that any were in the country. La Salle took new hope that Tonty had been able to hold out, for it was his presumption that if Tonty had left the Illinois he would have headed for Fort Miami.

On the plains along the Kankakee and the upper Illinois they saw thousands of buffalo and deer. They killed a number, halting long enough to dry the meat in thin flakes which they could take with them to Tonty and his companions.

As they went on down the river they became aware that the buffalo were becoming scarce, and soon they saw none at all. They passed Starved Rock. No bastion stood atop it. In the surrounding country they saw no smoke, no sign of human life.

The great town of the Illinois had vanished. Not a mat house stood. The ground was blackened by fire as far as the high bluffs that rose above the valley.

They stepped ashore to stand with white faces before a scene of inconceivable desolation. On the charred poles of houses were human skulls which had been picked clean by birds. Wolves ran from them dragging parts of human bodies. Buzzards rose from the large cemetery. Every grave had been rifled and the remains they contained had been scattered, providing a hideous feast for the birds of prey and the animals. The caches of the Illinois had been broken open and the stores they contained had been destroyed. The cornfields, which had been ripening in the autumn sun, had been burned.

Frantically, the men searched for a clue that would tell them of the fate of Tonty and the others. La Salle went himself to the crude fort which the Iroquois had built. More skulls had been mounted on its logs and protruding poles. He came upon several fragments of French cloth—nothing more. He examined innumerable skulls, but the bits of hair remaining on them showed that they were Indian.

As dusk settled, the men made camp on the bank of the river. Night hid the terrible scene from their eyes, but not from their thoughts—they would never forget it. La Salle would write that it was very cold, and though they feared that Iroquois might still be lurking in the area, "this did not prevent us from making a fire and lying down by it, each of us keeping watch in turn.

"I spent the night in a distress which you can imagine better than I can write it; and I did not sleep a moment with trying to make up my mind as to what I ought to do.

"My ignorance as to the position of those I was looking for, and my uncertainty as to what would become of the men who were to follow me with La Forest if they arrived at the ruined village and did not find me there, made me apprehend every sort of trouble and disaster.

"At last, I decided to keep on my way down the river. . . ."

In the dawn La Salle gave his orders. Three men would be concealed on an island with most of their baggage. If La Forest and the others arrived, they, too, were to wait there until he had returned. He and four men would descend the river until he was satisfied that Tonty had not gone that way.

La Salle identified the men he took with him in two canoes as

Dautray, Hunaut, You and Saget. They had not gone far before it became clear to them that the Illinois had attempted to escape by fleeing down the river, and had been systematically slaughtered by the pursuing Iroquois. They passed campgrounds that were littered with dead bodies, some of them cut to pieces.

Traveling rapidly, they passed Peoria Lake and the ruined Fort Crèvecoeur. The skeleton of the bark still stood on the ways, but the Iroquois had drawn all nails and spikes from its timbers and planks. No human being was seen as they went on. The howling of wolves was heard, but few other sounds broke the stillness of the forest.

Near the mouth of the Illinois they came upon another campground and were startled by the sight of several human figures standing erect and motionless. As they landed, they were revolted by the scene which met their eyes.

The erect figures were the partially eaten bodies of women, still hanging from stakes on which they had been tortured to death. About the campground were the bodies of scores of women and children, mutilated masses of rotted flesh. Eyes had been gouged out. Limbs and breasts and vital organs had been torn from them.

Here was the site on which the Iroquois had held their final orgy, a mass torture of women and children. Here they had turned back, their ferocity and demonic passions sated at last in a bloody bath and a feast of human flesh.

At least half the Illinois nation had been exterminated.

On December 6, 1680, La Salle once more looked out upon the broad eddying waters of the conjunction of the Illinois and Mississippi Rivers. From a bluff he gazed down the great river, in his thoughts seeing far beyond the reach of his sorrowful eyes.

Dautray, Hunaut, You and Saget came to him, and they told him that if he wanted to go on they were unafraid, they would go with him to the sea. He shook his head, thanking them for their loyalty. He would not give up the search for Tonty and his men. But even if their fate had been determined, he would not attempt the journey with such a small force. He would not permit his sadness and dejection, which were greater than he had ever known, to drive him to commit acts of desperation. He would not permit his profound disappointment to destroy his good sense.

On a tall tree near the Mississippi's bank La Salle fashioned a blaze. He carved on the smooth surface figures of men in a canoe and above them a calumet. To the blaze, which could be seen clearly from the river, he attached a letter to Tonty. It told Iron Hand that he had been there and was continuing his search.

On December 7, they started back up the Illinois.

Once more La Salle appeared to be seized by an uncontrollable impatience. Once again he fell into a dark mood, spoke seldom, and seemed to be absorbed by private thoughts.

He drove his men hard. On December 11, they passed the great ruined town. Paddling from dawn to dark, and sometimes into the night, they traveled more than two hundred miles in four days.

Reunited with the three men left on the island, they pushed on. With the beginning of the new year the weather turned extremely cold. Floating ice slowed their progress. On the sixth of January, with the temperature nearing zero, they found the Kankakee frozen. Abandoning their canoes, they shouldered packs and struck out overland.

It was January 26 when they saw Fort Miami ahead.

To La Salle it was a particularly cheering and comforting sight, but not alone because of the safety it provided. La Forest had arrived soon after his departure for the Illinois. In less than three months not only had the fort been restored, but timbers and planks for a new vessel had been sawn and a ways had been constructed on the bank of the St. Joseph. And nearby stood the huts of two score Indians, Abnakis, Shawnees, and Mohegans, with whom La Forest had made friends, and who were eager to acknowledge La Salle as their leader.

But there was no news of Tonty.

[169]

31 ❦ ❦ ❦

AT FORT MIAMI in the winter of 1680–81, La Salle was acutely aware that the Iroquois invasion of the Illinois Valley had created a problem not only more serious and ominous but of greater urgency than any other facing him. Failure to devise a means of effectively solving it would cause a costly, if not disastrous, disruption of his progress.

As the situation stood, both the Jesuits and the merchants opposing him had acquired in the Iroquois a most useful and powerful ally. They would encourage the Five Nations to hold the advantages gained while undertaking more bloody incursions in the west. Unless these were prevented, more Indian peoples would be destroyed or driven from their homes.

The Iroquois raiders already had turned on the Miamis, who had aided them in the attack on the Illinois, and had slain without warning a hundred Miami warriors. No one knew when or against whom they would strike next. The inhabitants of every village lived with the terrible fear that they would become victims of the eastern scourge.

In his reasoning on the involved question, La Salle once more demonstrated his incomparable skill as a wilderness ambassador. Gradually he eliminated all possible courses of action except one.

He could no longer influence the Iroquois. That power, which he had for several years enjoyed, had been taken from him. They would not listen to any appeal he might make. Any attempt to negotiate with them by traditional procedures would be futile.

The only means of halting them was by the creation of a new and potent force. And that could be accomplished only by the establishment of an alliance of nations.

The first barrier to be surmounted—in itself formidable—was

composed of the enmities which existed between the western tribes. These had to be dissolved. Each must be induced to forget grievances and rivalries and ancient controversies, to see the wisdom of uniting, to recognize the advantage of binding themselves together for their mutual protection. They must be made to realize that only by a strong coalition could the Iroquois be prevented from cutting paths of death and destruction through every section of the interior and be driven back to their own territory in Ohio, Pennsylvania, and New York.

La Salle's first step was to hold councils with the Abnakis, Mohegans, and Shawnees in the immediate vicinity of Fort Miami. These Indians, among them several score warriors, were refugees from New England and the Ohio River. Living in a strange country, in constant peril, they readily subscribed to his proposal, and acknowledged him as their leader. Some of them possessed guns, but he gave them more and supplied them with powder and ball. If there were not many of them, they nevertheless comprised a strong and stable nucleus of the defense force he hoped to organize.

Although the winter had not broken, by March 1 La Salle felt he could not afford to wait longer to open negotiations with the Illinois. Finding them might involve a long search. He set out with La Forest and fifteen men. They traveled on snowshoes, dragging canoes on runners, and striking directly across country toward the Kankakee.

The prairies of northern Indiana glared in a dazzling white brilliance. La Salle and several men became snowblind, and for three days suffered extreme pain as they lay in camp with covers over their eyes.

The delay caused by the affliction, however, was not unrewarding. While hunting, Hunaut came upon a band of Foxes who had come south from Green Bay to scout against the Iroquois.

They gave La Salle welcome news. Tonty and the others were safe in the village of his friend and admirer, the Potawatami chief

Onanghisse. Hennepin, Accau and Le Picard, accompanied by de Lhut (Duluth), had passed through Green Bay en route to Michilimackinac.

The Foxes thought well of La Salle's plan for an amalgamation, and gave him their word they would convey it to their own leaders.

With a great burden removed from his mind, La Salle and his small company moved on into northeastern Illinois. A thaw had opened the Kankakee, and the canoes could be floated. They had gone only a short distance down the river when they encountered a group of Illinois cautiously returning toward their village from the south. Among them were two influential chiefs whom La Salle understood would convey the news of his presence in the country and his words to other Illinois leaders.

He gave them presents and outlined his plan. He and his men and his Indian allies would stand by the Illinois if they would agree to an alliance of tribes by which the Iroquois could be defeated and driven back. He would build an impregnable fort in the Illinois country and would maintain a strong garrison in it that would be ready to join the Illinois and other peoples in defending themselves. But he would do more than that. He would bring them trade goods which would give the Illinois every advantage of civilization now enjoyed by the Iroquois and other tribes closer to the St. Lawrence and the Hudson.

The promises seemed to be music to the ears of the Illinois chiefs. They, too, swore allegiance to La Salle, and vowed that they would strive to obtain the acquiescence of all other Illinois leaders.

Satisfied that he had done all he could at the time, La Salle turned back. His next destination was a large camp of Miamis which he had learned had been established at the head of the Kankakee. Before reaching it, however, he dispatched La Forest and two men to Michilimackinac to tell Tonty to wait there for him.

With the Miamis were several Iroquois who had participated

in the slaughter and cannibalistic feast of the Illinois women and children. La Salle wrathfully confronted them, cursed them as cowards, and warned them that he would shoot them down without mercy unless they left the country at once. The next morning the Iroquois were gone, and La Salle was informed that they had fled eastward during the night. He was aware that his bold confrontation of the arrogant Iroquois and their hurried flight had made a deep impression on the Miamis. But he played his hand astutely and unhurriedly.

Near the Miamis was a large camp of eastern Indians, some of whom had come from Rhode Island and had fought in King Philip's War, and others who had wandered west from Massachusetts and Virginia. Ignoring the Miamis for the moment, La Salle called them together for a smoke. He urged them to join the other Abnakis and Mohegans in the alliance with the Illinois, with whom, he told them, he had formulated a pact. Knowing that Miamis were listening, he vowed that French arms would defend them and that in return for their allegiance they would have permanent homes in a land in which game was plentiful, and that they would be supplied with all trade goods and weapons they desired.

Neither his talk nor the enthusiastic response to it went unnoticed by the Miamis, and, early the next morning, messengers were speeding from lodge to lodge summoning all headmen to a grand council.

"Few men," said an official report to the Court of Versailles, the authors of which were unidentified, "are more adept than La Salle in the arts of forest rhetoric and diplomacy. He is the greatest orator in North America."

To which must be appended the remark that an oration delivered in the French language to an audience of Indians was only as great as its interpreter made it.

Yet, the assertion of the official report, if boastful, may not be justifiably described as an exaggeration. For historical records do not produce a man of the time who could sway the minds of stony-faced Indian chieftains, who could stimulate their imaginations and arouse their enthusiasm, who could hold their attention and open their hearts, better than La Salle.

He smoked the pipes of the Miamis, and then he spread before them a quantity of gifts. But the gifts were not for the living. They were for those who had gone in honor and glory to the spirit world—cloth and coats to cover their still bodies, hatchets with which grand new scaffolds could be erected, beads and bells and shiny buttons to place in their graves.

La Salle gave no indication that he knew full well these valuable gifts would be appropriated by the men before him. He took note of the delight in their eyes, but he did not stop with the knowledge that they were deeply appreciative of his tribute to their brave dead. He delivered an impassioned eulogy of one of their distinguished leaders whom he had learned had been recently killed, declaring that he would be honored to be called by his name, and that he would contribute generously to the support of his squaw and children. The chiefs applauded and made signs to show that La Salle was deserving of so great a name.

Still La Salle did not stop. He signaled to his men, and they brought in a canoe-load of goods, more coats, more cloth, more hatchets, knives, ironware pots, brilliant beads and bits of metal, shirts and vests and plumed hats, and six muskets. Hands were clapped to mouths to show astonishment, and wild cheers and arm waving destroyed the last vestige of solemnity.

La Salle's face grew serious and his eyes moved in an intent gaze from face to face. The chiefs became quiet.

Saget, a skilled orator in his own right, interpreted La Salle's words as he told the Miamis in a tone touched with sternness:

"He who is my master, and the master of all this country, is a mighty chief, feared by the whole world; but he loves peace, and the words of his lips are for good alone.

"He is called the King of France, and he is the mightiest among the chiefs beyond the great water. His goodness reaches even to your dead, and his subjects come among you to raise them up to life.

"But it is his will to preserve the life he has given. It is his will that you should obey his laws, and make no war without the leave of Onontio, who commands in his name at Quebec, and who loves all the nations alike, because such is the will of the Great King.

"You ought, then, to live at peace with your neighbors, and above all with the Illinois. You have had causes of quarrel with them; but their defeat has avenged you. Though they are still strong, they wish to make peace with you. Be content with the glory of having obliged them to ask for it.

"You have an interest in preserving them, since, if the Iroquois destroy them, they will next destroy you.

"Let us all obey the Great King, and live together in peace, under his protection.

"Be of my mind, and use these guns that I have given you, not to make war, but only to hunt and to defend yourselves."

Placing two belts of wampum on the ground, La Salle went to his camp. In the light of his fire he recorded his own words and wrote a report of the meeting.

He knew in the morning that his appeal to the Miamis had been successful. Summoned to a council, at which the chiefs were decorated with the goods he had given them, he was told:

"The Illinois is our brother, because he is the son of our father, the Great King.

"We make you the master of our beaver and our lands, of our minds and our bodies.

"We cannot wonder that our brothers from the east wish to live with you. We should have wished the same, if we had known what a blessing it is to be the children of the Great King.

"The feasting and the dancing to bind our agreement will begin."

The alliance of western tribes had been born, but to assure its growth and stability La Salle would need more money, unlimited goods, more men. It was imperative that these things be obtained before he did anything else. There was only one way to get them —return to Canada.

His discouragement was profound. The letters which he had spent so many nights answering—answers that were not yet mailed —left no mistake about the state of his affairs. Everything he owned was heavily mortgaged or taken over by creditors. His personal resources were virtually nil. Yet, he had no alternative but to try to recoup them, to secure enough financial backing to continue.

On a day late in May he set out with Nika and several *couriers du bois* for Michilimackinac.

Few things irritated La Salle more than complicated business procedures. He wanted none of them. This attitude spawned the conviction in many persons who lent him money that he had no business sense. That was not the truth. He was an able and, when he gave his full attention to the work, successful trader. His weaknesses lay in his willingness to take enormous risks, in his sanguine expectations, in the supreme confidence he had in himself, and in a tendency to place trust in men who did not merit it.

He was deeply hurt by the discovery that some of the letters he had written in the past had not reached their destinations. It was as if he could not bring himself to believe that his enemies would stoop to such dishonorable tactics.

"I cannot pardon myself for the stoppage of my letters," he told Thouret, "though I made every effort to make them reach you. I wrote to you in '79 and sent my letters to M. de la Forest who gave them in good faith to my brother."

Abbé Cavelier had gone out of his way to get hold of letters La Salle wrote to friends and government officials.

"I don't know what he has done with them," said La Salle. "His conduct towards me has always been so strange. . . ."

In a report intended to reach official eyes, La Salle somewhat angrily defended himself with the assertion that while he had reason to thank many persons for supporting his plans, it seemed to him that he had "done still more, since I have put everything at stake; and it would be hard to reproach me either with foolish outlays or with the ostentation which is falsely imputed to me."

His enemies had disseminated rumors that La Salle was stealing the money of his investors and living in a grand style on it. "Let my accusers explain what they mean," he said. "Since I have been in this country, I have had neither servants nor clothes nor fare which did not savor more of meanness than of ostentation. . . ."

Behind an impassive exterior there was deep in La Salle an enthusiasm he seldom revealed. There were in him, too, profound emotions, a sensitiveness, an almost naïve friendliness, warmth and intensity of feeling, that invariably brought suffering and injury on the rare occasion when he permitted them to surface. If he were not born a stoic, he had come to understand the wisdom of giving no indication that he was either enjoying pleasure or enduring pain.

When they met in Michilimackinac, he and Tonty and Membre threw their arms about each other, and with the greatest difficulty withheld their tears. La Salle's statement of their union was perhaps less restrained than those of the others. He was "overjoyed." Tonty said nothing of his own feelings, merely remarking with notable understatement that they "were very glad to see each other."

Tonty and Membre were in complete accord with La Salle's plan for a western alliance. It was clear to them, said Membre, that if "we wish to settle in these parts . . . it is absolutely necessary to maintain peace and union among all these tribes, as well as among others more remote, against the common enemy, that is the Iroquois, who never makes a real peace with any whom he has once beaten, or whom he hopes to overcome by the divisions which he artfully excites, so that we should be daily exposed to routs like that to which we were subjected last year."

Dallying not at all in the unfriendly atmosphere of Michilimackinac, La Salle, Tonty and Membre and a crew of *couriers du bois* set out late in June for Montreal. There La Salle left the others and pressed on swiftly for Quebec.

Frontenac had his orders from Versailles, and they differed not at all from his own sentiments. Despite financial difficulties and debts, La Salle's discoveries were not to be permitted to lapse.

However, if the King were agreeable to having La Salle continue the great Mississippi venture, he was not willing to finance it. Faced with this paradoxical situation, Frontenac relied on his own initiative, persuasive powers, and political influence.

La Salle's creditors were temporarily soothed by loans obtained from several wealthy persons. A number of merchants, seeing a possible advantage to themselves by subscribing to the official position of the French government, offered sufficient credit to let La Salle purchase the equipment, supplies and trade goods he required. One of these was his cousin, François Plet, who had as yet received only small returns on his previous large investments in the La Salle enterprises.

But being consummate men of business, these supporters were not unduly influenced by the prospect of gaining political favor. On the contrary, they extracted hard bargains. La Salle was obliged to surrender shares, proportionate to the funds each advanced, in his western trade monopolies.

La Salle did not quibble over terms. He would have surrendered every trade concession he possessed, if necessary to acquire the means to continue. There was nothing else in life for him.

On August 11, 1681, at Montreal, La Salle wrote a will, prefacing it with the statement that because of the "great dangers" he faced in wilderness voyages he wished to "acknowledge, as much as I am able, the great obligations I owe to M. François Plet. . . ." To his cousin he bequeathed his seignory of Fort Frontenac, all his patented trading rights, and all his property, both real and personal, in North America.

La Salle was obliged to spend only a few days in Quebec and

Montreal before completing his mission and starting out again with a large cargo convoy. Only a brief pause was made at Fort Frontenac, and, by mid-September, the canoes had reached the Humber River. Two weeks were occupied in portaging to Lake Simcoe.

October was gone by the time they had passed through Lake Huron and had left Michilimackinac behind them. The weather was favorable as they paddled day after day with little rest down the eastern shore of Lake Michigan. The forests were bare, and the feel of winter was in the air.

The last month of the year 1681 had begun when they beached their canoes before Fort Miami at the mouth of the River St. Joseph.

32 ⚜ ⚜ ⚜

"M. LA SALLE began with his ordinary activity and vast mind, to make all preparations for his departure. He selected twenty-three Frenchmen, and eighteen Mohegans and Abnakis, all inured to war. The latter insisted on taking along ten of their women. . . . These had three children, so that the whole party consisted of but fifty-four persons. . . ."*

These were the words in the official report, *Rélation de la Découverte*, which told of the start of the expedition that would win for France the vast empire, to be called Louisiana, in the interior of North America.

They were written by the Recollect, Father Membre, from notes he entered in his journal at Fort Miami in December, 1681.

The actual start of the voyage that would delineate a new course for the history of the western world took place four days

* Not including La Salle.

before Christmas. On December 21, six canoes carrying a score of men and heavily loaded with goods, supplies, tools, and camping equipment pushed out of the mouth of the River St. Joseph on the cold, gray waters of Lake Michigan. The dunes along the curving southern shore of the lake were under deep snow, and ice covered the dead silent marshes, but the lake was still open, and the paddlers bent to their task with the hope of making the crossing before it was closed against them. Snow, driven by a bitter wind, struck when they camped the third night on the Chicago River.

This was the first contingent of the expedition. Led by Tonty, it had been sent ahead to investigate the condition of the country. If it were found that the rivers contained too much ice to permit the passage of canoes, sleds were to be built.

It was a wise precaution. The snowstorm abated, but was followed by severe cold. When La Salle arrived at the Chicago with the others of the company on the fourth of January, 1682, the stream was frozen.

For the next twenty-three days they dragged their heavy canoes, traveling on river ice when feasible but taking every possible shortcut overland. They passed Starved Rock, which lifted a white mantle against a frigid blue sky. They passed the great Illinois town at Utica, where the terrible massacre had occurred, and found it deserted. They passed the island on which the Iroquois had held their orgy and cannibalistic feast. Over all lay a thick blanket of pristine snow, concealing the hideous scene from the eyes but not from the memories of the men who had witnessed it.

The Indian women and children had not been able to keep up, and some of the men had remained to protect them. Only the fringes of Lake Peoria were frozen, and the main group waited there, cheered by the sight of open water, until the stragglers had arrived. Then the sleds were abandoned and the entire company floated in milder weather down the Illinois. The village below the lake, where the agents of La Salle's enemies had sought to poison the Illinois against him, had been reoccupied, and a council was held in which he made another plea for a western alliance. He was disappointed by the apathetic attitude of the Illinois leaders, who promised only that they would give the proposal further consideration. They appeared to be people of broken spirit, and he left them fearing they would never recover from the catastrophe which the Iroquois had inflicted upon them.

The sight of the ruined Fort Crèvecoeur and the collapsing skeleton of his bark did nothing to bolster La Salle's own spirits. But he said nothing of his feelings, and the next bend of the river brought once more into view the unspoiled wilderness, the great rolling prairies and bare forests of Illinois still undefiled by the destructive and cruel hands of man. But uneasiness clung like a shadow to the optimism and the encouragement he had come to possess.

For the third time, he gazed on the confluence of the Illinois and Mississippi Rivers. Twice he had been obliged to turn back from it, but now, on the sixth day of February in the year 1682, he felt himself justified in harboring a new hope, the hope that at last the dream he had so long held would be fulfilled.

If that were to come, however, it would not be with the speed he would have liked. The great Mississippi was filled with immense chunks of floating ice. A week was lost in waiting for it to clear.

On the afternoon of February 13th they were able to embark once more. Here the Mississippi made a sharp bend toward the southeast, and, after traveling at good speed a few miles, they came suddenly upon a powerful flood sweeping in from the west.

It was the flood of the Missouri.

They encamped beside a village of Illinois Indians, who told them, said Membre, that the Missouri was "full as large as the river Mississippi into which it empties, troubling it so, that from the mouth of the Missouri the water is hardly drinkable."*

* Membre called the Illinois the Seignelay, and the Mississippi the Colbert, names which La Salle also had applied to them in his reports, not without a purpose. His name for the Missouri was Osage.

An inquiry as to the source of the Missouri brought intriguing replies from the Indians. They "assure us that this river is formed by many others, and that they ascend it for ten or twelve days to a mountain where it rises; that beyond this mountain is the sea where they see great ships; that on the river are a great number of large villages, of many different nations; that there are arable and prairie lands, and abundance of cattle and beaver."

The weather remained favorable. Each day game and fowl were killed and fish were caught, fresh nutritious foods to supplement the staples of maize and beans they had brought with them. It was not a journey of hardship, and they were making good progress. Yet, La Salle was not satisfied. Impatience as great as he had ever known surged in him. He wished that he had come with less equipment and fewer persons. The women and children were excess baggage, and he would have liked to send them back with some of the Indians, and make greater speed.

The Ohio, the "Beautiful River" of the Senecas, which he had found on his first wilderness voyage, was passed shortly after the middle of February. Some eleven years had gone by since he had stood at the falls [Louisville] struggling to suppress his impulse to continue down it, eleven hard and perilous years during which his enemies had made every conceivable effort to thwart him. As he gazed upon the junction he experienced a profound satisfaction— he had overcome every barrier placed before him.

But his final victory was yet to be won. That fact, he reminded himself, he must not forget. And the admonition brought him abruptly back to the reality of his situation.

Below the Ohio were immense swamps, dismal in aspect and reaching into the sky on each side of the river. Membre recorded that for several days they could find no good landing, for the banks were "low and marshy, and full of thick foam, rushes and walnut [?] trees." They paddled from dawn until darkness forced them to stop, eager to pass the depressing country. After traveling some hundred miles, they reached a pleasant region. The river was bordered by high bluffs, and prairies interspersed by thick forests extended to distant hills. Most of the company, enjoying good food and traveling with ease on the strong smooth current of the river, were gay and contented.

But the keen eyes of some of the scouts found signs—fresh tracks and distant smokes and the ashes of campfires which had not long been cold—which convinced them they were being watched. Campsites were selected which provided protection—on narrow strips of land between lagoons, or on islands, or in clearings—and sentinels were posted.

Early in March they stopped in the afternoon at the Chickasaw Bluffs. Four hunters were sent out. Only three of them returned. Each had found the fresh tracks of a number of Indians and had not fired a gun.

The missing man was Pierre Prudhomme, a Canadian capable in the use of firearms and an expert canoeist but with limited experience as a wilderness tracker. Throughout much of the night La Salle remained awake beside a large fire. Sentinels were concealed in the surrounding trees. In the first light of the dawn he sent Saget and several other men out to look for Prudhomme's trail, while he directed the construction of a redoubt made of logs, brush, and earth. The canoes were drawn from the water, and goods, ammunition, and foodstuffs were made secure within the walls of the hurriedly erected fort.

Five days and nights of watchful waiting passed. On the sixth day Saget brought in two Chickasaw Indians. They declared that they had not seen Prudhomme, but La Salle did not believe them. He gave them presents, and one of them offered to remain in camp while the other went to their village, twenty miles away, to determine whether any others of their band had met the missing man. La Salle gave him gifts for their chief, and the Indian departed.

For three more days the search was continued. On the ninth day, Saget came across Prudhomme wandering in the wilderness.

He had become lost while hunting and was half-crazed with fear that he had been left behind.

La Salle now saw an opportunity to decrease the size of the company. Prudhomme needed rest to regain his strength, if not his senses, and he ordered that five of the squaws, the three children, three Abnakis, and two Frenchmen who were indifferent workers, remain with him. They were to strengthen the fort—to which he gave the name Prudhomme—and await his return.

In a dozen canoes, the expedition—now consisting of thirty-six men and five women—departed from Fort Prudhomme on March 13 and were soon halted by an impenetrable fog. Through the eerie damp blanket from the right bank came the sounds of drums and the wild cries of a war dance. Unable to see ahead of them more than a few yards, they crossed slowly and quietly to the opposite side of the river. A defense works of brush and fallen trees was quickly erected.

In the morning the fog lifted and the Indians stared in astonishment at the strange scene. Presently, several warriors cautiously approached in canoes. Saget held aloft a calumet and gave them signs of peace. They landed, and La Salle presented them with tobacco. A Frenchman and two Abnakis returned with them, and soon afterward signaled that they had been well received and that the chief desired to entertain the visitors.

The entire company crossed. "The whole village," Membre wrote, "came down to the shore to meet us, except the women, who had run off. I cannot tell you the civility and kindness we received from these barbarians, who brought us poles to make huts, supplied us with firewood during the three days we were among them, and took turns in feasting us." These Indians were Quapaws, generally called Arkansas.

The largest village of the Quapaws stood on the west bank of the Mississippi near the mouth of the Arkansas River. To La Salle this was an especially significant milepost of the journey. It was the point at which Marquette and Joliet had turned back nine years earlier, believing themselves to be nearing the Gulf of Mexico—the Mississippi's mouth was still some seven hundred miles ahead of them—and fearing that they would be captured by Spaniards if they went farther.

The solemnity of the ceremony La Salle staged at the confluence was in sharp contrast to the wild dancing with which the Indians entertained their guests. The village leaders appeared to be entranced, but they would not have admired and enjoyed it as much if they had understood its meaning.

The program was opened by Membre. He felt that he made a hit with his attempts in the sign language "to explain something of the truth of God, and the mysteries of our redemption. . . . They showed that they relished what I said by raising their eyes to heaven, and kneeling as if to adore."

Next, with La Salle and Tonty leading them, the Frenchmen marched with dignity to the center of the village. There a hole was dug and a tall cross was erected. On it had been carved the fleur-de-lis. Membre stepped forward and sang a hymn. To shouts of *Vive le Roi*, La Salle pronounced the land a possession of France and all its inhabitants subjects of Louis XIV. The watching Indians, understanding not a word of what he said, responded with loud applause and cries. Several of them came forward, giving signs of their appreciation of the ceremony, and, to Membre's great satisfaction, "rubbed their hands over their bodies after rubbing them over the cross."

Almost the entire valley of the Mississippi between the Illinois and the Arkansas had delighted every member of the expedition, its beauty and abundance exceeding all their expectations. The swamps and areas in which the river overflowed were forbidding and unpleasant, but between and behind "these drowned lands you see the finest country in the world . . . there are vast fields of excellent land, diversified here and there with pleasing hills, lofty woods, groves through which you might ride on horseback, so clear and unobstructed are the paths."

[185]

It was a rich, bountiful, lovely land, and below the Arkansas it knew full spring. The air was balmy as the company floated along through the twistings of the mighty river. Great oaks were adorned with streamers of moss. The hardwood forests were bright with new foliage. Flowers made colorful palettes of meadowlands. Birds flashed brilliant plumage along the tall rushes. Alligators sunned themselves on the banks. They shot several, finding them delectable, and Membre was astonished to learn that the monsters, some of which exceeded twenty feet in length, were born of eggs.

La Salle had obtained two guides from the Quapaws, and on March 22 they stopped on the west bank and indicated they were near a large tribe with which they were on friendly terms. La Salle was indisposed, and assigned Tonty, Membre, and several canoe-men to visit the village which the guides said was located on an adjacent lake.

The Indians were Taensas, who belonged to the Natchesan linguistic family, and at the time of the La Salle expedition were living on a body of water (in Tensas Parish, Louisiana) that had once been a part of the main Mississippi but which had been isolated when the river changed its course.

A canoe was carried on a foot trail through a swamp to a lagoon, and Tonty and Membre were paddled to the village. The Taensas were apprised of their approach and a committee was waiting to receive them. Tonty was astonished by the size and structure of the houses. They were built of mud mixed with straw, covered with arched roofs of cane, and stood in precise rows about a cleared rectangular area. He and Membre were escorted to the dwelling of the chief which was "40 feet square, the wall 10 feet high, a foot thick, and the roof, which was dome shape, about 15 feet high."

Near the chief's house was another equally large building, a Temple of the Sun, "surrounded with strong mud walls, in which are fixed spikes, on which they place the heads of their enemies whom they sacrifice to the sun."

[186]

The Taensas knew of white men, but in the time of the oldest among them none had come to their country. They had heard that to the southwest there were bearded men who rode great animals, and far to the east and to the south were others who vanished into the sea in ships, but they had never seen them. Yet, it was apparent that in the years gone white men had been in their land, for they had found breastplates of metal and knives and sabers and buttons and several guns, all made useless by rust, and it had come down to them in a legend that at one time a grand army in armor and plumes and mounted on horses had passed over the Mississippi and disappeared in the sky.*

The chief of the Taensas graciously accepted the gifts La Salle had sent to him. If because of illness the white chief was unable to come to his house, he would honor him with a visit the next day.

Preceding the chief the next morning were two men bearing white fans, sent ahead to prepare the place of meeting. Next came a warrior carrying a disc of burnished copper, a symbol of his ancestor, the sun. When the chief appeared, he was accompanied by tambourine players, a group of women singing his glories, and naked warriors waving white fans. A cane mat was placed on the ground for him. La Salle "received him with much politeness, and gave him some presents." The chief reciprocated with "plenty of provisions and some of their robes." It was Membré's impression that while the chief "maintained a very grave demeanor" his visit was "full of confidence and marks of friendship."

The Quapaw guides turned back, fearful of encountering enemies of their tribe, and on March 26 the company continued down the river. In the afternoon they met several Indian fishermen

* This was not a legend. They were speaking of the army of De Soto which had passed through the region a century and a half before on a disastrous hunt for treasure. They were the first white men to cross the Mississippi north of its delta.

[187]

who invited them to their village. Although it was "three leagues inland, the sieur de la Salle did not hesitate to go there with a part of our force."

Membre was a member of the party. The night was spent in the village, and the Frenchmen "received as kindly a welcome as we could expect; La Salle, whose very air, engaging manners, and skillful mind . . . so impressed the heart of these Indians,* that they did not know how to treat us well enough. . . ."

To this point, almost to the confluence of the Mississippi and Red Rivers, the journey had the aspect of a triumphal march. La Salle's success in winning the friendship of Indians had been extraordinary, but he was not infallible. Troubles were in the making, and they began on April 2.

Indians were seen on the bank, and La Salle sent a canoe containing four men to meet with them. The Indians fled into the trees. As the emissaries landed, even though they displayed a calumet, they were forced to "return in hot haste, because the Indians let fly a shower of arrows at them."

La Salle ordered the company to proceed, and, a few miles below, a village came into sight. It appeared to be unoccupied. A landing was made. It was then discovered that only a few days before the village had been sacked and plundered. In three huts were bodies "lying on one another," stacked like cords of wood.

Immediately the grisly scene was put behind them. For the next three nights they rested uneasily beside their arms, and during the daylight hours held as much as possible to the center of the stream.

The last of their dry staples had been consumed, and hunting in the seemingly endless swamps was difficult and unproductive. They welcomed the discovery by one of the scouts in a deserted cabin of what appeared to be a quantity of venison. It had been

* They were Koroas, whose home was on the west bank of the Mississippi near Natchez.

dried and smoked in thin strips and was well preserved. As he nibbled on it, Membre pronounced it "good and delicate."

Nodding in agreement, an Abnaki informed him that he was eating human flesh.

"We left the rest to the Indians," said Membre, "and lived on wild potatoes and alligators."

On the sixth of April the river branched out in three channels of almost equal size. Perplexed as to which course to follow, La Salle divided the company into three groups. He took the west channel, Tonty followed the middle passage, and Dautray commanded the canoes on the other one.

All three branches of the river ran with a strong current between low, marshy shores. All were, in Tonty's words, "very fine, wide, and deep."

And all led to the sea.

The fresh water became brackish, then turned to brine. The wind carried the smell of the ocean. At last, they saw ahead of them the vast Gulf of Mexico shimmering under a clear spring sky, and they heard the roar of combers breaking on the shore.

On the ninth of April, 1682, the province of Louisiana was officially established.

On that day, twenty-one Frenchmen, fifteen Indian men, and five squaws assembled on a small palm and cypress island near the mouth of the Mississippi and conducted a ceremony which made France the greatest colonial power in North America.

The empire they created reached from the ridges of the Appalachians to the towering walls of the Rocky Mountains, from the Great Lakes to the Gulf of Mexico, an empire of inconceivably vast forests, of great plains that rolled against the sky, of immense rivers whose sources were lost in unknown frigid realms and desert wastes and alpine vastnesses, an empire of incalculable natural bounties, of wild red peoples whose numbers were indeterminable, an empire that was in every way one of the richest regions on the face of the earth.

The Spanish had found the Mississippi gateway, but they had made no effort to hold it. They had established colonies on each side of it, in Florida and in Texas, but they had failed to link them together. La Salle had driven, with the force of international law, an indestructible wedge between the two.

A tree was trimmed. From it the flag of France waved in the sea breeze, and on it were carved the words:

LOUIS LE GRAND—ROI DE
FRANCE ET DE NAVARRE—
REGNE—LE NEUVIÈME AVRIL
1682

A cross was planted, and beside it was buried a copper plate on which had been inscribed:

LUDOVICUS MAGNUS REGNAT

Father Membre led the Frenchmen in chanting the *Te Deum*, the *Exaudiat*, and the *Domine salvum fac Regem*.

La Salle moved to stand by the flag tree. He opened a parchment, and in a voice that disclosed the emotion within him he proclaimed:

"In the name of the most high, mighty, invincible, and victorious Prince, Louis the Great, by the Grace of God King of France and of Navarre, Fourteenth of that name, I . . . in virtue of the commission of his Majesty . . . do now take, in the name of his Majesty . . . possession of this country of Louisiana, the seas, harbors, ports, bays, adjacent straits, and all the nations, peoples, provinces, cities, towns, villages, mines, minerals, fisheries, streams, and rivers . . . hereby protesting against all who may hereafter undertake to invade any or all of these aforesaid countries, peoples, or lands, to the prejudice of the rights of his Majesty. . . . I hereby take to witness those who hear me, and demand an act of the notary here present."

In planning the ceremony before he had left Fort Frontenac

the previous fall, La Salle had not neglected to take with him a man who held a commission as a notary. He was Jacques de la Metarie, and he stepped briskly forward and signed the parchment, giving it the status of a legal document.

Membre lifted his arms, and the voices of the Frenchmen rang out in the Hymn of the Church, *Vexilla Regis.*

When the signing ended, shouts of *Vive le Roi* rose, accompanied by musket shots.

And then the stillness, disturbed only by bird calls and the stirring of the wind in the rushes, settled once more over the delta of the Rivière Colbert, the Mississippi, that now belonged to France.

The next day, April 10, the expedition started back up the river, leaving the fleur-de-lis flying in lonely splendor on the tiny island.

33 ⚜ ⚜ ⚜

IN MAY, 1682, La Salle lay dangerously ill in the crude log stockade, called Fort Prudhomme, under the shadow of the Chickasaw Bluffs.

The journey up the Mississippi had been extremely arduous. Except for the Arkansas, the Indians encountered had displayed an unfriendliness they had not previously exhibited. Several times the company found itself in danger from large war parties. Two serious fights had occurred. Forced to defend themselves, the white men and their red companions had killed a dozen attacking warriors and wounded a large number. The clashes had dashed La Salle's hope of establishing peaceful relations with all the river tribes.

Membre and others spoke of La Salle's illness as "strange" and "mysterious." It was probably a stroke. At times he appeared to lose consciousness. At other times, although he could see and hear and speak in a whisper, his strength seemed to have completely left him, and he was unable to move on his bed of buffalo robes. At still other times, he was delirious, rambling incomprehensibly, his eyes glazed and sightless.

Some of the medicines which the Indian women prepared seemed to calm him and induce undisturbed sleep. Either these potions or the natural course of his illness brought periods in which, although too weak to rise, he was composed and alert, in full possession of his faculties. At such times he gave orders, straining to explain the trend of his own thinking, struggling to make clear his own attitude toward his responsibilities and obligations, as if he feared that he would not have time to divulge all the thoughts and reveal all the concerns in his mind before he lapsed once more into unconsciousness.

He ordered Tonty to take half the company to Fort Miami, then push on to Michilimackinac and send dispatches telling of his discovery to Quebec. It was vital that the Governor be enabled to send the news to the King and the Marquis de Seignelay before winter had halted waterborne traffic in the St. Lawrence.

Tonty was to recruit as many additional men as possible in Michilimackinac, Green Bay and other posts, and return with them to Starved Rock on the Illinois. Tonty also was to send requests to Frontenac for more men and supplies.

At Starved Rock would be built the first of the settlements he had planned to establish in the interior. It would be called Fort St. Louis. A strong bastion would rise atop the high rock. Below it would be warehouses and dwellings and more defense works, surrounded by fields. It would be the uppermost part of a chain that would reach to the Gulf of Mexico. To Fort St. Louis would be brought the Illinois and all other tribes that wished to join La Salle's alliance and share in the advantages of the commerce which would flow to and from Europe. Fort St. Louis would be the first of the installations that would make France impregnable in the

[192]

interior of the Continent and make impossible any advance by either the British or the Spanish.

May and half of June passed before La Salle was able to take a few halting steps. Membre, Saget, and Nika ministered to him day and night during this time, fearful that each hour would be their beloved leader's last. They anointed him with animal oils, and fed him the strong gruels which the squaws prepared from choice bits of game meat, corn, nuts and wild herbs, roots and bark.

Late in June they helped him into a canoe and made him comfortable on skins, and Fort Prudhomme was left to stand deserted in the wilderness of the Mississippi. For a number of days they traveled only short distances, but as his strength gradually increased they extended their daily journeys. They had not ceased to marvel at La Salle's determination to live. They had seen no sign nor heard a word to indicate that his courage had failed him or that he had given up hope of surviving.

In mid-August, they reached Fort Miami. Several hundred tepees stood along the banks of the St. Joseph. It was a sight which gratified and encouraged La Salle, for it meant that his plan of a western confederation to stand against the Iroquois was being accepted by Indians from various parts of the country. Bands had come from as far away as New England, Pennsylvania, Virginia, and Ohio, and had been joined by groups from Wisconsin and other regions adjacent to Lake Michigan.

He might have rested there and made a full recovery, while awaiting Tonty's return, but in so doing he would not have found peace within himself. He could not be content until he had made certain that the dispatches informing Frontenac of the successful voyage to the Gulf of Mexico had been sent by special courier to Quebec. Taking the best canoeists available, he set out again.

The forests of northern Lake Michigan were displaying the colors of fall when La Salle stepped ashore at Michilimackinac. Tonty had bad news for him.

Frontenac had been recalled. A former naval officer, Le Febvre de la Barre, had been named to succeed him.

Also, reports had reached Michilimackinac that the Iroquois had sent another army to attack western tribes.

Tonty had succeeded in enlisting a few *couriers du bois* and had been able to trade a good stock of furs, which had accumulated at Fort Miami, for supplies and powder. He was ready to leave for the Illinois, and La Salle did not hold him.

Weakness again pervaded La Salle, and he was forced to rest a large part of each day. Tonty had turned over to him a number of letters which had reached Michilimackinac during the summer with trading parties. They augmented the burden of his poor physical condition with anger, disappointment, and frustration. He taxed his strength in replying to them and completing others he had started months earlier. No time could be lost in getting them on their way. The northern rivers would soon be locked in snow and ice. A courier would be obliged to travel by way of the lakes, across the Niagara portage, through Lake Ontario to Fort Frontenac, then by land through deep snow and bitter cold to Quebec. Further, this route might be made impassable by storms before it could be traversed.

Even if he had been in good health, La Salle would not have gone on to Quebec. A meeting with the new governor could be postponed without the situation becoming more adverse to him. He felt that his "presence was absolutely necessary" with Tonty on the Illinois. Not only the reports that the Iroquois were moving to another assault had brought him to that decision. The organizing of the western alliance and the building of the Starved Rock settlement were responsibilities he could not leave to others, not even to the loyal and capable Tonty. They required his personal direction and leadership, and he was unwilling to assign these vital tasks to anyone else. Others would share in his success, if it came, but he must bear the weight of failure alone.

The recall of Frontenac could mean only that his supporters had been outmaneuvered, but he refused to believe that they would not regain the ground lost. They were too politically influential, too ambitious, too wealthy, to be contained, to endure passively an ignominious defeat. Yet, that some fears existed in him was apparent, for he wrote appealingly to Bernou: "I pray you, my dear sir, to give me once more all the help you can. I have great enemies, who have succeeded in all they have undertaken. I do not pretend to resist them, but only to justify myself, so that I can pursue by sea the plans I have begun here by land."

La Salle had no way of knowing whether La Barre had already been installed, and, hoping that Frontenac might still be in Quebec, he wrote him, imploring him to send more troops to Fort Frontenac to protect it against the Iroquois.

He wrote nothing to La Barre, for he feared that if Frontenac had not yet departed he might offend him by corresponding prematurely with his successor. There would be time enough to report to La Barre, and in the spring he would have more news of developments in the Illinois Valley.

Abbé Bernou had informed him of new malicious charges and criticisms of his character which his antagonists had made against him. La Salle's reply was more a confession than a defense, a remarkable portrayal of a man struggling to conceal beneath an austere manner and a cold reserve weaknesses born in him and which he understood could never be overcome.

"You write me that even my friends say that I am not a man of popular manners," he told Bernou. "I do not know what friends they are. I know of none in this country. To all appearance they are enemies, more subtle and secret than the rest."

Admittedly his pride was grievously wounded by the "stabs," but he had long suffered them, and as a result he thought it was "not surprising that I open my mind to nobody, and distrust everybody."

He appeared to be profoundly disturbed by the reflections upon his personal habits.

"I do not know what you mean by having popular manners," he said. "There is nothing special in my food, clothing, or lodging, which are all the same for me as for my men."

The accusation that he remained aloof and that he refused to talk with those under him was without foundation, for "how could it be? I have no other company. You do not know the men one must employ here, when you exhort me to make merry with them. They are incapable of that; for they are never pleased, unless one gives free rein to drunkenness and other vices. If that is what you call having popular manners, neither honor nor inclination would let me stoop to gain their favor in a way so disreputable; and, besides, the consequences would be dangerous, and they would have the same contempt for me that they have for all who treat them in this fashion."

And then La Salle turned a mirror on himself:

"If I am wanting in expansiveness and show of feeling towards those with whom I associate, it is only through a timidity which is natural to me, and which has made me leave various employments, where without it I could have succeeded."

As the cold winds of the late fall of 1682 swept across the gray reaches of Lake Michigan, he was on his way to rejoin Tonty and his company at Starved Rock.

34 ⚜ ⚜ ⚜

BY THE SPRING of 1682, Louis XIV had become extremely weary of attempting to reconcile the factions which kept both Canada and the French court in an uproar with their bitter clashes over colonial policies. The brilliant Colbert, who had for so many years protected him from the barrage of charges and countercharges, had retired and was nearing the end of his earthly road. Colbert's son, the Marquis de Seignelay, who had succeeded him as Colonial Minister, was dedicated and enterprising, but the King was not convinced that Seignelay would be able to withstand the pressures and resolve the conflicts which were the responsibility of the office as shrewdly and as competently as his father.

Precipitate changes, the King reasoned, would not effect a lasting peace—it was hardly possible that could be achieved by any action he might take—but they would bring a lull in the fighting. This desirable state would endure at least until the antagonists had time to reevaluate the situation and regroup their forces. He thoroughly distrusted the Canadian Intendant Duchesneau, yet he saw nothing to be gained in removing him and leaving in Quebec Governor Frontenac, whose policies and projects, not the least of which were his program of expansion and his unqualified support of La Salle, were so strenuously opposed by powerful men whose opinions and demands could not be ignored.

Louis XIV cleaned house in Quebec, recalling both Frontenac and Duchesneau, as well as the chief aides of each.

To Canada he sent as governor La Barre, and as Intendant Jacques de Meules, Sieur de la Source. Both men were acceptable to the anti-Frontenac forces.

La Barre, sixty years of age when he reached Canada, was pompous, greedy, ambitious, and corrupt. By profession he was an attorney, but his accomplishments as a legal practitioner were not to be compared with his success as a salesman of political favors and a specialist in circumventing the law. With the help of influential politicians he had secured an appointment as commander of military and naval forces in the French West Indies, a post for which he was totally unfitted. During his brief tenure there, while he was busy dishonestly enriching himself, professional and experienced French officers were successful in repulsing assaults by the

English. La Barre got credit for the victory. Thereafter in France he insisted on being addressed as *Monsieur le Général*.

As Governor of Canada, La Barre was precluded by statute from engaging in the fur trade. This was a stumbling block which he adroitly got around by organizing a trade syndicate with several prominent merchants who had commercial establishments in Montreal and Quebec. For the purpose of increasing the syndicate's profits, La Barre issued an order which prohibited *couriers du bois* from trading as individuals among western tribes. This directive endeared him not only to the St. Lawrence traders but to the Jesuits, who had long struggled to halt the traffic in liquor which the unscrupulous *couriers du bois* conducted with the western Indians.

La Barre's enmity for La Salle, whom he had never met, stemmed not only from the fact that he was the colonial representative of La Salle's opponents. It had a source as well in personal jealousy. He was envious of La Salle because of the favor shown him by the King. He resented La Salle's trade monopolies and the royal authority granted him to build settlements and develop commerce in the Mississippi Valley.

The instructions given La Barre by the King had increased his bitterness toward La Salle and caused him to vow to thwart him in every possible way. He was not to permit any more journeys of discovery for the time being in the country west or south of the Great Lakes, but the restriction was not to be applied in any manner to La Salle. La Salle was to be permitted to make any explorations deemed to be of value to France, and was to continue his enterprises as long as he complied with the terms of the patent given him.

A letter La Salle had sent to Frontenac, in which he had requested that, because of the Iroquois danger, the small number of troops stationed at Fort Frontenac be increased, fell into La Barre's hands. It offered the first opportunity he had received to strike directly at La Salle. Instead of reinforcing the garrison at

Fort Frontenac, La Barre withdrew the few soldiers who were there. He then seized the property and turned it over to two of La Salle's most vigorous opponents, the Montreal merchants La Chesnaye and Le Ber. La Barre's excuse for this clearly illegal action was that by leaving the fort defenseless La Salle had failed to live up to the provisions of the seignorial grant.

La Chesnaye and Le Ber promptly sent a contingent to occupy Fort Frontenac. La Barre ignored the protests registered by La Salle's cousin, Plet, and other investors. The agents of La Chesnaye and Le Ber not only took over La Salle's trade but sold the stores at the fort, some of which had been sent there on orders from the King, and divided the revenue with La Barre. La Salle's lieutenant, La Forest, who was present at the time of the seizure, was informed that he could remain in command if he gave his allegiance to La Barre. He refused, and departed for France. Settlers were forced to leave. Cattle were allowed to pasture on growing crops until they were butchered. The settlement was ruined.

Upon his arrival in Canada, La Barre had boasted that he would quickly put an end to the bloody aggressions of the Iroquois. "They have twenty-six hundred warriors," he wrote the King, "but I will attack them with twelve hundred men. They know how roughly I handled the English in the West Indies." When he had become more familiar with the situation, however, his confidence vanished and he sent urgent appeals to the Colonial Minister for more French troops.

Meanwhile, he dispatched the eminent *voyageur,* Charles Le Moyne, to invite the Iroquois chiefs to a conference in Montreal. Some forty, representing all Five Nations, accepted.

La Barre had neither the dignity nor the diplomatic ability of Frontenac, and he did not possess the great Onontio's showmanship. The chiefs were unimpressed by him, although they cordially accepted the gifts, valued at two thousand crowns, he showered on them.

Two promises, neither of which they intended to keep, were

extracted from the Iroquois. They would maintain peace with the French, and they would not launch an attack on other tribes without first notifying the Quebec government. La Barre asked why they had slaughtered the Illinois.

"Because they deserved to die," a chief told him.

It was not a satisfactory reply, and La Barre sought further information on the matter. This elicited responses which greatly pleased him. They had invaded the west, said the chiefs, because La Salle had been arming the Illinois for the purpose of attacking them.

La Barre knew that any claim of self-defense made by the Iroquois could have no foundation in fact. He understood the purposes of the alliance La Salle was attempting to establish in the west, and he realized that, if it were successful, not only would France secure territorial acquisitions of inestimable value but La Salle and his supporters would enjoy incomparable commercial advantages. He knew the truth, but he closed his ears to it, for it stood in the way of the designs he had been sent to Canada to carry out, in the way of the plans of the faction he represented, in the way of his own machinations.

Neither he nor the colonial government, he told the Iroquois, could be held accountable for the diabolical schemings of La Salle. The Iroquois had his permission to deal with La Salle, their great enemy, in whatever manner they wished. In any case, La Salle would be punished by the King for his irresponsible and unauthorized actions.

Behind their stony countenances the chiefs were laughing at La Barre. The pledge of amnesty they had given was broken almost at once. On Lake Erie, Iroquois warriors attacked and captured a French convoy carrying goods valued at more than fifteen thousand *livres*. It was en route to Michilimackinac, and it had been sent out by the syndicate of merchants La Barre had organized.

Stunned by the treachery of the Iroquois, and infuriated by

the loss, La Barre sought an explanation from them. He got it, and it did nothing toward alleviating the intensity of his feelings. The Iroquois had mistakenly assumed that the convoy belonged to La Salle, and La Barre had told them they might strike against him whenever an opportunity arose.

La Barre would sit in more councils with the Iroquois, and he would lead troops to Fort Frontenac, to no avail. His threat to exterminate the Senecas because of their attacks on French traders was answered with an invitation to make the attempt. Well supplied with guns and powder by the English, and assured of trade outlets on the Hudson, the Iroquois openly defied the French.

Perhaps because La Barre would not share his illegal profits with him, or perhaps because he was too timid to violate laws he had sworn to uphold, the Intendant Meules turned against La Barre. He kept Seignelay informed of La Barre's trading enterprises, and truthfully recounted the failure of La Barre's negotiations with the Iroquois. But Meules did not disclose La Barre's schemes to injure La Salle. That would have displeased his own political supporters.

Meanwhile, more than a thousand miles west of Fort Frontenac, in the wilderness of the Illinois Valley, La Salle had made more progress than he, even in his most optimistic moments, had permitted himself to expect. From Fort St. Louis, on the bold uplift of Starved Rock, he could look down on thousands of skin lodges, bark huts, and log dwellings. On each side of the river were great fields cultivated in the crude Indian manner. Corn, squash, and melons were showing their first green in the warm spring sun. At night, campfires dotted the prairies and forest clearings like bright yellow jewels.

Responding to La Salle's call for a strong western alliance to stand against the Iroquois, more than fourteen thousand red people belonging to scores of tribes, large and small, had migrated, some of them great distances, to the country of the Illinois. And the

Illinois, numbering more than six thousand, had returned to live once more in the homeland from which they had been driven. Their lodges stood once more on the sites where so many of them had been slaughtered.

Stark terror no longer haunted these twenty thousand men, women, and children. They looked upon La Salle as a messiah who had led them to a land of hope and peace, a leader upon whom they could depend for the security and material advantages they had long dreamed of enjoying but which they had never known.

The initial phase of La Salle's plan to create a new French colony in the West—the league of tribes—had been completed. He had under his command some four thousand warriors, many of them possessing guns, and all of them imbued with the spirit and determination that welded them into a formidable fighting force, a savage and dedicated army that the Iroquois could not hope to destroy. Now the time had come for him to take the next steps vital to the continued success and progress of his great enterprise.

The storehouses at the colony of Fort St. Louis were filling up with furs. He had to provide the goods he had promised to exchange for them. And until he could open traffic from the mouth of the Mississippi, those goods could come only from Montreal and Quebec.

Had Frontenac not been recalled, he would have been assured of the support and the supplies he required. Frontenac was gone, and in his place was a man of whom La Salle knew nothing, but who he had every reason to expect would refuse the unqualified cooperation he must receive or meet with failure.

He did not, however, allow misgivings that sprang from nothing more substantial than imagination to deter him. When the rivers opened he sent a convoy of *couriers du bois* and trusted Abnakis and Mohegans to the St. Lawrence for goods, weapons, and food supplies. With them he sent a letter to La Barre in which he expressed the fervent hope that the new colonial government would respect, and aid in fulfilling in every manner, the rights granted him by the King, "although I know my enemies will try to influence you against me."

He gave La Barre an account of his journey to the Gulf of Mexico. The Valley of the Mississippi had become a French possession, the province of Louisiana, and the gate had been opened to commercial development. He explained that he had laid the foundation for a French settlement on the Illinois, portal to the west, by granting lands to the Frenchmen of his company. And he told La Barre:

"I am now going [sending emissaries] four hundred leagues south-southwest of this place to induce the Chickasaws to follow the other tribes and settle at [Fort] St. Louis. I hope you will not detain my men as *couriers du bois* [operating without government sanction] when they come down to Montreal to make necessary purchases. I am aware that I have no right to trade with the tribes who descend to Montreal, and I shall not permit such trade to my men; nor have I ever issued licenses to that effect, as my enemies say that I have done."

He informed La Barre of Indian reports that the Iroquois were again expected to invade the western country, and "last year the Miamis were so alarmed by them that they fled, but at my return they came back, and have been induced to settle with the Illinois at my fort of St. Louis. The Iroquois have lately murdered some families of their nation. . . . Some of the Hurons and French [traders at Michilimackinac] tell the Miamis that I am keeping them here for the Iroquois to destroy. I am afraid they will take flight, and so prevent the Missouris and neighboring tribes from coming to settle at St. Louis, as they are about to do."

Here La Salle revealed that he was attempting to enlarge the alliance to include tribes living west of the Mississippi and on the lower Missouri River, a part of his plan he had not previously mentioned.

In June, La Salle had gone to the Chicago portage to negotiate with Indians who were considering joining the Fort St. Louis colony. There he met some wandering *couriers du bois* who told him they had heard—presumably by way of the wilderness grapevine—that his supply convoy had been detained at Fort Frontenac on orders from La Barre. He at once dispatched a second contingent, pleading with La Barre: "Do not suffer my men who have come down to the St. Lawrence to be longer prevented from returning. There is great need here of reinforcements. . . . I have postponed going to Michilimackinac, because, if the Iroquois strike any blow in my absence, the Miamis will think I am in league with them; whereas, if I and the French stay among them, they will regard us as protectors.

"I pray that you will let me hear from you, that I may give these people some assurances of protection before they are destroyed in my sight."

Now the depth of La Salle's apprehension that La Barre would fail him became fully apparent. "But, Monsieur," he told the Governor, "it is in vain that we risk our lives here, and that I exhaust my means in order to fulfill the intentions of his Majesty, if all my measures are crossed in the settlements below, and if those who go down to bring munitions, without which we cannot defend ourselves, are detained under pretexts trumped up for the occasion."

He excoriated the traders and the Jesuits who were attempting to defeat him, reminding La Barre once more of his letters patent from the King, which would be "useless if I am prevented from bringing up men and supplies." It would be very hard for him and his creditors, he declared, "to have our efforts frustrated by obstacles got up designedly."

The summer days passed. The Indians hunted and found game plentiful. Buffalo and deer hides mounted in the storehouses of Fort St. Louis. The corn ripened and was harvested. The nights were filled with the beating of drums and the chants of dancers.

And each day La Salle and his men watched from their aerie on Starved Rock for a sight of heavily loaded canoes coming down the Illinois. But the canoes did not come.

There was a good reason for the emptiness of the river. La Barre had ordered that La Salle's men were to be held on charges of conducting illegal traffic with northern tribes, and that no supplies were to be sent to him. He further charged that La Salle had engaged in trade with the English in the Mohawk-Hudson region, and therefore had become a traitor to his own country.

The Jesuits took advantage of the situation by persuading La Barre that La Salle's explorations were meaningless. La Salle, they declared, had discovered nothing. Marquette and Joliet had discovered the Mississippi, and La Salle had done no more than follow the trail they had broken. La Salle was an impostor. But the Jesuits said nothing about their failing to take credit for discovering the Mississippi until after La Salle had reached the Gulf of Mexico. For several years after the journey of Marquette and Joliet they had remained silent, hoping to keep the world from knowing that the Mississippi had been opened, and thus forestall an influx of *couriers du bois.*

But La Barre was only too willing to believe the Jesuits, and he sent to Seignelay his own opinion of the value of La Salle's explorations: nil. And he added: "The Iroquois have sworn La Salle's death. The impudence of this man is about to involve the colony in war."

La Barre's pen was busy. La Salle, he told the Colonial Minister, had spent the winter not on the Illinois building a settlement, but carousing with a bunch of vagabonds at Green Bay and robbing legitimate traders as well as Indian allies of France.

He sent to Paris copies of La Salle's letters, declaring that from them it could be "perceived that his head is turned, and that he has been bold enough to give you intelligence of a false discovery."

Louis XIV appeared to have swallowed whole the propaganda

of the anti-La Salle faction. "I am convinced, like you," he told La Barre, "that the discovery of the Sieur de la Salle is very useless, and that such enterprises ought to be prevented in the future, as they tend only to debauch the inhabitants by the hope of gain, and to diminish the revenue from beaver skins."

But it would be seen in time that the King's expressed view was not in accord with his private opinions. Indeed, his assertion that such enterprises as La Salle's (that is, settlement and development of the resources of interior North America) ought to be prevented in the future was in direct conflict with secret plans for conquest to which he was then giving his personal attention.

However, the constant attacks on La Salle gave rise to false reports in Paris that he had fallen out of the King's favor, that his seignorial rights would be withdrawn, and his ambitious program would be discontinued. Neither the King nor Seignelay issued denials—they kept silent.

But the accusations and rumors brought the Abbé Bernou roaring to La Salle's defense. The charges were false, the slander iniquitous. La Salle's morals were "irreproachable," his conduct was "unassailable," he was "wise, judicious, diplomatic, vigilant, indefatigable, sober, fearless." He was an incomparable New World ambassador, speaking fluently the languages of the savages, a great patriot struggling only to bring riches to the empire and to win new glories for his King.

In the salons of Paris the battle of words raged. In the wilderness of the Illinois another kind of battle was being waged.

Autumn had come, but still no supply canoes appeared, none of the men who had gone to the St. Lawrence returned, no messengers arrived with letters.

La Salle could wait no longer. La Barre's silence was intolerable. His position was untenable. Without trade goods and ammunition he could not hope to hold the tribes together much longer. His alliance was on the brink of disaster.

Desperate, and mystified by the failure of his supporters to come to his relief in any manner whatsoever, La Salle saw as his only recourse a personal appeal to Seignelay. Only by going to Paris could he learn the truth of things.

In early September he placed Tonty in command of Fort St. Louis, and set out for Quebec. He took with him only six men in three small canoes. The long journey—by way of Lakes Michigan, Huron, Erie, the Niagara portage, Lake Ontario to Fort Frontenac and the St. Lawrence—had to be accomplished with all possible speed in order for him to reach Quebec before the last ships of the season had sailed.

In large measure, the truth La Salle sought was brutally delivered to him at the Chicago portage. There he met the Chevalier de Baugis of the King's Dragoons and a contingent of soldiers and *couriers du bois*. La Barre had sent de Baugis to take possession of Fort St. Louis and seize all furs and hides stored there.

And at last La Salle received a letter from La Barre. De Baugis delivered it, and it ordered him to report forthwith to Quebec and explain his failure to fulfill the provisions of his letters patent from the King.

La Salle exploded in a mad rage. So intense was his fury that his eyes bulged and appeared to be filled with blood, he trembled violently, the muscles of his face became so taut that they were like white thongs lacing his deeply browned chin and cheeks. He sat down, spewing vicious curses, gripping his head in his hands, as if he were suffering excruciating pain. Nika and Saget ran to him, fearing he had suffered another stroke.

Suddenly he became very still, his anger vanished, and was supplanted by cold calmness. His voice was quiet and without a trace of emotion as he asked for ink, quill and paper. With a steady hand he wrote a letter to Tonty, directing him to extend a cordial welcome to de Baugis, to obey the surrender order, but to remain at the fort as his representative until he had received further word from him.

Then he and his men shouldered their canoes, carried them to the Chicago River, and set out for Lake Michigan.

La Salle reached Quebec early in November. He ignored La Barre, and conferred with no one. He, Nika, and Saget sailed for France on the first available ship. On the twenty-third of December they landed at Rochelle and took seats in a coach for Paris.

35 ❧ ❧ ❧

DIEGO DIONYSIO de PENALOSA, a native of Peru who had become politically prominent in Mexico City, was appointed Governor of the colony of New Mexico in 1660. He was tyrannical, unscrupulous, malicious, morally corrupt, and defiant of all church authority. Threatened with excommunication by the Father President of the colony for his abuses of padres and his violations of religious laws, he retorted that he recognized no judge in New Mexico, "neither ecclesiastic, bishop, nor archbishop," who could excommunicate him. To this arrogant assertion he added the boast: "I was a cleric in my own country, a padre, and I married when I was ordained as subdeacon, and I sang and intoned nicely a *gloria*, a *credo*, and a *prefacio*."

In 1663, he resigned and returned to Mexico City. There he found that charges had been filed against him in the Holy Office, and that he would have to stand trial. The sentence Penalosa received was one of the heaviest ever imposed by the Inquisition in Mexico. He was made to don a penitent's robe, walk barefooted through the streets, and carry a lighted green candle. In addition to this punishment, he was fined 500 *pesos*, stripped of all rank, barred forever from holding political or military office, and banished from New Spain.

Penalosa became a revolutionary, dedicated to overthrowing the Spanish government in the New World. He went first to

England, calling himself the Count of Santa Fe, and sought to interest Charles II in his traitorous scheme. The British King had enough troubles to occupy his attention at home without starting another war with Spain, and sent him on his way. Penalosa then went to Versailles, and there found in Colbert and Louis a more attentive audience.

But the mills of the French Court ground slowly. Penalosa, impecunious, existed by the sufferance of a few men who saw merit and practicality in the plan he proposed. It was to invade northern Mexico from the Gulf, establish a French colony at the mouth of the Rio Grande, send raiders inland to capture mines which he claimed existed in Durango and other provinces, and continue the invasion until all of Texas, Mexico, and New Mexico had fallen to France.

The years passed, and, while nothing was done to execute Penalosa's scheme, it was not forgotten. In January, 1684, with France and Spain at war, he proffered a new proposal. It was to raise some twelve hundred buccaneers in Santo Domingo, capture the town of Panuco on the central Mexican coast, and cut directly across Mexico. In this way, the northern Spanish provinces could be quickly isolated. They could be held while other incursions were launched to the south and Mexico City.

Penalosa was familiar with the geography of Mexico, to be sure, and that gave him some value as an advisor, but he had put no new ideas in the minds of either Colbert or the King. All during the time that Penalosa was in France, plans not dissimilar in scope or purpose were being advanced in North America. When he went to French Canada as Governor, Frontenac had carried instructions to make every effort to find a transcontinental water route. And Louis had written to Intendant Talon: "After the increase of the Colony, nothing is of greater importance for that country and for the service of his Majesty than the discovery of a passage to the South Sea."

Frontenac and Talon had proceeded to execute these orders.

As they saw the situation, the first important step was to reach the Mississippi and follow it to its mouth, for they, as did everyone else in Quebec, believed that it would lead them to the goal they sought, an arm of the Pacific.

"And it is by this same great river," Talon wrote the King, "that we can hope some day to find the opening to Mexico."

The statement leaves little, if any, doubt that both Frontenac and Talon were apprised of the thoughts in the mind of Louis XIV regarding the New World possessions of Spain.

Talon recommended that La Salle, who had already found the Ohio and knew that it joined the Mississippi, be sent with an expedition to explore the Mississippi, and Fontenac, although he did not yet know La Salle, agreed. But where was La Salle? He was somewhere in the western wilderness. Perhaps he would not return for a year. Perhaps never. Talon and Frontenac felt they could not postpone the expedition for no better reason than the mere hope that La Salle would soon come back. They chose Louis Joliet, who, as Talon said, "has already been near this great river." The Jesuits, with spies in every official chamber in Quebec, asked that Father Marquette be allowed to accompany Joliet. Frontenac objected, but was finally persuaded to agree by Talon. Joliet had gone out to St. Ignace, where Marquette was then stationed, in the summer of 1672. In May, 1673, Marquette and Joliet started.

Talon and Frontenac had no way of knowing at the time that La Salle already had reached the Mississippi by way of the Illinois, had descended it to the 39th degree, and had learned from Indians that it emptied not into the Vermilion Sea but into the Gulf of Mexico. But they would hear of La Salle's great discovery long before Marquette and Joliet had returned.

Penalosa was still hoping to lead an invasion of Mexico when La Salle arrived in France two days before the Christmas of 1683. The chances that he would have an opportunity seemed better than ever to him, for France and Spain were at war.

It wasn't much of a war in Europe—centering largely in the

Spanish Netherlands—but it had provided Louis with good reasons to send French men-of-war to the West Indies and the Gulf of Mexico. Besides attacking Spanish vessels, the French ships were to chart the coast of Mexico and investigate the defenses of Spanish colonial ports.

In Paris La Salle took lodgings once again in the little hotel in Rue de la Traunderie. He was somewhat shabby, in need of money, and dispirited. Within a few days, to his astonishment, these unpleasant conditions had undergone changes for the better. Renadout, Bernou, Conti, and others rallied their forces to assist him. He was welcomed and entertained as a long-lost friend. Funds and credits were supplied to him; loans, of course, not gifts or charity. His melancholy was dissipated, and, by the time he had had several audiences with Seignelay, he was confident that the adversities he had faced when he left Canada would be removed.

When or how La Salle met Penalosa is not a matter of documentary record. Whatever the circumstances, however, he had one or two conferences with the renegade Spaniard, and he neither liked him nor was he willing to exchange confidences with him. At last, he bluntly informed his friends that under no consideration would he become associated with him in any kind of venture whatsoever.

His supporters, especially Bernou and Renadout, as usual, were thoroughly informed on current affairs, and professed to understand the trend of the thinking at Court, even to the extent of looking inside the King's head. They began the preparation of a long and explicit memorial to be placed before His Majesty. It contained a record of La Salle's explorations, cited the reverses he had suffered at the hands of La Barre and others, and requested full restitution of the property illegally taken from him.

That subject exhausted, the document set forth La Salle's proposal "to return by way of the Gulf of Mexico and the mouth of the Mississippi to the countries he has discovered. . . ."

The principal result which La Salle expected, it stated, "from the great perils which he underwent, was to satisfy the wish expressed by M. Colbert of finding a port where the French might establish themselves and harass the Spaniards in those regions from whence they derive all their wealth." La Salle had found a suitable place "sixty leagues above the mouth of the Mississippi. . . . It could be fortified, and a colony could easily be founded there, as the land was very fertile and produced all the articles of life, and a fort there would provide the means of attacking an enemy or retreating in case of necessity. Its distance inland would prevent enemies from sending fleets to attack it. The river was narrow there and could be defended by fire-ships. The coasts and banks to the south were overflowed, making it inaccesible by land."

The Indians of the lower Mississippi detested the Spaniards, and had "eagerly made peace with La Salle, whom they loved and trusted . . ." (somewhat of an exaggeration, indeed) "and by uniting these peoples under the French flag it would be possible to form an army of more than fifteen thousand savages."

Now, La Salle and his authors disclosed their ignorance of the geography of Texas and northern Mexico, making errors that Penalosa could have corrected, had they consulted him. Actually, they eliminated the vast expanses of Texas, writing that the most northern province of Mexico was New Biscay and that "it was only forty or fifty leagues from the Red River, and was inhabited only by four hundred indolent and effeminate Spaniards."

New Biscay was the most advantageous place to launch an invasion, for defenders would have great difficulty reaching it from Mexico City. It was bordered on the south and west by immense chains of mountains and on the north by great forests inhabited by *Indios bravos y de guerra*, whom the Spaniards greatly feared and had never been able to subdue.

After giving a glowing description of the Mississippi Valley, La Salle warned that since he had opened it to the world and had made known its great resources, other nations would be eager to seize it, and should "foreigners anticipate us, they will complete the ruin of New France, which they already hem in by their establishments of Virginia, Pennsylvania, New England, and Hudson's Bay." Yet, with no more than two hundred and fifty Frenchmen and one or two forts strategically located, La Salle could control the inconceivably vast and rich interior of North America for eight hundred leagues on each side of the river.

To give even greater assurance that the invasion of Mexico would be successful, La Salle would bring down the Mississippi an army of four thousand savage warriors whom he had assembled within the structure of his western alliance.

La Salle already had prepared battle plans. He would send three forces to attack the Spaniards simultaneously "on the two extremities of the province, and on the same day the center of the country would be entered." Each of the divisions would include fifty Frenchmen and several thousand Indians, all well armed, while others would be held in reserve to give support when and where needed.

Penalosa's plan was thoroughly discredited in the memorial. The River Panuco, where Penalosa advised that the landing be made, was "populated from its mouth by Spanish settlements." Thus, the invading forces would encounter strong opposition at the beginning, and would also be open to attack at sea by Spanish war vessels. The initial assault should be made by land, which would give it the invaluable element of surprise. A few men could hold the mountain passes, after which the seaports could be taken, and the silver mines captured. Moreover, in land advances from remote areas, containing few inhabitants, the thousands of Indian warriors could be most usefully employed.

The memorial did not neglect to touch upon a side of the matter in which the writers knew Louis would be especially interested—costs. They stressed that there "never was an enterprise of such great importance proposed at so little risk and expense." Most of the expenses would "be repaid in a short time by the duties which his Majesty could levy on the articles which would enter into the commerce that would be carried on," and His Majesty's coffers would be greatly enriched by the silver and gold from the Spanish mines.

Indeed, His Majesty could not lose a *livre*, under any circumstances, for if there would be peace with Spain and the invasion of Mexico be abandoned, La Salle himself "would repay to his Majesty all that may be advanced, or forfeit the property and government of the colony which he shall have created."

The establishment of a colony near the mouth of the Mississippi, the memorial stated, was a project La Salle had struggled to complete for more than a decade, at great personal sacrifice to himself. He had given Louisiana to France. The proposal of Penalosa encompassed nothing more than aggression. If that were His Majesty's desire, La Salle would, of course, do everything within his power to aid His Majesty in achieving it. But it would be a disastrous mistake to give it precedence.

Could not the two plans be combined under a single authority—his? Seignelay answered the question. They could very feasibly be combined. It was a most practical idea, and he would work toward that end.

The Colonial Minister did not dally, for he understood that the time was most opportune to ask the same question of the King.

Louis had long before declared it to be his policy that all the seas of the world must be open to French commerce. The Spanish, even in time of peace, had defied him with the pronouncement that the Gulf of Mexico was closed to French vessels. Profoundly aggravated, he had dispatched a naval squadron to penetrate the barrier. Spasmodic fighting had followed. Several French merchantmen had been seized on the high seas, their cargoes confiscated, their crews held in Spanish ports. With the declaration of war, Louis determined to resolve the Gulf controversy by doing what he had wanted to do for many years—invade Mexico.

On a spring day in 1684, La Salle answered a knock on the door of his humble Paris lodgings. Before him stood the resplendent figure of a King's courier. In an envelope that bore the royal

seal was a summons to appear at eleven o'clock the next morning
at the Palace of Versailles.

36 ⚜ ⚜ ⚜

AN OBSERVER of the two men sitting in the small, paneled and
exquisitely furnished room might well have been fascinated by the
striking contrasts they presented. Even in the dissimilarities of their
physiques and their garb, there was sheer drama. As for their
inherent qualities and their instincts, the diversities left no basis for
comparison.

Always as punctual as a clerk in fear of losing his post, the
Sun King was ready to receive La Salle when he was announced.
Splendrous in his morning coat of brocade with its raised patterns
of gold, he slumped comfortably in a gilded arm chair behind an
ornate escritoire. As La Salle bowed he waved him to a seat.

The man who with a stroke of a pen could send an army
crashing across Europe or a battle armada to the farthest seas of
the world, who could decree death or preserve life, in whom was
embodied the awesome powers of one of the great nations of the
earth, was stoutish, paunchy, florid, and given to fingering objects
on his desk, as if to relieve a tension pressing for release. Dark eyes
swept over La Salle, appearing to take in every detail of his appearance, and came to rest in a penetrating gaze on his face. Louis's
voice was firm and quiet, but the forthright manner in which he
spoke left no doubt that he knew very well what he intended to say.

Literally and figuratively, it might have been said, the man
opposite the King was from another world. Wearing a new suit
of plain dark worsted, in which he appeared to be somewhat
uncomfortable, La Salle was spare, and burned almost to a negroid
darkness by wilderness winds and suns. Broad shoulders, roughened
hands, a muscular face and throat, suggested extraordinary hard-

ness of body and great physical power. It was his eyes that held Louis' gaze, as they held the gaze of everyone who had ever seen them, dark and brooding eyes, silhouetted by changing lights and frequently appearing to be fixed on incalculable distances. His cold calmness, his impenetrable reserve, were broken only to a slight degree, only by courteousness and by the sincere respect he displayed.

There were papers in an embossed leather folder on the desk. They were La Salle's memorial. Seignelay had presented them. The King declared he had gone through them, and that he agreed in principle with most of the proposals set forth, but there remained much to be discussed. He had questions to ask. First La Salle would read a letter he had written to La Barre, and he pushed it across the desk.

The letter was dated April 10. "I hear," it said, "that you have taken possession of Fort Frontenac, the property of the Sieur de la Salle, driven away his men, suffered his land to run to waste, and even told the Iroquois they might seize him as an enemy of the colony.

"You must make reparation for the wrong, and place all of the Sieur de la Salle's property, as well as his men, in the hands of the Sieur de la Forest, as I am satisfied that Fort Frontenac was not abandoned, as you wrote to me that it had been."

Seignelay would send a similar letter to Intendant Meules. It would instruct Meules that La Forest was to "suffer no impediment" upon his arrival in Canada. La Forest would go, of course?

Of course, said La Salle, and expressed his gratefulness. He would tell La Forest to pay himself his own wages out of the revenues of Fort Frontenac. And should His Majesty approve of the plan to transport the warriors from the Illinois to the Gulf, it would be the loyal and trustworthy La Forest who would lead them.

That was settled, then. Now La Salle would elaborate on his plans, repeating details if necessary, and taking all the time he wished. It was an important matter. It had to be thoroughly understood.

La Salle talked. Louis listened and he was not only impressed, he was convinced. La Salle would not only get what he asked, he would get more than he asked. Orders would be forthcoming, but they would be secret orders. La Salle must keep his own lips tightly closed.

It was rumored after La Salle had left the King's private conference room that his proposals had been rejected. La Salle was a ruined man. The King had sent him back to live in obscurity among his beloved savages. It was no more than he deserved—a gloomy, cold-faced clod of a man who belonged in some dirty fur trading post. How was it that His Majesty wasted time with him?

The King was silent. He conferred on the matter only with Seignelay. And Seignelay saw that the orders were carried out. The gossipy courtiers of the court knew nothing of what was going on.

The commission which Louis gave to La Salle complied with his request that he be given supreme command of the expedition. It could be construed in no other way. Yet, Seignelay was reluctant to adhere strictly to it, and—presumably with the King's acquiescence—he decreed drastic revisions.

"Having resolved to cause some expeditions to be undertaken in North America," wrote Louis, "to subject to Our dominions divers savage tribes, and to convey to them the light of the Faith and of the Gospel, We have been of the opinion that We could not make a better choice than of Sieur de la Salle to command in Our name all the Frenchmen and Indians whom he will employ for the execution of the orders We have entrusted unto him."

The language with which Louis made known his intent was precise and unmistakably clear: "We have by these presents constituted and ordained Sieur de la Salle to command under Our authority, as well in the country which will be subject anew to Our dominion in North America, from Fort St. Louis, on the River of the Illinois, unto New Biscay, as well among the French and

Indians." La Salle would "cause them to live in unison and concord, keep the soldiers in good order and police according to Our rules, appoint governors and commanders in the places he shall think proper, maintain trade and traffic, and generally do and exercise for Us in the said country all that shall appertain to the office of Commandant, and enjoy its powers, honors, authorities, prerogatives, preeminences, franchises, liberties, wages, rights, fruits, profits, revenues, and emoluments during Our pleasure.

"We command all Our said subjects and soldiers to acknowledge, obey and hear you in things relating to the present power: FOR SUCH IS OUR PLEASURE."

The orders which Seignelay issued:

(a) A distinguished navy captain, Sieur de Beaujeu, would command the ships of the expedition at sea.

(b) La Salle would select the course to be taken.

(c) La Salle would command troops and colonists on land.

Seignelay need have done nothing more, had it been his design—which it was not—to launch the enterprise under adverse circumstances. Both Beaujeu and La Salle went to the port of embarkation, La Rochelle, prepared to dislike each other, and they did—from the first moment they met.

La Salle, resentful that he was obliged to share his command, even at sea, withdrew into himself, becoming cold and impenetrable. When Beaujeu demanded to know their destination, so that he might study the course to be taken, La Salle told him bluntly "Canada." A few days later, La Salle informed him that he had changed his mind, and that they would sail for the West Indies. Shortly afterward he informed Beaujeu that he had not yet decided which direction they would take and that he would not give him any information until they were at sea.

Beaujeu, justifiably angered and disgusted, wrote several strong letters of protest to Seignelay. They forcefully portrayed the unpleasant situation and graphically described not only his own feelings but the attitude of La Salle.

La Salle, declared Beaujeu, "never commanded anybody but schoolboys." But what aggravated the old sea dog the most was La Salle's refusal to confide in him. "He has not told me his plan," Beaujeu complained. "He is a man so suspicious, and so afraid that one will penetrate his secrets, that I dare not ask him anything."

La Salle's secretiveness, however, did not stem from pique alone. He had been informed by Abbé Renadout that Madame de Beaujeu was head of a women's organization dedicated to supporting the Society of Jesus.

In view of his sad experiences with the Jesuits, he might have been forgiven for distrusting an associate whose wife was passionately devoted to them.

There was more evidence to substantiate La Salle's fear that the plans of the expedition would be made known to the Spanish. Renadout also informed him that Beaujeu was in correspondence with Cabart de Villarmont in Paris. Villarmont was one of La Salle's supporters, but he was as well a relative and confidant of an influential Jesuit archbishop. La Salle's suspicions were increased by Villarmont's indiscreet act of showing Beaujeu's letters to Renadout and other acquaintances.

Not only Beaujeu was irked and mystified by the deceptiveness and vacillation of La Salle. La Forest, preparing to sail for Canada, complained that La Salle changed his plans overnight. First La Salle had ordered him to reoccupy Fort Frontenac, then go to Fort St. Louis and prepare to lead four thousand warriors down the Mississippi. Next, La Salle told him to remain at Fort Frontenac until he received further orders. A short time later, La Salle expressed the fear—to both La Forest and Seignelay—that La Barre would attempt to use the Iroquois war as an excuse for preventing La Forest from going to the Illinois. In this event, La Salle declared, he would attempt to go himself up the Mississippi and conduct the warriors to the Gulf to fight against the Spanish.

La Forest left France not only perplexed but saddened by

the fear that the chief whom he so greatly admired and had duti-
fully served for so many years had suffered an aberration. Perhaps
the ordeals, the frustrations, and the serious illness La Salle had
undergone had taken a greater toll of his mind than anyone had
suspected.

La Forest had been too long in the wilderness, knew too well
the conditions existing there, and too well the ways of Indians, not
to understand that the scheme to transport four thousand warriors
down the Mississippi from the Illinois was not only impractical but
logistically impossible of execution. Even if the warriors could be
induced to join in the attack on the Spanish, they would not
abandon their women and children and the elderly to be slaughtered by the Iroquois. The very thought of attempting to move no
less than ten or twelve thousand people such a great distance and
through strange lands inhabited by traditional enemies was itself
fantastic. Moreover, he believed that La Salle himself was fully
aware that the proposal was nothing but a pipedream, and had
advanced it only to deceive the King and the Colonial Minister
into believing that the invasion of Mexico would be supported by
tribes loyal to France. Either that was true, or La Salle had lost
his power to reason. It was all very painful to think about, but
La Forest departed determined to do the best he could to recover
La Salle's property and carry on his fur trade, to obey His
Majesty's instructions.

Advice from Seignelay that he cease his protestations against
a divided command increased Beaujeu's wrath and prompted him
to write more letters derogatory of La Salle.

"I think him a good, honest Norman," he told Villarmont,
"but Normans are out of fashion. There are very few people who
do not think that his brain is touched. I have spoken to some who
have known him twenty years. They all say that he was always
rather visionary."

Both Beaujeu and La Salle frequently became haughty, petty

and childishly stubborn, engaging in bitter exchanges over problems that were actually simple of solution.

A decidedly different view of La Salle was etched by the Recollect, Father Le Clercq. La Salle's "first care," wrote Le Clercq, "was to provide for the spiritual, to advance especially the glory of God in this enterprise."

La Salle had asked both the Sulpicians and the Recollects to assign priests to the expedition. He expressed his feeling of gratitude to both orders. The Sulpicians, notwithstanding the machinations of his brother, had given him his start in Canada when he arrived there poor and homeless. The Recollects had steadfastly supported his enterprises in the American wilderness, had accompanied him on several of his explorations, and had shown themselves to be his true friends.

He was delighted when the Recollects named his old wilderness companion, Father Membre, to accompany him. With Membre came Father Le Clercq, who had served for five years at Canadian stations, and Fathers Douay and Morguet from the Province of St. Anthony.*

The Sulpicians assigned "three ecclesiastics, full of zeal, virtue and capacity to commence new missions in Louisiana." When they arrived in Rochelle, La Salle censured himself scathingly for his incautiousness. Two of the Sulpicians, Fathers Chefdeville (a distant relative of La Salle) and Dainmaville had had little experience in foreign missionary work. The other was his brother, the Abbé Cavelier.

La Salle's disappointment was not alleviated by the information that Father Cavelier had requested the duty so that he might "keep an eye on his brother." La Salle complained that Jean Cavelier was succeeding in his purpose, for wherever he went he felt "the suspicious eyes of the abbé stabbing him in the back." Yet,

---

* Illness would prevent Morguet from going with the expedition.

he resolved to make no attempt to have Father Cavelier recalled, and to bear his misfortune to the best of his ability.

While preparations for the voyage were under way at Rochelle, La Salle went to Rouen for a last reunion with his family. His mother was frail but alert. Tears flowed as they embraced and she told him of the joy he had brought her. She was not only proud of him for his accomplishments and the fame he had achieved but of his rectitude and his adherence to the high principles she had sought to instill in him as a youth.

Both his brother, Nicholas, and his sister, Madame Crevel, gathered their own large families for his homecoming. They urged him to take two of his nephews with him on the great journey, which they felt certain would result in bringing him greater honors than he had received and would make of him the most powerful man in the New World. La Salle demurred, citing the dangers of the voyage, but at last agreed to let Cavelier, only fourteen years of age, and Moranget, no more than sixteen, his godson, sail with him as aides.*

In Rouen, La Salle met Henri Joutel, whom he had known well as a youth, and whose father had been gardener for Henri Cavelier, La Salle's uncle. Joutel had served for sixteen years in the French Army. He was eager to go with the company, and La Salle had no hesitancy in accepting him.

Louis had lived up to his promise to give La Salle more than he had requested. He authorized the use of not two vessels but four, and the recruitment of not two hundred men but four hundred. When July came and the convoy had not sailed, Louis became irritated and demanded of the naval intendant at Rochefort to know the cause of the delay. After that the docks of Rochelle

---

* Records of the time and accounts of the expedition do not provide further identification of these two young men, speaking of them simply as Cavelier and Moranget, La Salle's nephews.

bustled with activity. Quarrelsome voices went unheard in the greater noise accompanying the loading of stores, arms, munitions and tools.

By the middle of the month, the ships were crowded. Besides the regular crews and a hundred soldiers, some three hundred other men and a few women and children were jammed into poorly ventilated spaces below the decks. Among them were craftsmen and laborers, a dozen families to be established on farms of the projected colony, and a score of unattached young women from the bordellos and bistros of Rochelle and Rochefort, lured by the almost certain prospect of obtaining the husbands and security that were unavailable to them at home. In addition to this heterogeneous assembly and the few persons invited by La Salle, was a motley group of some thirty volunteers. It included adventurous but impecunious gentlemen, ex-soldiers recruited from the gutters of Paris, burghers whose records made it advisable for them to escape the country, and several degenerates who had spent more of their lives in cells than in freedom.

On July 18th, La Salle wrote the last letter he would post in France to "Madame My Most Honored Mother."

"We all have good hope of a happy success," it said. "I passionately wish, and so do we all, that the success of this voyage may contribute to your repose and comfort. Assuredly, I shall spare no effort that it may; and I beg you, on your part, to preserve yourself for the love of us.

"You need not be troubled by the news from Canada, which are nothing but the continuation of the artifices of my enemies. I hope to embrace you a year hence with all the pleasure that the most grateful of children can feel with so good a mother as you have always been. Pray let this hope, which shall not disappoint you, support you through whatever trials may happen, and be sure that you will always find me with a heart full of the feelings which are due to you.

[223]

"My brother, my nephews, and all the others greet you, and take their leave of you.

"Madame my Most Honored Mother, from your most humble and most obedient servant and son."

The favorable wind for which they had waited a week came on July 24, 1684. Twenty-four vessels of all sizes and types stood out into the Bay of Biscay. Twenty of them would soon swing onto a course for the Gulf of St. Lawrence, their destination French Canada.

Four of them—a formidable man-of-war carrying forty guns, *Le Joly*, a frigate, *La Belle*, a merchantman, *La Amiable*, and the ketch *St. Francis*—would point for Cape Finisterre.

On the bridge of the *Joly* stood a fuming and disgusted Captain Beaujeu. He did not yet know whether, after passing the Spanish promontory, he should sail directly for some French port on the Island of Hispaniola or chart a route around Cuba for the Gulf of Mexico. And La Salle would not tell him which to do. La Salle stood beside him, gazing far across the tossing blue Atlantic, his face a mask of ruddy marble, silent, and revealing nothing of the thoughts occupying him.

37 ✤ ✤ ✤

THREE DAYS after Rochelle had disappeared over the stern, the *Joly's* bowsprit was smashed by large waves. In a conference of officers, La Salle accused Beaujeu of poor seamanship and carelessness. He demanded that the fleet put into Portugal for the repairs. Beaujeu thought it more sensible to return to the navy yard at Rochefort. His officers agreed with him. "We made back for the river at Rochefort," said Joutel, "whither the other three vessels followed us, and a boat was sent in to acquaint the intendant with this accident. The boat returned some hours after, towing along a bowsprit, which was soon set in its place."

On August 1, the ships were again at sea. Eighteen days later they were approaching Madeira, and Beaujeu proposed that they anchor there to replenish water casks and obtain a supply of the wines for which the island was famous. La Salle objected, declaring that the landing would disclose to the Spanish the size and purpose of the expedition. The argument had little plausibility, for all France knew that the venture had been undertaken, and this intelligence doubtlessly had been reported by Spanish agents.

A heated debate ensued. The naval and army officers sided with Beaujeu. Seamen muttered imprecations against La Salle, and even civilians who properly should not have participated in the row openly cursed and threatened him. His demand that they be silenced and punished brought only a laugh from Beaujeu. The captain capitulated, however, when La Salle warned that he would construe the landing as a traitorous act designed to aid and comfort the enemy; Madeira was left behind.

As they neared the Tropic of Cancer, early in September, the crew of the *Joly* prepared for the customary ceremony of ducking passengers who had never before crossed it. Only by generous gifts of liquor or money could the victims escape being thrown into a large cask which had been placed on deck and filled with sea water.

La Salle refused to permit the celebration, terming it folly, which, Joutel recorded, gave the sailors "occasion to mutter again, and rendered himself privately odious. Assuredly, they would gladly have killed us all."

Rough seas, driven by winds of gale force, were encountered in mid-September. The crowded and poorly ventilated bunk areas of the soldiers and colonists were fetid with the odors of vomit and excreta. Even when the weather calmed, and portholes and hatches could be opened, the cabins and holds were made unbearable by the tropical heat. Several score persons, some fifty on the *Joly* alone, were stricken with dysentery, heat prostration, fever, and various other disorders. On the *Belle* a gunner died.

Fights in which heads were smashed and blood flowed occurred, the constant bickering between La Salle and Beaujeu, and the general dissension among the officers, brought the morale of all persons aboard to a dangerously low level and made it all but impossible to maintain necessary discipline. Joutel saw the clashes, which he inappropriately termed "misunderstandings," as "being no way advantageous to his Majesty's service" and foreshadowing of more "tragical events."

La Salle had, at last, named Port de Paix on the Island of Hispaniola as their destination, and had disclosed that he had orders from Seignelay to the Marquis de Saint-Laurent, Governor-General of the French West Indies, who resided there, to "furnish such necessaries as he needed."

In a storm that raged through September 19 and 20 the ships became separated. La Salle was confined to his berth with sea sickness and suffering from fever. When Beaujeu advised that the *Joly* continue alone, without attempting to find the other vessels, so that fresh water might be obtained as soon as possible, he was in no mood to argue.

He was still indisposed on the night of September 25, during which Beaujeu deliberately passed Port de Paix.

It was not until twenty-four hours later that La Salle discovered the deception. Beaujeu's excuse was that adverse winds had made it impossible to approach Port de Paix with safety. Nor could he turn about because the same conditions prevailed. On the 28th, the *Joly* entered the small harbor of Petit Goave, some hundred miles by land from Port de Paix.

Seething with anger, and still suffering from fever, La Salle dispatched a messenger to Saint-Laurent, advising him of the orders and requesting him to come to Petit Goave. He ordered that a camp be established for the soldiers on a small adjacent island, and instructed Joutel to remove the sick, "who were suffering very much, by reason of the heat and being too close together," to a place on shore in which they might receive proper attention.

La Salle then collapsed.

"I was walking with him," said Joutel, "when he was seized of a sudden with such a weakness that he could not stand, and was obliged to lie down on the ground."

La Salle was taken to the nearby house of a goldsmith. There Joutel, Nika, Saget and the Abbé Cavelier attended him around the clock. For several days he was delirious. His imagination "pictured to him things equally terrible and amazing." Joutel thought that the "posture of La Salle's affairs, want of money, and the weight of a mighty enterprise, without knowing whom to trust with the execution of it, made him still more sick in mind than he was in his body."

Petit Goave was a filthy, steaming, rat-infested town inhabited by poverty-stricken natives of Indian and Negro blood, escaped criminals, renegade seamen, beachcombers, all manner of degenerates and prostitutes, and a few shopkeepers and shippers of somewhat better station who derived meager livings from the small seaborne commerce in tropical products and the sale of stores to the few ships which put in there. Venereal diseases were rampant, and the soldiers and sailors, said Le Clercq, "having plunged into every kind of debauchery and intemperance, so common in those parts, were so ruined and contracted with dangerous disorders that some died and others never recovered."

Beaujeu appeared to find a diabolical satisfaction in La Salle's condition, and not averse to aiding in bringing about his early demise. A group of sailors from the *Joly* appeared before the house in which La Salle was near death and staged a drunken orgy, dancing with wenches from a nearby brothel and howling throughout the night. Beaujeu rejected a request by Father Cavelier to stop them, and, said the Abbé, "The more we begged them to be quiet, the more noise they made."

The other three ships had put in first, as ordered, at Port de

Paix, and had then set out to rejoin the *Joly* at Petit Goave. Only the *Belle* and the *Amiable* arrived. In the Gulf de Gonaives, the ketch *St. Francis* was captured by Spanish pirates.

General Saint-Laurent and several of his aides had arrived at Petit Goave to confer with La Salle. Saint-Laurent criticized Beaujeu severely for disobeying La Salle's orders. Joutel quoted Saint-Laurent as saying that "the misfortune would not have happened had Beaujeu put into Port de Paix, and did not spare to signify as much to him and to complain of that miscarriage."

The loss of the *St. Francis* was serious, for she was "laden with provisions, ammunition, utensils and proper tools for the settling of our new colonies." The men ministering to La Salle attempted to keep the bad news from him, fearing it might interrupt the progress of his recovery. One of Beaujeu's officers, however, spoke of the disaster in La Salle's presence.

La Salle suffered a relapse. His delirium returned, and once more it was thought he would die.

But after a few anxious days his mind again cleared, and, as Joutel wrote, "through the excellent constitution of his body he recovered."

La Salle slowly regained his strength. In early November, he was able to move from his bed a few hours each day. He was burdened in his convalescence by new troubles. A number of men had deserted, several had died, and others chose to return to France. At mid-month he ordered that all soldiers and colonists be confined to the ships. Beaujeu announced that when they sailed the *Joly* would not be held back by the *Amiable*, which was a slow ship. The *Joly* and the *Belle* would go ahead and leave the *Amiable* to make out as best she could. Beaujeu sought to agitate La Salle further by declaring he had learned from other mariners in Petit Goave that the mouth of the Mississippi was laced with perilous shoals, could not be entered by a sailing vessel, and that the surrounding country was dismal and unsuitable for a settlement or a fort.

Captain de Aigron of the *Amiable*, who had been a strong partisan of Beaujeu throughout the voyage, did his bit to disturb matters by declaring that he wanted nothing more to do with La Salle. He soon regretted the remark, for La Salle responded to it by transferring himself, Fathers Cavelier, Membre and Douay, and Nika, Saget, and Joutel from the *Joly* to the *Amiable*. This, in effect, made it the flagship from which Beaujeu was obliged to receive instructions.

On November 25th, La Salle, although emaciated and still in a weakened condition, felt himself strong enough to embark and to withstand the rigors of the sea, and he ordered the three ships to sail. He commanded that the *Joly* and the *Belle* follow the *Amiable*.

By nightfall the three ships were standing in that order under a fair wind toward the south coast of Cuba.

Tonty and his little band of Frenchmen and Abnakis had held Fort St. Louis on the Illinois with great difficulty through the fall of 1684 and the following winter. For six days in November they had been besieged by a band of Iroquois, but, with the help of some Illinois warriors had succeeded in repulsing them and driving them from the region. After that the Miamis and the Illinois, traditional enemies, had broken their amnesty and had taken to the warpath. The Illinois had been badly defeated. Tonty, striving to prevent La Salle's western alliance from being completely destroyed, was able to negotiate a tenuous peace, but "it cost us 1,000 [dollars worth of trade goods] to reconcile these two nations, which I did not accomplish without great trouble."

In the autumn of 1685, Tonty and several *couriers du bois* set out for Montreal with the hope that they would hear news of La Salle. Tonty was overjoyed to discover that the King had ordered all La Salle's property restored, that La Barre had been succeeded by the Marquis de Denonville, that La Forest was in command at Fort Frontenac, and that La Salle was en route with a strong expedition to establish a colony at the mouth of the Mississippi.

Governor Denonville wanted Tonty to lead a force against the Iroquois, but Tonty had other plans. Upon receiving the information about La Salle, "I resolved to go in search of him with a number of Canadians, and as soon as I should have found him, to return back to execute the orders of Denonville." He gave no consideration to La Salle's idea of sending several thousand warriors down the Mississippi from the Illinois, agreeing with La Forest that it was a totally impractical and utterly fantastic proposal.

Tonty's eagerness to rejoin La Salle would not allow him to spend the winter in idleness in Montreal, and on October 30, 1685, unaware that La Salle lay near death in Petit Goave, he started back to the Illinois. He had enlisted twenty-five Frenchmen, and the company made a winter journey by land, reaching Fort St. Louis late in January, 1686. They rested there three weeks to recuperate from the ordeals of the trip. Adding five Abnakis to their number, they set out on February 13, dragging canoes and supplies on sleds until they reached open water below Lake Peoria.

In Holy Week [April 10] Tonty stood on the site where La Salle had taken possession of the Mississippi and all its tributaries in the name of his King. The fleur-de-lis and the column had fallen, and he moved them "five leagues further up, and placed them in a higher situation."

He sent canoes along the Gulf coast, but they came upon no sign of the expedition. On Easter Monday, his men opposed to making further searches for fear of encountering Spaniards, he sadly turned back up the Mississippi.

After traveling a short distance he reached Indians with whom La Salle had engaged in a skirmish. They received him in friendship, and he left there a letter for La Salle.

"Sir," it said, "having found the column on which you placed the arms of France thrown down, I caused a new one to be erected.

. . . It gives me great uneasiness to be obliged to return under the misfortune of not having found you."*

Still hoping, if not believing, that La Salle would reach the lower Mississippi, Tonty arranged with six *couriers du bois* to remain in a post at the mouth of the Arkansas. If they heard from Indians any news of La Salle's whereabouts, they were to send a message to him at once. Then he went on with his company up the Mississippi.

38 ⚜ ⚜ ⚜

FOR AT LEAST one hundred and seventy-two years before 1685, the location of the Mississippi delta had been known. The river was not then called by that name, but its mouth was depicted with considerable accuracy on a Venetian map printed only twenty-one years after the landing of Columbus in America. The identity or nationality of the navigator (or navigators) who supplied the information has been forgotten, but it remains obvious that two decades after the discovery of the New World some daring pilot (or pilots) examined the coast of the Gulf of Mexico.

Others followed during the ensuing years, but not until 1519 do the records contain a desirable completeness. In that year, Francisco Garay, Governor of Jamaica, sent Alonso de Pineda to explore the entire Gulf coast. Pineda performed the remarkable feat of sailing close to shore from the Florida Keys to the River Panuco, on the central coast of Mexico [Tampico]. He, too, charted

*Fourteen years later in an Indian village then called Bayagoulis, an Indian chief handed Tonty's letter to the Sieur de Iberville, colonizer of Louisiana and brother of Sieur de Bienville, governor of the territory and founder of New Orleans. It had been carefully preserved by the chief all that time.

the mouth of the Mississippi. Nine years later the river was noted by the men in the five makeshift boats of the disastrous Narvaez expedition to Florida who were desperately trying to reach Panuco.

I was taught as a boy that De Soto discovered the Mississippi in 1542, but I soon came to know that was not true. He was the first to cross it north of its mouth. After his death, however, his lieutenant, Luis Moscoso, led the expedition on barges some seven hundred miles down the river to the Gulf and along the coast to Panuco.

The Spanish made no attempt to establish a colony at the Mississippi's mouth, but in the passing decades numerous ships sighted it. As the Spanish conquests were extended, seaborne commerce steadily increased in the Gulf of Mexico.

Cartographers continued to make mistakes. An old Spanish map La Salle had obtained showed the Mississippi flowing into Mobile Bay. But if some maps contained errors of this type, all were correct in one respect: the Mississippi's mouth was on the Gulf.

The failure of Captain Beaujeu of the *Joly* to find the Mississippi delta was inexcusable.

He had discussed its location and its physical aspects with pilots and buccaneers in Petit Goave who had seen it. Its latitude, if not its longitude, was known to him. If he had sailed along the northern coast of the Gulf of Mexico, he could not have missed it. No other river poured such a great flood into the Gulf. No other delta was of comparable size, nor extended farther out from the mainland.

Instead, after leaving Cape San Antonio, at the western end of Cuba, he sailed in first one direction and then another, and several times in circles. On December 14, said Joutel, Beaujeu came aboard the *Amiable*, "and having conferred with La Salle about the winds being contrary, proposed to him to return to Cape St. Antony, to which La Salle consented . . . though there was no great occasion for so doing, and accordingly we went and anchored in the place from whence we came."

At Cape San Antonio, the *Amiable* and the *Belle*, anchored an improper distance apart, were driven together by a squall. The *Belle* was badly damaged, losing her mizzenmast, her anchor, and a hundred fathoms of cable.

When favorable winds came on December 18, the three ships again set sail. Instead of passing through or rounding the Florida Keys, and steering north so that they might strike the arching north coast of Apalache Bay, they held to a course that took them almost directly northwest across the Gulf of Mexico.

For thirteen more days and nights, the ships zigzagged westward, and on January 1, 1686, they saw ahead a low coast. Beaujeu and Aigron were of the opinion, after allegedly consulting their charts, that they were in Apalache Bay.

They were off the coast of Texas.

One may only speculate as to the cause of La Salle's actions. Either he had no knowledge that he was being deceived, or he had become incapable of bearing the burdens which fell upon him. He appeared to be a man pervaded by an extreme weariness, to have lost all stomach for quarreling, and at times to be almost indifferent to the problems confronting the expedition. He seemed to hold only a single thought: to find the Mississippi, to land, and to commence the building of the establishment to which he would give his favorite name, Fort St. Louis. All other matters were irrelevant.

After attending mass sung by Father Douay on New Year's Day, he went ashore. He found nothing but endless coastal marshes and some distance behind them low plains that touched the sky. If this was the shore of Apalache Bay, as Beaujeu and Aigron said, then they were still far east of their destination, and there was only one thing to do—go on westward.

For five days the ship sailed, sometimes tacking long distances seaward, southwestward along the coast. Through almost every moment of daylight, La Salle, on the bridge of the *Amiable*, strained his eyes watching the shore for some sign of a great river pouring its flood into the Gulf. On January 6 he was excited by the sight of a wide opening between two low points of land. Father Cavelier said that La Salle "thought this was the Mississippi." He urged that small boats be sent to examine the pass, but Aigron objected. The *Joly* had disappeared, and Aigron demanded that they keep on in search of her. La Salle yielded to him, and said no more about landing.

They were, in fact, off Galveston Island.

Aigron held the *Amiable* in the area for five days. At last, when the *Joly* had not reappeared, La Salle agreed with Aigron that Beaujeu must have continued along the coast. The *Amiable* and the *Belle* went on to the southwest.

In the course of the next week, two landings were made and several attempts to reach shore were halted by heavy surf. They saw only more low islands guarded by shallow waters and shoals. One day, naked Indians were seen, and they anchored and signaled to them. The "savages made signs to us with skins to go to them," said Joutel, "but we could not get ashore because of the sea running high. . . . At last some of them fetched a large piece of timber, which they threw into the sea, placed themselves along both sides of it . . . and in that manner reached our boat. La Salle was pleased to see them, imagining they might give him some account of the river he sought after; but to no purpose, for although he spoke to them in several of the languages he knew, and made many signs; they still understood not what he meant. . . . We gave them some knives and strings of beads, after which they were dismissed. . . ."

La Salle proposed to put ashore at the first opportunity a party of thirty men to march along the coast, but, said Joutel, he was opposed "by brutish people [meaning Aigron and other officers] and altered his design to avoid giving offense. In that particular he committed an irretrievable error. . . ." Joutel was convinced that they were near the Mississippi, and that a shore party might have found it, but La Salle was "refused that success," and appeared to be satisfied with sending a small landing party, instead of a large group, which "returned without having seen anything, because a fog happened to rise." One of the men who went ashore on this occasion declared he "believed there was a river there, yet La Salle took no notice of it nor made any account of that report."

The morning of January 19 brought a fog that concealed the shore, and the *Amiable* and the *Belle* anchored. When the mist cleared, the *Joly* was seen approaching. "Our joy, however," declared Joutel, "was short, and we soon wished that Beaujeu had not joined us again, but that he had rather gone away for France without ever seeing of us."

Beaujeu accused La Salle of intentionally deserting him, and a bitter argument took place on the *Amiable*. It was La Salle's contention that if he had wanted to leave Beaujeu he would not have permitted the *Amiable* to move along the coast in the course that had been recommended by both Beaujeu and Aigron. While the argument did not appease Beaujeu, he changed the subject with the declaration that he wished to talk about their situation.

La Salle quickly made it apparent that he had not given up hope of finding the Mississippi delta, but that he believed they had passed it. He proposed that they turn about and re-examine the coast.

Beaujeu as promptly refused, and gave his reasons. First, he believed the Mississippi was ahead, that is, southward, and would be found if they followed the coast in that direction for only a short distance. Second, the voyage had taken longer than expected. The soldiers he carried on the *Joly* were consuming his provisions, and soon there would not be enough to supply his crew on the return trip to the West Indies. He would agree to sail back along the coast only if La Salle gave him the necessary quantity of stores.

La Salle offered to transfer enough rations from the *Amiable* and the *Belle* to supply the crew and passengers of the *Joly* for fifteen days. That, declared Beaujeu, was not an acceptable offer.

The stalemate continued for several days, during which the vessels moved slowly southward along the coast. At last, La Salle resolved the problem with a new proposal which not only astonished Beaujeu but left him no alternative but to accept.

If Beaujeu would not agree to return northward along the Gulf Coast, he would land at the first suitable place, build a fort and prepare to invade the Spanish possessions, as the King had commanded him to do.

Father Dainmaville thought that La Salle appeared to be "very perplexed." That may not be denied, but it should be said as well that La Salle was also very resolute, that his courage had not failed him, and that he was determined to found his colony, if not at the preferred location, sixty leagues above the mouth of the Mississippi, then somewhere else on the Gulf of Mexico.

From the *Amiable*, La Salle could see long lagoons separated from the sea by narrow strips of land. He again proposed that a contingent be sent ashore to examine the resources of the country and to discover an advantageous site for a fort. And this time he met with no objection.

The landing was made in the first week of February on Matagorda Island. In command was Joutel. His lieutenant was La Salle's nephew, Moranget. They had under them twenty men. La Salle, said Joutel, "furnished us with all sorts of provisions for eight or ten days, as also arms, tools, and utensils, of which every man made his bundle."

For three days the little company trudged northeastward along the sandy barrier lying between San Antonio Bay and the open Gulf. On the fourth day they were stopped by what Joutel called "the mouth of a great river." It was not a river. It was Cavallo Pass, the entrance to Matagorda Bay.

A crossing was necessary. None of the ships was in sight, and, therefore, no small boat could be obtained. They built a fire and kept it going night and day. Dangerously short of fresh water, and fearing that the ships had missed them, they set about constructing a raft which they might propel across the wide bay west of them to the mainland, where they would find both water and game. They accumulated a few large pieces of driftwood, lashing them together with reeds, thongs, and clothing, but three days later, as a few men prepared to push off, a strong wind blew seaward, making it impossible to use the rickety float.

"We were put out of our pain," said Joutel, "when the *Joly* and the *Belle* were discovered at sea." The smoke from the fire had been sighted by lookouts on the ships. Small boats were sent in. On the following day La Salle landed.

It had been his contention that they had sailed beyond the Mississippi's mouth, but, now, after a brief observation of the surroundings, he appeared to change his mind. He expressed the belief that they had reached the westernmost prong of the Mississippi delta, and that the main river could not be far to the northwest.

La Salle's attitude and his reasoning are incomprehensible, and must remain a mystery, for he neither spoke nor wrote words which might serve to explain them. The coast on which he had landed in no way resembled the delta of the Mississippi. No great flood of fresh water poured into the sea. They had sailed both south and north of Matagorda Bay, and had come upon no river, or series of rivers in close proximity to each other, that might be mistaken for the mouth, or mouths, of the Mississippi, which he had seen. It is possible that he was attempting to bolster the spirits of his men, give them new courage, but that seems unlikely, for it would not have been in keeping with his way of doing things. Perhaps his judgment, even his good sense, was impaired by his eagerness to rid himself of Beaujeu, to escape the quarreling, and

[237]

to be fully in command—alone. If neither of these suggestions is acceptable, then he was, for reasons known only to himself, being deliberately deceptive.

The pass to Matagorda Bay was sounded, and it was learned that at high tide the water was deep enough for the *Belle* to enter without difficulty but that the *Amiable* drew slightly too much to pass the bars. Over the strenuous objections of Beaujeu, who maintained that the currents of the pass were too strong to attempt a passage, La Salle ordered a large part of the *Amiable's* cargo brought ashore in small boats.

The *Belle* came in safely, and La Salle instructed Aigron not to attempt to enter the bay under sail but to tow the *Amiable* through the pass. He sent the *Belle's* pilot, a most competent seaman, to assist the pilot of the *Amiable*. Aigron refused to allow him on board, declaring angrily "that he could carry in his ship without help."

La Salle had sent eight men to build a canoe out of a large tree that stood a mile distant along the shore. Three of them were soon seen running back. The little group had been surprised by Indians, and five had been made prisoners. With a score of soldiers, La Salle set out at once to rescue them.

As he hurried in pursuit of the Indians, La Salle saw to his dismay that the *Amiable* was moving under full sail toward the pass, and he yelled to Joutel in anguish that she "was steering wrong and was standing toward the shoals."

But La Salle did not stop, and pressing on, they lost sight of the *Amiable*. A village was soon seen on a rise ahead. It "consisted of about fifty huts made of rush mats, and others of dried skins, and built with long poles bowed round at the tops, like great ovens." This was not a new experience for La Salle. He ordered ten men to lay down their arms to signify that they came in peace, and "seeing this most of the Indians laid down their bows and arrows and came to meet us, caressing us and stroking first their own hearts and then ours."

La Salle was in no mood for a lengthy parley. He profferred some knives, hatchets and various trinkets, and demanded that the prisoners be released. The report of a cannon was heard, and many of the Indians fell to the ground in terror. The captured men were brought quickly from a hut, and the rescue party started back at once.

When they came in view of the bay entrance, La Salle stopped abruptly and stood immobile, his face "a mask of horror." The *Amiable* lay careened on her starboard, her stern smashed.

Joutel wrote that stakes had been planted to guide Aigron through the channel, but that he ignored them, and "took a contrary course. This wicked captain's carelessness in not dropping his anchor as soon as the ship touched, the folly of lowering his mainsheet and hoisting out his sprit-sail, aided him all the better to fall into the wind and secure the shipwreck." Bitterly Joutel added: "Several other circumstances reported by the ship's crew and those who saw the ill management, were infallible tokens and proofs that the mischief had been done designedly and advisedly, which was one of the blackest and most detestable actions that man could be guilty of."

The accusation was supported by Le Clercq, who wrote: "La Salle had ordered Aigron to follow exactly the channel staked out; none of his orders were executed, and the faithless man, in spite of the advice given him by a sailor who was at the maintop to keep off, drove his vessel on the shoals, so that it was impossible to get off."

Quite in contrast to what might have been expected of him, La Salle remained calm as he surveyed the wrecked vessel. Nor did he castigate Aigron; he ignored him. He became again the cold, inscrutable, withdrawn La Salle that every member of the expedition had come to know so well, and that everyone, especially the ignorant men of the ranks, detested and mistrusted.

The *Amiable* carried "almost all the ammunition, utensils, tools and other necessaries for a settlement," and Joutel thought that "while La Salle needed all his resolution to bear up against the loss, his intrepidity did not forsake him, and he applied himself without grieving, to remedy what might be."

All members of the expedition who were to remain were on the beach. "They were all sick with nausea and dysentery," said an engineering officer named Minet. "Five or six died every day, in consequence of brackish water and bad food. There was plenty of oysters. There was nothing to make ovens, so that they had to eat flour boiled into messes of porridge with this brackish water."

The cargo lost in the *Amiable* included the larger part of the food staples brought from France, sixty barrels of wine, four cannon, sixteen hundred balls, four hundred grenades, four thousand pounds of iron, five thousand pounds of lead, most of the carpenters' tools, a forge, a mill, several score crates of arms, bales of cordage and barrels of spikes, surgical supplies and medicine, and most of the personal baggage of the soldiers and settlers.

Laboring furiously and always under dangerous circumstances, crews directed by La Salle managed to recover some of the food-stuffs and equipment. Two longboats were used to transport boxes, bags, and casks to the shore, but one of these was deliberately smashed by someone at night. The arduous work was halted "when wind blowing in from the offing made the waves run high, which, beating violently against the ship, split her, and all the light goods were carried out."

Several times Indians sneaked in under cover of night and made off with stores piled on the beach, despite efforts to guard them. In a fight with the red raiders, two men, Oris and Deslages, were killed, and two, Gayen and Moranget, were badly wounded by arrows. The Indians, Karankawas, like other tribes living along the Texas coast, were cannibals.

While a temporary rampart was being constructed of drift-wood and timbers from the *Amiable*, La Salle, with several men in two canoes obtained by trading from Indians, set out to explore the bay. They reached a stream to which he gave the name La Vache, (now Lavaca), because of the great number of buffalo in the area.

Returning from his brief exploration, he announced that he had found an advantageous site for a settlement, and he instructed Joutel to prepare the company to move inland to the *Rivière La Vache*.

Beaujeu thereupon declared that inasmuch as La Salle had assured him they had reached an arm of the Mississippi delta, his own job was completed. He would sail for France. Some twenty craftsmen and volunteers asked for passage, and he took them aboard. One was the engineer named Minet, who complained that La Salle had treated him "as if I were the meanest of mankind." The excuse for leaving given by the others was that they had lost faith in La Salle and thought the expedition was doomed to failure.

The *Joly* sailed on March 12, 1685. Beaujeu also took with him Captain Aigron and the entire crew of the wrecked *Amiable*.*

39 ⚜ ⚜ ⚜

SPANISH TEXAS had been invaded by the French.

This inane exploit was performed by some two hundred men and twenty or thirty women and children.

This was the force that was to capture the gold and silver mines of Mexico, the force that was to take possession of a territory larger than western Europe, a territory that could be, and eventually would be, defended by thousands of Spanish colonial troops.

At the head of this force was a man who had long been

---

* In France, Aigron was charged with intentionally wrecking his ship, and sentenced to a long term in prison. Minet, the engineer, also was jailed for deserting La Salle. Beaujeu, with the help of influential Jesuits, managed to escape incarceration, but he was publicly criticized by Seignelay, and his long naval career came to an abrupt end.

obsessed by a single and quite different plan, a plan noble in its scope, meritorious in its design, and laudable in its purpose, a plan to build for his country prosperous settlements in a rich land he had discovered. But he was a man who had been constantly frustrated, defeated in every effort he had made to bring it to fulfillment. Now he had been defeated once more. Now he had been put ashore in a wilderness, over which waved an enemy flag, with a pitifully small company composed largely of incompetents, wastrels, degenerates, and degraded females.

Now every quality inherent in La Salle, every characteristic and every force he possessed, became stronger, more pronounced, more intensified. Always incapable of gayness or of sharing with others commonplace pleasures, always sober, moral, and devout, he became uncompromisingly melancholy, withdrawn, grave, prudish, strict, and profoundly pious.

His written words throw light beneath the cold dark exterior. Accused by disappointed creditors of being brutal to the men under him, he once had vigorously protested that the kindness and understanding he was said to lack would be "out of place with this sort of people, who are libertines for the most part; and to indulge them means to tolerate blasphemy, drunkenness, lewdness, and a license incompatible with any kind of order. It will not be found that I have in any case whatever treated any man harshly, except for blasphemies and other such crimes openly committed. These I cannot tolerate: first, because such compliance would give grounds for another accusation [against me], much more just; secondly, because, if I allowed such disorders to become habitual, it would be hard to keep the men in subordination and obedience, as regards executing the work I am commissioned to do; thirdly, because the debaucheries, too common with this rabble, are the source of endless delays and frequent thieving; and, finally, because I am a Christian, and do not want to bear the burden of their crimes."

The only men La Salle appeared willing to take into his confidence were Joutel, Membre, Nika, and Saget. To all other persons he displayed an attitude which clearly bespoke his suspicion and distrust of them. Only to the four, the two Indians and the priest who had been with him on his wilderness journeys and had never deviated in their loyalty to him, and to the ex-soldier who had been his boyhood friend and who had proved himself a competent leader, did he reveal his thoughts and his plans.

It was vitally necessary that they establish defenses with all possible speed. No one could say how long they would have to remain in the region. No one could say how near they were to a Spanish settlement. The Indians were unfriendly and would continue to make trouble. Moreover, they might send word of their presence to the Spanish authorities. A strong fort must be constructed in which they would be able to withstand indefinitely a siege by either red or white adversaries. He had found a cove in the bay in which he believed the *Belle* could be safely concealed. Not until these tasks had been accomplished could he give thought to making a search for the Mississippi.

The site La Salle had chosen for Fort St. Louis was at the head of Lavaca Bay. He marked out the ground lines of the structure to be erected and the palisade that would surround it. Always a disciplinarian, he now drove both men and women in the work of building with the relentlessness of a brutish slaveowner. From dawn to dark he stood over them directing the cutting and squaring of logs, the clearing of fields, the planting of grain, the construction of magazines and storehouses.

It was good country. There were buffalo and deer and other game on the plain that rose gradually beyond the bay. There were ducks and geese in the marshes. There were oysters and crustaceans on the tidal flats. There were many kinds of fish in the fresh and brackish and salt waters.

But full bellies were not a panacea. They were not cures for demoralization, depravement, disease, not a prescription that could defeat death.

The minds and hearts of everyone, with the exception of La

Salle and a few indomitable men who could be counted on the fingers of the hands, were ruled by terror and hopelessness.

"Build and secure yourselves," he told them. "Have faith. And I will find the Mississippi. That is our country, the land of France. We will go there on the *Belle*. And there we will be safe."

His words were wasted. They believed he had brought them to disaster, to perish in a godforsaken wilderness, that he had deceived them, and that he would desert them.

If a restoration of the confidence they had once held in him had been possible, it was precluded by his dark moods, his self-containment, his dour expressions, his cold reserve, his austerity, his strictness. And loathing of him was added to the fear and depression which filled them.

Under a sailcloth, spread to shield them from the burning Texas sun, twenty men lay dying in agony from syphilis and gonorrhea contracted in Petit Goave.

Ten soldiers died during the summer from food poisoning.

A carpenter, pursuing game into a wood, vanished and was never found.

A craftsman, described by Joutel as a "man of character, and very serviceable by reason of his general knowledge and fidelity towards La Salle," was bitten by a rattlesnake. When poultices failed to halt the swelling of his leg, it was amputated. Two days later he died.

Illicit sexual affairs troubled not only the priests but La Salle, and at last, in an effort to halt them, he directed Joutel to confine all unattached women in a separate hut. Deprived of their love-making, at least at nighttime, several men asked permission to marry, and the ceremonies were performed. The restrictions La Salle invoked brought little improvement in conduct. Men and girls constantly slipped away together into the surrounding marshes.

Always the Karankawas watched the fort. They sneaked in close at night, howled dismally, and shot arrows over the stockade.

The mutilated bodies of half a dozen hunters and workers caught off guard were found during the course of the summer.

Six men deserted, but their fate was never learned.

La Salle, taking with him Nika, Saget, and a few capable gunners, made several brief trips of exploration. He gave no indication of what he hoped to discover, but Joutel believed that he feared a Spanish patrol might be searching for the colony, and that he hoped to destroy it in a surprise attack.

La Salle and his scouts came, one day, upon a small band of Indians belonging to a tribe not previously encountered. They were friendly people engaged in gathering crayfish, and they invited the white men to their village. "My brother," said Father Cavelier, "accepted the offer and made them some presents." The village, only a league distant, consisted of some twenty huts, "surrounded by a kind of wall made with a potter's clay and sand, fortified with little towers at intervals."

Attached to a stake in front of one of the dwellings was a copper plate, and "on it were engraved the arms of Spain, with the date 1588."

By October, the fort had been completed, a large supply of meat had been cured, and the crops from the fields had been stored. The most valuable tools, a quantity of ammunition and weapons, and part of the provisions were transferred to the *Belle* for safekeeping. Ten men were assigned to live on the little vessel and guard it. La Salle now felt that he could safely leave on a search for the Mississippi, the "fatal river," as Joutel called it. With him he would take fifty men, one of them his brother. They would attempt to follow the seacoast to the north.

Joutel would be in command of Fort St. Louis. "This left me," he said, "with thirty-four men, three friars, a number of women and children, including two young orphan daughters of a Canadian who had lately died." There were also ten sailors and a priest on the *Belle*.

[245]

La Salle suspected that some men would desert him, and "he instructed me," said Joutel, "not to receive any man of those he took along without an order in writing from him. He and some of the others constructed corselets of small lath, to secure themselves against arrows."

On the morning of October 31, 1685, five cannon shots were fired at Fort St. Louis. A long file of men, with La Salle in the lead, twisted along the north shore of Lavaca Bay. The search for the Mississippi had begun.

Where, in the four months they were gone, La Salle and his company actually went cannot be determined. It is known only that they pushed northward from Matagorda Bay. Abbé Cavelier wrote an account of the journey, but it is far more fanciful than factual.

Somewhere along the coast of Texas in February, 1686, he says, "we came to a pretty large river, which my brother thought might be the Mississipy, although its course was just the opposite." Presumably he means that this river ran more eastward than southward. A few days later they came upon three Shawnees whom "my brother lost when he descended to the mouth of the Mississippy by the Illinois," a most improbable story. However, according to Father Cavelier, the Shawnees fell upon La Salle and "almost stifled him by their embraces in the transport of pleasure which they experienced on seeing him again."

It is not beyond the realm of possibility that La Salle had met some wandering Indians who had seen him before. But even this theory becomes dubious with further consideration. The conversations with them were conducted by means of the sign language, in which both Nika and Saget were proficient. If they had been Shawnees, Nika, a Shawnee, would have been able to talk with them in their own language. And if they had seen La Salle, the meeting could have taken place only on the Mississippi. Therefore, that being the case, they could have told him how far he was from the river, and they could have led him to it. Apparently this thought occurred to Father Cavelier, and he recognized it as a weakness in his fiction, for he has the Shawnees explaining that they "were not unnatural enough to abandon their wives and children," by going with La Salle to the Mississippi, and "moreover, being in the most fertile, healthy, and peaceful country in the world, they would be devoid of sense to leave it and expose themselves to be tomahawked by the Illinois or burnt by the Iroquois in an insufferably cold land."

Now, to liven his narrative, Father Cavelier discovers gold. The Shawnees assertedly led La Salle to "some holes from which we took some specimens of stone," and declared that a short distance away, "gold was found in large grains and dust; that the Indians used it only to make collars and bracelets, but that they valued it less than certain red stones which they put to the same use." Father Cavelier states that he kept some of the nuggets, had them assayed in Paris, and they proved to be "gold ore, which had only half waste."

That Father Cavelier's account was designed to discredit La Salle, and to make it appear that La Salle had failed to obey the orders given him by the King, becomes clear when he writes about fighting the Spanish with the support of the Texas Indians. The Shawnees, he avers, urged La Salle to lead them in an invasion of Mexico, but that La Salle refused.

La Salle had failed His Majesty, but his brother does credit him with finding the "fatal river," writing: "On the 10th of March we descried the River Mississipy, where we left some men in a little redoubt of pickets."

Strangely enough, indisputable records show that La Salle had returned to Fort St. Louis on Lavaca Bay only five or six days later.

Several men were left in a redoubt on a river, but its location or the name of the stream [it was probably the Colorado] remains unknown, for it was never found and the men were never heard from again.

One man had deserted on the journey. He was known as the Elder Duhaut, and he had returned to Fort St. Louis with a tale that he had become separated from the company and had been unable to find their trail.*

"About the middle of March," wrote Joutel, "I spied seven or eight persons coming toward us. I ordered eight men to follow me to meet them, and as soon as we drew near we recognized La Salle, Cavelier, his brother, Moranget, his nephew, and several others. They were in bad condition, their clothes ragged. Cavelier's short cassock hung in tatters; most of them had no hats, and their linen was no better; however, the sight of La Salle rejoined us all, though he had not found the fatal river."

La Salle was anything but "rejoiced." The *Belle* had disappeared. It was his belief at first that the men he had stationed aboard her had sailed for the West Indies. But the truth would soon be learned.

Being short of water, five of the men on the *Belle* had gone ashore with several casks. A gust of wind overturned their boat and they were drowned. Stranded on board, and forced to quench their thirst with wine and brandy, the remaining men were obliged to wait several days before they judged the weather calm enough to attempt to move the vessel to the fort.

They had no sooner raised the moorings before a violent wind swept upon them. The ship was driven upon a shoal and sank. Two sailors and the priest reached shore by clinging to pieces of wreckage, but three more men were lost.

La Salle, said Joutel, had put aboard the *Belle* "his clothes, his linen, his papers, and all his best effects, all of which he was

---

* First names seldom appear in any of the accounts of La Salle's explorations and expeditions. There were two Duhaut brothers at Fort St. Louis, and they were distinguished by being called Elder and Younger. The Younger Duhaut was seldom mentioned, but the Elder, a vicious, cowardly, degraded ex-convict, would, as will be seen, be ever remembered in history.

then in the utmost need. Besides, he was planning to send the *Belle* to the islands for assistance and then to sail in it to look for his river."

La Salle collapsed. The delirium and fever he had suffered first on the Illinois and then in Petit Goave returned. For a fortnight he was seldom more than semiconscious. Expecting him to die, Joutel stood prepared to leave Fort St. Louis and attempt to save the company by traveling overland toward his "fatal river."

40 ✣ ✣ ✣

WHEN LA SALLE was absent from Fort St. Louis, and when he was ill, Joutel had demonstrated his ability as a leader under constant pressure of adversities and hardships that would have broken a man of less stamina and courage. He permitted no one able to work to remain idle. Each day both men and women were assigned tasks—hunting, fishing, gardening, curing meat, constructing canoes, strengthening the fort, cooking. He built a small chapel and a cellar.

"We did what we could to amuse ourselves and drive away care," he wrote. "I encouraged our people to dance and sing in the evenings; for when La Salle was among us, pleasure was often banished. Now, there is no use being melancholy on such occasions. It is true that La Salle had no great cause for merry-making, after all his losses and disappointments; but his troubles made others suffer also.

"Though he had ordered me to allow to each person only a certain quantity of meat at every meal, I observed this rule only when meat was rare [in short supply, which was seldom]. The air here is very keen, and one has a great appetite. One must eat and act, if he wants good health and spirits. I speak from experience. . . . If I was busy hunting or anything else, I was not so dull. So I tried to keep the people as busy as possible."

His efforts to bolster spirits were not altogether successful. Depression and fear were malignancies eating upon spirit and reason and faith.

Elder Duhaut sought to foment an uprising, declaring that La Salle had run away to save himself and would not send help for them. He urged them to reject Joutel, refuse to obey his orders, and make him their leader. He would, he vowed, save them by leading them to the nearest Spanish settlement. Imprisonment by the Spanish was better than death at the hands of savages.

Joutel pressed a pistol against Elder Duhaut's ribs, and threatened to shoot him if he made further disloyal and traitorous statements or in any way contributed to the "rising discontent of the colonists."

"In view of what happened," Joutel wrote, "I would have done La Salle a singular service had I put Duhaut to death."

Father Le Clercq proved himself unable to withstand the strain. He prepared a scurrilous attack on La Salle, maligning his character and condemning his motives, and permitted several persons to read the paper. Joutel took it from him, and burned it "on the urgent treaty of the other clerics, who dreaded what might ensue, should the absent La Salle become aware of the aspersions cast upon him."

After lying desperately ill for nearly three weeks, during which time Membre and others had despaired of saving La Salle's life, he began a remarkable recovery. By the middle of April, although still weak and somewhat unsteady, he declared his intention to make a second search for the Mississippi. If he reached it, he would either go himself or send men to the Illinois to enlist the aid of Tonty and friendly Indians. From the Illinois, couriers would be sent to Montreal, so that the King might receive a report of the disasters which had befallen the expedition.

He chose twenty men whom he believed could endure the rigors of the journey. Among them were Fathers Cavelier and Douay, Nika, Moranget, Saget, Clerc, Hurie, Younger Duhaut,

Biborel, Heins, Ruter, Grollet and Dumesil. The names of the other six do not appear in the accounts kept by Douay and Cavelier, nor are they mentioned by Joutel.

Douay wrote that they started on April 22, 1686, "after celebrating the divine mysteries in the chapel of the fort." Each man carried a pack containing eight pounds of powder and lead, and they had with them "two axes, two dozen knives, as many awls, some beads, and two kettles."

Having learned from experience the difficulties of attempting to travel northward along the coastal plain, which was laced with innumerable rivers, swamps and inlets, La Salle elected to follow a route farther inland. It took them across the Colorado, the Brazos, and northwest of the present site of Houston.

Douay speaks of their passage through a "beautiful country, with delightful fields and prairies, skirted with vines, fruits, and groves," and "meeting everywhere so prodigious a quantity of Cibola, or wild cattle, that the smallest herds seemed to contain two or three hundred."

In this region they met large numbers of Indians, many of them mounted, riding Spanish saddles, and wearing Spanish boots and spurs. They were bands belonging to the Caddoan Confederacy.

In every village, some of which contained as many as three hundred cabins, states Douay, they were received "with all possible friendship, even the women coming to embrace our men. They made us sit down on well-made mats near the chiefs, who presented us the calumet. . . . La Salle so won them by his manners and insinuated so much of the glory of our King, telling them that he was greater and higher than the sun, that they were all ravished with astonishment."

Cavelier wrote that when the Caddos were asked by signs where they had obtained the Spanish articles, "they took a coal and depicted a Spaniard, houses, steeples, and showed the part of the heaven under which New Mexico would lie."

In one village described by Douay, from which the Caddos

emerged to greet them "with ears of corn in their hands and a polished, honest air," they were told of "white men living toward the west, a cruel, wicked, nation, who depeopled the country around them." When La Salle informed the Indians that the French were at war with "that people, they pressed us to stay and go to war with the Spaniards of Mexico." But La Salle "put them off with fair words, and made a strict alliance with them, promising to return with numerous troops."

At some point on the Brazos, probably in the vicinity of Navasota, La Salle turned eastward. By this time—late May or early June—the little company had experienced a number of serious troubles. Only nine of the twenty men were still with him.

Five had become sick and exhausted and had asked permission to return to Fort St. Louis. La Salle had granted it. They were never seen again.

Five had deserted.

La Salle and his brother had narrowly escaped drowning in crossing the Brazos on a raft.

Nika had been bitten by a rattlesnake, and they had waited a week for that hardy warrior to recover.

One man became lost while hunting, and their efforts to find him failed.

The Indians continued to be friendly, and they were enthusiastically welcomed in each village along the way. The line of their march indicates that they had been informed of the most direct route to the Mississippi. Well established intertribal trade trails passed through this region, running from both the Red River and Mississippi valleys, crossing the Brazos, reaching the Colorado, ascending it to the vast sweeps of the southern Great Plains, and going on to the Pueblo country of New Mexico.

It may be logically assumed that La Salle now knew where he was, and how far he was from his goal.

But once again he was to be defeated in his quest.

The Trinity River was crossed, and Douay speaks of the "fine country" and the "great trees." But a few days later their trail came to an abrupt end.

La Salle was stricken with a "violent fever, which brought him to extremity."

Cavelier would write that "My brother was so affected and weakened by it that we did not dare to proceed."

The seriousness of La Salle's attack may be judged from Douay's passage that the "length of this sickness disconcerted all our plans. It kept us back more than two months."

One of the puzzling aspects of the journey was the failure of La Salle to obtain horses when the Caddos were first encountered. Had he done so, he might well have reached the Mississippi, or perhaps the Red River on which he could have descended to the Mississippi. Douay told of seeing "mounted troops of Indians," and makes the flat statement that "horses are common." They could have been obtained "for an axe," and one warrior offered the priest a horse for the hood of his habit, "to which he took a fancy."

Yet, it was not until they had neared the Trinity River, or perhaps not until they had crossed it, that they obtained a horse, and it was a gift from "a very honest Indian returning from the chase with his wife and family."

During La Salle's long convalescence, Nika and Saget traded knives and weapons for more horses, and by the time La Salle was able to travel there was a mount for each man. Now, however, they were faced with an insoluble problem. Their supply of powder was almost exhausted. Douay says that all were agreed it would have been foolhardy to have attempted to reach Fort St. Louis on the Illinois without sufficient ammunition to protect themselves against dangerous savages. Fort St. Louis on Lavaca Bay was much closer, no more than "a hundred and fifty leagues in a straight line."

And "in so distressing a crisis, La Salle resolved to retrace his steps."

Douay says that on the return journey "nothing happened worth note, except that one of our men was carried off by a crocodile of prodigious length and bulk." The man was Biborel, and the tragedy occurred on the Colorado River. Douay might have mentioned, also, that five of their horses were lost, and that during the last three weeks of the journey nine men rode the remaining five scrawny mounts.

But this situation was recorded by Joutel. On a day late in August, nine men with five horses were seen approaching, and Joutel was one of the first to run towards them, "and we were extraordinary glad to see our commander-in-chief return safe, though he had not found his river, nor been towards the Illinois, as we had hoped. This was a very dismal and deplorable account, but the even temper of our chief made all men easy and revived the lowest ebb of hope."

This was a man speaking whose loyalty to La Salle was un-qualified, whose own spirit and faith were indestructible. Father Cavelier painted a different picture, portraying the dejection of the men and women at Fort St. Louis as bordering upon complete despair, men and women whose last hope was that "the King might send aid from France." But even that hope was soon gone, "and banished, as it were, to the uttermost parts of the earth, we regarded this agreeable country as an abode of weariness and a perpetual prison."

41 ✢✢✢

IT WAS TWELFTH NIGHT, the year 1687.

On the earthen floor of the little log chapel, the men, women and children knelt together and crossed themselves, and the inton-ing of the priests could be heard by the sentries peering into the darkness of wood and marshland and water that reached away on every side from the palisade of Fort St. Louis.

And when the ceremony ended they filled their cups, not with wine, for there was none, but with water. And they held the cups aloft, crying:

"The King drinks! Long live the King!"

And the gravity, the disconsolation, the sorrow of their faces was revealed in the weak unsteady light of the candles. And their eyes reflected the fear, and the hopelessness, and the despair, weighing upon their hearts.

Regretfully, it cannot be said how many were gathered in the rough little room, before the rude altar adorned with torn and faded cloths and few ornaments. They numbered no more than fifty. Only twenty-seven names have been remembered, and most of them are incomplete.

It can be said that, whoever they were, they were the last of the living who had been abandoned there, nearly two years before. Little wooden crosses, more than a hundred of them, braving the winds that swept the sandspits of the wild Texas coast, told their own stories. But there had been others who were gone, some three score of them, who lived only in memory, whose eternal resting places were unmarked by holy symbols.

La Salle spoke that Twelfth Night. He leaned forward a bit, for some weeks before he had strained his groin—Joutel said he had suffered a hernia—and he was not fully recovered from the painful injury.

Tomorrow he would leave again. Surely this time he would reach the Mississippi. He would take with him no more men than he thought necessary. Barbier, a skilled hunter and woodsman, who had been born in Canada and had fought Indians, would be left in command. Twice before, said La Salle, he had learned of the perils and hardships of the journey. They were too great for women and children to endure. If the entire company attempted it, with only game to sustain them, and neither canoes nor horses to carry them, few would survive.

Surely some of those who would accompany him would reach Canada. If he lived, he would be the first to return, either with a strong troop of Frenchmen and warriors down the great river, or in a vessel, to save them. Have strength. Be brave. Do not abandon hope. Have faith in him.

And in the early light of the morning, the five Indian horses were loaded with packs of utensils and ammunition. The wind blowing in from the sea was chill and damp, and the men who would go wrapped themselves in skins and coats made from the sails of the *Belle*.

There was weeping, loud sobbing born of desolation. And the men followed the bent La Salle along the north shore of Lavaca Bay. And as long as they could see each other, the groups waved.

And then the men on the shore vanished, and at the gate of the palisade eyes gazed after them, but they saw only emptiness, and they heard only the silence of the wilderness.

Left at Fort St. Louis were thirteen men (including three priests), eleven women, one teenage youth, and six boys and girls, a total of thirty-one persons.

Most of them lived only through the summer. Sometime in the autumn, a horde of Karankawas swept upon them from the forest. Four children were carried off by Indian women. The youth and one young man also were taken as prisoners.

All the others were butchered.

Since the capture of La Salle's ship, the *St. Francis*, in the West Indies, the Spanish had been searching for the colony. The wrecks of the *Amiable* and the *Belle* had been found, but Fort St. Louis, wisely built farther inland, where it could not be seen from the bay, had not been discovered.

But in January, 1689, one of the men who had deserted La Salle guided a company of Spanish troops, commanded by Alonzo de Leon, to it. They found the palisade and the buildings all but destroyed. Broken crates and barrels, rusty weapons and utensils, books and pieces of clothing, lay scattered about the small courtyard. Among them were the rotted remains of several bodies.

Captain de Leon forcefully rescued the four children and the youth from the Karankawas. He learned of the young man's capture, but could not find him. To his surprise, among a band of traveling Indians he found two white men dressed and painted like savages. They confessed to having deserted La Salle, and he put them in chains.

With the seven survivors, de Leon took his company back to Coahuila, where he sent a report to the Viceroy at Mexico City—the final tragic chapter of the story of France's irrational and badly devised attempt to invade New Spain.

42 ✤ ✤ ✤

THEY KNEW the best trail to the north, for some of them had traversed the country four times. Yet, the best trail was difficult, and for a month they made slow progress, suffering greatly from the need of adequate footwear. Few had shoes of any kind. The feet of most of them were encased in raw hides. And they left blood stains on the rough earth and rocks and sharp marsh grasses. Storms swept in from the Gulf of Mexico, driven by gale winds and deluging the country, and the rivers and streams and gullies were in flood.

With La Salle were sixteen men. The names of fifteen of them are known. They were the Abbé Cavelier, his brother; Cavelier, his nephew, now 17; Joutel; Liotot, a surgeon; Moranget, his nephew; Father Douay; Elder Duhaut; Heins; De Marle; L'Archevêque; Saget, the Mohegan; Barthelmy; Teissier; Nika, the Shawnee; and Talon.

When they reached the Colorado they found it flooding over the surrounding country, and they were forced to travel upstream for four or five days before finding a place where they could construct rafts and safely cross. Hunger was banished by buffalo and deer meat and marrow bones. In mid-February they were able to obtain from Indians a number of dressed deerskins with which they made moccasins. And a few days later they reached people who owned a large number of horses and who possessed numerous articles of Spanish origin, which they said they had obtained in trade "far to the west." With knives, hatchets and awls, thirty mounts were purchased.

One day the company reached a large village, were feasted, offered lodgings in mud and thatched huts, and more than a score of young women were assigned to entertain them. It was raining, and the dry shelters would have been most welcome, but La Salle ordered that their camp be established some distance from the village. He posted guards to keep the "handsome maidens" out and the men from straying into the wet night. This, said Joutel, was his custom, and "he forbade us to have any communication with the natives, which was very prejudicial to us," and made "the men angry with him."

From the Colorado, they struck northeastward, following much of the same route they had traveled the previous year. On most days Indians accompanied them, and Father Cavelier recorded that on one occasion "thirty well-mounted young warriors took us by as well-beathen a road as that from Paris to Orléans," and reaching away to the sky "was a most level country, extremely well adapted to pasturage."

With those words, Father Cavelier's account of the journey ended. He dated his last entry "Feb. 16, 1687." (It should have been March 16th.) In view of the events which took place, his reticence to commit himself on paper after that date may easily be understood.

The Brazos had been reached on March 13, and crossed the following day, the horses swimming and the men transported against the strong current in canoes provided by Indians. On the 15th they followed a clearly marked trail toward the northeast, entering what Joutel called "a pleasanter country than that we had passed through."

[258]

It was on this day, March 15, La Salle remembered that "on the previous journey he had hid some Indian wheat [maize], beans, and beads, not far away, that he wanted to recover." Saget and Nika knew the location of the cache, which was three leagues from their present position, and he sent them with Elder Duhaut, Heins, Teissier, L'Archevêque and Liotot to pick up the goods. Several warriors accompanied them on the mission. As it was late afternoon, La Salle made camp to await their return.

The provisions were spoiled, and, taking the beads, the group turned back. Shortly buffalo were encountered, and two were shot. Nika was sent to inform La Salle that they would remain away overnight and to bring back horses to carry the several hundred pounds of meat.

The next morning, March 16, Nika, Moranget and De Marle set out leading two packhorses. La Salle had instructed Moranget to "send back a horseload of meat immediately, that they might eat it fresh, and to have the remainder smoked and dried."

This is Joutel's statement: "Moranget found that both buffalo were already being smoked, but were not yet sufficiently dried to be moved, and that Liotot, Heins and Elder Duhaut were roasting the best marrow bones for themselves."

Cursing them for their greediness, Moranget flew into a violent "rage, and told them they would not eat as much of the finest parts as they had imagined. He seized the marrow bones, and declared he would take all the meat back to La Salle and the others."

Although Joutel was not present, there were witnesses to give him a detailed account of the heated row, in which Moranget and Elder Duhaut almost came to blows. He thought Moranget's "passionate behavior contrary to reason," but that Elder Duhaut and Liotot also "had other causes of complaint."

With this assertion, Joutel is referring to past incidents which had augmented Elder Duhaut's and Liotot's bitterness against La Salle. Elder Duhaut's brother and a nephew of Liotot had been killed by Indians, and they both felt that La Salle's carelessness and poor leadership had been responsible for their deaths. Elder Duhaut had attempted to overthrow La Salle and take command of Fort St. Louis, but had been stopped by Joutel. When Moranget had been seriously wounded by an arrow, Liotot had attended him, and claimed that he had saved the life of La Salle's nephew. Instead of expressing his gratitude for the attention and care he had received from the surgeon, Moranget had cursed him as an incompetent physician and had charged him with performing a clumsy operation. Moreover, both Elder Duhaut and Liotot had extensive property holdings in France, and they had become convinced that they would not live to see them again unless they escaped from the dominating La Salle and resorted to their own devices to save themselves.

The curing of the meat had not been completed as dusk settled, and Moranget announced that they would wait until morning before rejoining La Salle. Night fell. Moranget, Nika, and Saget prepared their beds beside each other. Elder Duhaut, Liotot, Heins, L'Archevêque and Teissier sat together in darkness beyond the reach of the firelight. Several Indians made their own camp some yards away.

It was after midnight when Liotot crept silently and cautiously toward the sleeping Moranget. Behind him he held a hatchet. Suddenly he sprang forward.

He struck three quick blows. Nika and Saget instantly died, but Moranget struggled to arise, blood streaming over his face. Viciously Liotot struck him again, smashing in his head, and killing him.

The Indians had leaped up, but they found the guns of Elder Duhaut and Heins aimed at them, and they fled into the blackness.

Throughout March 17, La Salle waited for Moranget and the others to return, and, says Joutel, "That evening, while we were talking about what could have happened to the absent men, La Salle seemed to have a presentiment of what was to take place.

He asked me if I had heard of any machinations against them, or if I had noticed any bad design. I answered that I had heard nothing, except that they sometimes complained of being found fault with so often. We were very uneasy all the rest of the evening."

When daylight came, La Salle resolved to go with an Indian guide and Father Douay to learn why the men had not returned. As they neared the meat camp, the Indian pointed to vultures circling ahead.

"On the way," writes Douay, "La Salle conversed with me of matters of piety, grace, predestination, expatiating on all his obligations to God for having saved him from so many dangers during the years that he had traversed America. He seemed to be peculiarly penetrated with a sense of God's benefits to him.

"Suddenly I saw him plunged into a deep melancholy. He was so troubled that I did not know him any longer."

They came to a small stream. L'Archevêque was seen standing on the opposite bank. La Salle dismounted and called out, asking where Moranget might be found. L'Archevêque replied only with a wave of a hand, as if to say: "Somewhere farther along the stream."

La Salle rebuked him for his insolence, and started ahead, leading his horse. He had taken only a few steps when two shots were fired from a clump of reeds. One bullet narrowly missed its mark. The other struck La Salle in the temple, instantly killing him.

Douay and the Indian stood still in terror as Liotot and Elder Duhaut rose from the reeds and came toward them.

"Don't fear," Elder Duhaut told them. "You're not going to be hurt."

Liotot stood over La Salle. *"Te voilà, grand Bacha, te voilà!"*

Douay stumbled forward and knelt beside La Salle, and "his face was full of blood. I watered it with my tears."

Douay maintains that he buried La Salle and placed a cross

on his grave. Joutel, who reached the scene of the murder shortly afterward, tells a different story:

"Elder Duhaut, Liotot, and L'Archevêque barbarously stripped La Salle's corpse, and vented their malice in vile and opprobrious language. They dragged the naked corpse into the bushes and left it to the wild beasts."

Perhaps Father Douay simply wanted to believe that La Salle had received a decent burial with proper religious rites. "La Salle had confessed and fulfilled his devotions just before we started," he says. "I gave him absolution. Thus died our wise commander, constant in adversity, intrepid, generous, engaging, dexterous, skilfull, capable of everything."

La Salle was eight months less than 44 years of age.

Joutel's eulogy was somewhat more realistic, if no less heartfelt: "La Salle died at a time when he might entertain his greatest hopes, as the reward of his labors. He had a capacity and talent to make his enterprise successful. His constancy and courage, his indefatigable body, would have procured a glorious end to his undertakings, had not all those excellent qualities been counterbalanced by too haughty a behavior, which sometimes made him insupportable, and by a rigidness towards those under his command, which at last drew on him implacable hatred and was the occasion of his death."

When, a few hours later, Father Cavelier was informed of the tragedy, his only words were:

"My poor brother is dead. We shall be next."

La Salle's grave—if there was one—was never found. The most that may be said about the location of the scene of his murder is that it was on or near the Trinity River in southeastern Texas.

Epilogue

ELDER DUHAUT proclaimed himself commander, and none disputed him.

Continuing on toward the northeast, the eleven men passed through a number of large Caddo towns. In one they found three Frenchmen who had deserted La Salle the previous year. Two of them were Grollet and Ruter. The other was identified only as a Provençal.

In a fight over trade goods—a few beads, hatchets, and knives —Heins shot Elder Duhaut to death, and Ruter wounded Liotot. The surgeon lived for several hours in terrible agony, before Ruter finished him off by exploding a pistol loaded with a charge of powder against his head.

Heins now became the leader.

Father Cavelier proposed that they continue on to the Mississippi. Heins refused to go, but agreed to let the Abbé and others

[263]

who wished to accompany him depart only if they promised not to involve him in the murder of La Salle. Father Cavelier solemnly swore that Heins would not be implicated.

The company separated.

With Father Cavelier went Father Douay, Joutel, young Cavelier, De Marle, Teissier, and Barthelmy.

Left with the Caddos were Heins, L'Archevêque, Talon, and the one man whose name is not known. With them were the three deserters, Grollet, Ruter, and the man identified only as a Provençal.

L'Archevêque and Grollet would be captured by the Spanish the next year. Heins, Ruter, the Provençal and the unidentified man were not heard of again.

Mounted and guided by Indians, Father Cavelier's party traveled toward the Red River.

De Marle was drowned in a stream in northwestern Louisiana.

Late in July, the Indians led the six weary men to the junction of the Mississippi and Arkansas Rivers. A large village stood there. They wept with joy at the sight of a cross standing before one of the houses.

They were soon being embraced by three of the *couriers du bois* Tonty had left at the confluence, Couture, De Launey, and Carpentier.

The winter of 1687–88 was spent at Fort St. Louis on the Illinois. Father Cavelier had extracted from the others a promise to conceal the news of La Salle's death. The anxious Tonty was told that La Salle had been left alive and well on the Gulf coast and might arrive at any time on the Illinois with the remainder of the colony.

The Jesuit, Father Allouez, had been ill for several weeks at Fort St. Louis. When he heard that La Salle was en route north, he gathered his strength and fled in haste.

In March, 1688, Father Cavelier's group departed for Canada. Before leaving the Abbé obtained from Tonty furs valued at more than four thousand *livres*. These, he told the trusting Tonty, were to be sold and the money for them would be deposited in Montreal so that La Salle would have some ready cash when he arrived there. The furs were sold in Michilimackinac, but Father Cavelier pocketed the money and with it bought new clothes and a ticket to France.

The contingent—Fathers Cavelier and Douay, Joutel, young Cavelier, Teissier, and Barthelmy—traveling by way of the French River and the Ottawa, reached Quebec in August. They sailed for home a few weeks later.

In Paris, Father Cavelier disclosed for the first time that La Salle had been murdered. Joutel pleaded with the Colonial Ministry to send a ship to save the men, women, and children at Fort St. Louis. When the proposal was placed before Louis XIV, he rejected it.

In the early summer of 1688, Couture, one of the men Tonty had left at the confluence of the Mississippi and the Arkansas, arrived at Fort St. Louis on the Illinois, and told Tonty the truth.

The famous voyageur with the iron hand unabashedly wept. "One of the greatest men of the age is dead," he sobbed.

Couture knew nothing of the fate of the colonists left on the Texas coast. With five *couriers du bois* and three Indians, Tonty sped down the Mississippi to rescue them.

When he reached the Caddos, his men, fearing to go farther, deserted him.

Alone, he turned back. But he had learned from the Indians that the Spanish had found the destroyed settlement on Lavaca Bay—a scene of desolation and death.

Bibliographical notes

It would serve no good purpose to compile a complete bibliography of the scores of volumes I have consulted in my research on La Salle. Some of them contained only material that may be found in histories of the period in which he lived. Others recounted tales about him that were unsupported by documentary evidence, and not a few were hardly more than fictional accounts of his exploits.

The narrative I have written was derived largely from seventeenth-century records, reports, correspondence, private journals, and government documents. These may be of interest to a serious student of the subject, and, with some other carefully selected sources, they appear below.

BANCROFT, HUBERT HOWE. *History of the North Mexican States and Texas.* 2 vols. San Francisco: A. L. Bancroft and Co., 1886. Excellent general history.

BERNOU, ABBÉ. *Mémoire pour Monseigneur Le Marquis de Seignelay.*
Paris: 1672. In Margry, *Découvertes* (q.v.). This memorial to
the Colonial Minister of France contains La Salle letters, praises
his character, and commends his motives and actions. Extensively
used by Parkman.

BREBNER, JOHN BARTLET. *The Explorers of North America, 1492–
1806.* London: A. & C. Black, 1933. An excellent general history
of the subject.

CAVELIER, JEAN. *Account of La Salle's Voyage to the Mouth of the
Mississippi.* Paris: Gouvernement François, 1688. A report by La
Salle's brother to the Colonial Minister. Printed in Margry (q.v.).
Translations in Shea, French, Parkman, Cox (q.v.). Thoroughly
unreliable, and fanciful in large part.

CHESNEL, PAUL. *History of Cavelier de La Salle.* New York: G. P.
Putnam's Sons, 1932. Translated from the French by Andrée
Chesnel Meany. Afflicted by generalizations and poor chronology,
but contains useful biographical details.

COSTAIN, THOMAS B. *The White and The Gold, The French Regime
in Canada.* New York: Doubleday & Company, Inc., 1954. Valuable details on Frontenac and La Salle in Canada, and their association in the fur trade. Highly favorable to missionaries, and
omits Jesuit machinations against La Salle.

COX, ISAAC JOSLIN. *The Journals of La Salle and his Companions.* 2
vols. New York: Williams-Barker Co., 1905. Reprinted New
York: Allerton Book Co., 1922. Volume I contains accounts by
Le Clercq, Tonty, Membre, Hennepin, and Jean Cavelier, La
Salle's brother. Volume II contains journal of Joutel (q.v.), and
translations of La Salle's patent of nobility; La Salle's will; grant
to La Salle of Fort Frontenac by Louis XIV; letters patent given
by King to La Salle; and the Louis XIV Commission to La Salle
to establish colony—all of which first appeared in Margry (q.v.).

DOUAY, ANASTASIUS. *Narrative of La Salle's Attempt to Ascend the
Mississippi in 1687,* contained in the works of Le Clercq and
Margry (q.v.). Translations in Shea and Cox (q.v.). Accounts of

[268]

the Texas colony and of La Salle's murder. Not substantiated in many respects by other accounts of the same events.

FAILLON, ETIENNE MICHEL. *Histoire de la Colonie Française en Canada.* 3 vols. Montreal: Bibliothèque Paroissiale, printed by de Poupart-Davyl, Paris, 1865. This history of French Canada contains excellent material on La Salle and other explorers. Parkman drew heavily on it for his revised edition of *La Salle.* Faillon was an indefatigable researcher, and discovered many original documents in Canadian archives that threw light on La Salle's enterprises.

FRENCH, BENJAMIN FRANKLIN. *Historical Collections of Louisiana.* 7 vols. New York: Wiley and Putnam, 1846–75. Devoted in a large part to La Salle, and containing documents translated from French, many of which were reprinted in part in Shea, Parkman, Cox, and other works.

HENNEPIN, LOUIS. *Description of Louisiana Newly Discovered to the Southwest of New France by Order of the King.* Translated from the French by Marion E. Cross. Minneapolis: University of Minnesota Press, 1938. The first edition of this "travel book" appeared in Paris in 1693. It is valuable only because of Hennepin's journey, under orders from La Salle, from the Illinois to the upper Mississippi, and his descriptions of Indians. In a later book, thoroughly dishonest, Hennepin claimed he had preceded La Salle to the mouth of the Mississippi.

JOUTEL, HENRI. *Historical Journal of Monsieur de La Salle's Last Voyage to Discover the Mississippi River.* Paris: D. Jouast, 1876. The most accurate and complete account of the last three years of La Salle's life. Joutel was his most trusted lieutenant. His journal first appeared in Margry (q.v.).

LE CLERCQ, CHRÉTIEN. *Établissement de la foi.* Paris: Aimiable Auroy, 1691. The third part of this work is about the Mississippi voyage of La Salle, and was based on the journal of Father Membre, La Salle's faithful companion on several of his journeys who perished in Texas. A translation appears in Shea (q.v.).

MARGRY, PIERRE. *Découvertes et Établissements des Français dans*

l'ouest et dans le sud de l'Amérique septentrionale, 1614–1754.
6 vols. Paris: D. Jouast, 1876–86. Published at the expense of the
French and American governments, this is an invaluable collection
of documents pertaining to French explorations in America. The
first three volumes relate almost entirely to La Salle. Translations
of the most important La Salle documents appear in Parkman,
Shea, French, Cox, and numerous other works. Margry spent
thirty years compiling the volumes. He was director of the Archives of Marine and Colonies. In this depository he discovered
numerous original letters and *papiers famille* of La Salle, and made
them available to historians for the first time. He was the first to
publish the valuable journal of Henri Joutel. A storehouse of La
Salle material was also found by Margry in the Bibliothèque Na-
tionale in Paris. Were it not for the indefatigable efforts of this
dedicated scholar, much of the history of La Salle's explorations
and of his personal life might never have been brought to light.

MEMBRE, ZENOBE. *Narrative of the Adventures of La Salle's Party
at Fort Crèvecouer, in Illinois, from February, 1680, to June,
1681.* Paris: Aimiable Auroy, 1691. Translations in Shea and Cox
(q.v.).

———. *Narrative of La Salle's Voyage down the Mississippi.* Paris:
Aimiable Auroy, 1691. Translations in Shea and Cox (q.v.).

O'CALLAGHAN, E. B. *Documents Relative to the Colonial History of
New York.* 10 vols. Albany: Weed, Parsons & Co., 1855. Volume
9 contains La Salle material found in numerous other works.

PARKMAN, FRANCIS. *La Salle and the Discovery of the Great West.*
Boston: Little, Brown & Company, 1879. Parkman lists as the
main source of his material the collections of documents made by
M. Pierre Margry (q.v.). Many of the most important of these
papers were not available to Parkman when he published the first
edition of his *La Salle* in 1869. Ten years later he had access to
them, and issued a revised edition. Many of the quotations in Parkman's distinguished work are paraphrased and not accurate translations; i.e., they present the sense of a passage rather than repeating language obsolete in his time. Being a French scholar, he could

employ this device with accuracy and to good effect. I consulted the centenary edition of his historical works. He also drew material from Sparks, Faillon, and Shea (q.v.).

PHILLIPS, PAUL CHRISLER. *The Fur Trade.* Norman, Okla.: University of Oklahoma Press. 1961. Contains excellent material on La Salle, especially his activities in the fur trade.

RENADOUT, ABBÉ. *Histoire de Mr. de La Salle,* in Margry (q.v.). This paper tells of La Salle's discovery of the Ohio, Illinois, and Mississippi Rivers. Renadout interviewed La Salle on numerous occasions in Paris.

SHEA, JOHN GILMARY. *Discovery and Exploration of the Mississippi Valley.* New York: J. S. Redfield, 1853. Contains journals and accounts, some of which are incomplete, of La Salle's associates and contemporaries, among them the missionaries Claudius Dablon, Claude Allouez, Chrétien Le Clercq, Louis Hennepin, Zenobe Membre and Anastasius Douay. Other valuable material in the work includes La Salle's patent of nobility; his second commission from Louis XIV; and a Spanish account of the destruction of La Salle's Texas colony.

SPARKS, JARED. "La Salle," in *Library of American Biography.* 25 vols. Boston: Little, Brown, and Company, 1834–48. Sparks, a president of Harvard University and a noted editor, opened to Parkman his private collection of La Salle papers.

Index

LEE COUNTY LIBRARY
SANFORD. N. C.